BUSINESS INFORMATION PROCESSING WITH BASIC

GEORGE STRUBLE

University of Oregon

ADDISON-WESLEY PUBLISHING COMPANY

Reading, Massachusetts · Menlo Park, California

London · Amsterdam · Don Mills, Ontario · Sydney

Sponsoring editor: William B. Gruener
Production editor: Martha K. Morong
Designer: Catherine L. Dorin
Illustrator: Kenneth Wilson
Cover design: Ann Scrimgeour

Library of Congress Cataloging in Publication Data

Struble, George.
    Business information processing with BASIC.

    Includes index.
    1.   Business—Data processing.   2.   Basic
(Computer program language)   I.   Title.
HF5548.2.S834   001.6′424   79-1423
ISBN 0-201-07640-3

ISBN 0-201-07640-3
ABCDEFGHIJ-HA-89876543210

PREFACE

As computer technology makes computer facilities increasingly accessible to all of us, it is increasingly important, especially for those students planning careers in business, to understand business information processing. It is not enough to be able to play blackjack with a computer.

The primary objective of this text is to introduce the concepts of business information processing. We pursue this objective on several levels. First, we speak directly to the purposes and structure of business information systems. We explore analysis methods, the design of business information systems, and the controls necessary to the integrity and accuracy of a system. Second, we concentrate heavily on the development of computer programs that accomplish business information processing tasks. We attempt to develop computer programming skill in the students, and focus that skill on example programs that are representative of the tasks we ask computers to do in business information systems.

There are several reasons for developing computer programming skills. One is to enable students to use a computer as a tool in further study. Courses in many disciplines are finding that examples carried out by students with the help of a computer deepen the students' understanding of their disciplines; we want to help to implement this kind of computer use. Second, the explosion of minicomputers and microcomputers has created an awesome need for computer programming. The competition for programmers is fierce, to the great enjoyment of students preparing for careers in information processing. Since there are not enough programmers to go around, anyone who can do even minor programming tasks in conjunction with his or her regular responsibilities has a great advantage and is worth more. Such tasks include modification of programs already working in the organization, adaptation of programs working in other organizations, troubleshooting when something goes wrong, and writing programs to do special analyses. A third reason is that even if one does no actual programming, an understanding of the process makes it much easier to work with professional programmers (and especially not-so-professional programmers!).

But perhaps the strongest reason for learning programming is that it reinforces the student's understanding of business information systems: their structure, capabilities, operation, flexibilities, and rigidities, control, output, input, and development. The student who has learned how to program representative tasks will have a grasp of the relative difficulty of various tasks, the ability to specify what ought to be done in a form understandable to programmers, and the ability to extend his or her understanding to new situations.

This text can be used in several different courses. It is designed primarily for use in a first course in computing or information processing for students majoring in business administration. The material can also be combined with broader survey material for an introductory course that integrates "computer literacy" with a concentration on business information processing.

This text also supports a reasonable first course for a business-oriented data processing or information systems curriculum. We want to teach students in such curricula how to program in COBOL and RPG. Yet I believe that BASIC is a much better vehicle for a first course than either COBOL or RPG. Since the BASIC language is far simpler than COBOL, it permits the student to progress faster through the concepts of business information systems and business information processing. And since BASIC is procedural, it enables a real understanding of the procedures. Furthermore, BASIC is a live language in business information processing systems, especially in minicomputer and microcomputer systems, so BASIC is worth learning in its own right.

No previous computing or data processing background is required or expected of the students. Some elementary algebra is useful, but not essential. There are a few mathematical examples, which can be skipped with no loss of continuity. However, I do presume an interest in and at least an introductory awareness of the structure of business and its financial systems and management.

One of the primary features of this text is its attention to the logical structuring of procedures. We develop the ideas of top-down procedure design, and structured programming concepts and control structures. Because garden-variety BASIC is itself not at all structured, we introduce control structures in a pseudocode first, then present the transcription into BASIC. In all examples, we develop a procedure in the pseudocode first, and then the program from the pseudocode. We take this approach for several reasons. First, it is the only effective way to develop structured programming concepts when working in BASIC. Second, it emphasizes the *logical structure* of programs and the programming skills that develop clear, unambiguous, and *correct* programs. Third, it makes the programming skills more easily transferable to other languages; the logical thought and conceptual program design go into the procedure in pseudocode, and the transcription from that procedure is a fairly mechanical process into BASIC, COBOL, PL/1, assembly language, or any other procedural language. I have found that this emphasis on logical structure requires a mental discipline and precision beyond what many students are accustomed to. For these students especially, it is valuable to separate the logical development of a program from its transcription into a computer language; we can concentrate on developing the analytical and problem-solving skills. As a result, I have found that the number of students who cannot do a computing project because "I just don't know where to start" has fallen almost to zero. I am convinced that development of the students' analytical and problem-solving skills will be valuable to the students far beyond the immediate subject matter of this course!

The second of the two primary features of this text is its attention to reading and writing files. Business information processing is based entirely on the use of files, and I am amazed at the number of texts that claim to present business data processing but that introduce discussion of files only in the last chapter! This text begins early to talk about processing information in files, and after Chapter 6, almost all examples illustrate the use of files and attempt to show the place and function of files in business information systems.

Another feature of this text is its introduction of the structure of a computer. We describe the internal structure and even, at an elementary level, programming in machine language. The intent is certainly not to make machine language programmers of the students, but to establish a fundamental understanding of how a computer does elementary tasks; this establishes a context in which the students can readily accept the components of pseudocode procedures and BASIC statements and their place in the overall structure.

One of the big problems in writing any text using BASIC is the great variety of versions of BASIC. Vendors' willingness to tamper with and extend in conflicting ways the features of the BASIC language is one of the scandals of the industry. I especially feel the problem since the use of files is probably the greatest area of nonstandardization. My approach to the problem consists of the following.

1. Use a fairly minimal BASIC in the main text. Most of the details are those of the DECsystem-10, but I expressly do not use or cover all features even of this system, and I give warnings of potential differences between the student's system and mine, and sometimes a suggestion for taking advantage of the differences.

2. The structured pseudocode helps. First, it reduces the area of the incompatibility problem to the transcription from pseudocode to BASIC. Second, the more advanced features of some BASIC versions are actually closer to the pseudocode than is the BASIC I present, so the student will find it *easier* and more direct to transcribe procedures into his or her BASIC than into the minimal BASIC that I introduce.

3. A family of workbooks supplement the text itself. One version of the workbook maintains the use of the minimal BASIC of the text. Other versions of the workbook are specific to the versions of BASIC available on some of the most common computers that the students are likely to use. The initial family of workbooks includes versions directed toward the HP-3000, the DECsystem-11 (PDP-11) using BASIC-PLUS, and the TRS-80. I hope that one of these will be close enough to each student's version of BASIC that the remaining adjustments the students must make are minimal. There may also be additions to the family of workbooks, as the need develops.

The first three chapters are a brief introduction to the applications of computers, the organization of computers, and some of the details of using a computer. They may be surveyed briefly as background for the later material. If the instructor wishes, an alternative is to use the first three chapters as foundation for a more extended study of computer applications and the philosophical basis for business information systems, of computer organization and hardware, and of communication with a computer through its operating system.

Chapter 4 begins the study of procedures, and the use of structured pseudocode. Though this is not a long chapter, it is one of the most important, and is fundamental to nearly everything that follows. The background of computer structure and the capabilities of the computer given in Chapter 2 help to motivate the language elements used in the pseudocode and the procedures developed.

Chapter 5 introduces the BASIC language and the transcription of procedures into BASIC. By the end of this chapter the students should be able to write elementary but nontrivial programs, first expressing the logic of the program in a pseudocode procedure, of course.

Chapter 6 introduces data files, both the philosophy of their organization and use in business information processing and the procedures and BASIC statements that read sequential files.

Chapter 7 continues with the development of procedures and programs in BASIC, introducing more complex structures and programming techniques.

Chapter 8 discusses testing and debugging. The student or instructor may wish to jump ahead to portions of this chapter from earlier in Chapters 5, 6, or 7. On the other hand, an instructor may wish to defer some of the topics of this chapter until later. I consider the discussions of the design of test data and of verification of programs to be very important, perhaps more important to students who are going to do serious computer programming than to those seeking only a management-oriented understanding of business information processing.

Chapter 9 discusses programs that write files, introduces the concept of subroutines, and dives into merge-type update programs. This last is the most difficult topic in the text, and an instructor may wish to undertake it last or even skip it altogether. The topic is included because it represents a very common type of business information processing program and its general concept is essential to an understanding of business information processing systems, at least those that maintain sequential files.

The last four chapters (and, indeed, most of Chapters 8 and 9) are independent and may be taken in any sequence. Chapter 10 discusses arrays, which are probably the second most difficult major topic in the text. Chapter 11 discusses systems analysis and design in an elementary way, since these are topics of large books in their own right. Still, a student needs at least a little perspective on the processes, and the realization that there is much more to bringing up a business information system than writing programs! Chapter 12 introduces functions: first, the concept of a function, then the usual numeric functions, and then the string functions and an exploration of some text processing tasks. Chapter 13 discusses forms layout and formatted output. This topic especially may reasonably be considered earlier. Its placement in the last chapter is not a judgment of unimportance; it reflects my decision to emphasize the logical development of programs as early as possible to give that the maximum time to sink in, while formatted output is a much easier topic that can be grasped quickly at the end of a course.

This text owes much to a number of people. Among my colleagues, Peter Moulton and Stephen Hedetniemi made especially valuable suggestions. Barbara Korando did a marvelous job of reading my writing and typing the manuscript. My thanks go to Hewlett-Packard Corporation, El-jay, Inc., and the University of Oregon for making their computers available for trying and lifting example programs for both text and workbooks. I also wish to acknowledge the contributions of the students and instructors who used the text in its preliminary forms.

Finally, and by no means least, I am grateful to my family for their patience and their willingness to assist in typing and proofreading.

Eugene, Oregon   G.S.
December 1979

CONTENTS

CHAPTER 1
AN INTRODUCTION TO BUSINESS APPLICATIONS

In this chapter we introduce business information processing. We attempt a definition, but the term must, for the most part, gather meaning as you study this book and beyond it. We attempt to characterize the uses of business information processing partly by dividing the uses into categories, partly by summarizing the reasons for using a computer in business data processing, and finally by outlining some of the specific applications. We can barely begin a task of cataloging the breadth of data processing applications, and do not claim to do more. Still, the outlines should provide a frame of reference, and we will explore several of the application areas in more depth later. The chapter concludes with a somewhat more detailed, but still superficial, exploration of one of the application areas: payroll processing.

1.1 WHAT DO WE MEAN BY INFORMATION PROCESSING?

The focus of this text is *information processing*. The term *data processing* is used more often. What is the distinction?

A distinction between *data* and *information* can be helpful. Data are facts, and by themselves may not be of much use. Information, on the other hand, is a fact or conclusion that *informs*—that is, tells us something we want to know. The distinction leads to my point that one reason for processing data is to retrieve or distill information. We take a series of data that is not directly very informative, and by processing it we produce information that we can use. For example, the complete set of a store's sales slips for the month is data, but if we want to know how these sales compared to last month's, we will process the data into a summary, and put last month's sales figures on the same page for comparison; the result is information.

What kind of data and information will we be considering, and what kind of processing will we talk about? The words on this page are data, and it is my hope that your eyes and brain can process it into information. But this book is not about that kind of processing. Not that we restrict attention strictly to numeric data; text data, made up of letters, digits, and punctuation and other special characters, are important, too. The processing we will explore is that carried out by an electronic digital computer and the equipment that goes with it, but we will expand the focus slightly to include manual procedures that prepare data for computer processing and use the information after processing. So the data we will consider are those that are used in a computer-supported process.

Have we defined information processing? Not really. What I have tried to do instead is to set an orientation or scope for this book. One of the lessons of the dramatic development of information processing in the 1960s and 1970s is that our definitions expand continually as we develop new ways to process data and produce information.

We can be a little more specific about business information processing, and the role of a computer in it. As we have said, the computer processes data in order to produce information. Another function is to organize and store data for later use. The detailed sales data for the current month may be stored in a computer file in an organized fashion, so that further programs could analyze those data. These analyses could produce reports of fast- or slow-moving products, reports of productivity of individual salespeople, or summaries of sales made to in-town versus out-of-town customers. Obviously, what data or information to store and how to organize it will be determined by the planned uses for the data.

Let us also distinguish among three kinds of output from an information processing system. The first is *action documents*, such as checks, invoices, and bills, which are used directly in facilitating the day-to-day work flow of the organization. Is this producing information or merely reproducing data? The action documents contain information if they are helpful to the clerks, customers, vendors, etc., for whom they are designed, but to a higher level of management these documents are merely data, since they do not directly contribute to the management's decision processes.

This brings us to the second kind of output, which is designed to facilitate *managerial control*. The daily or weekly transactions may be summarized so that bookkeepers can verify that the sales reported balance to cash (plus checks, etc.) received, or so that supervisors can discover strengths and weaknesses and deploy resources (production facilities, salespeople, newspaper ads, prominent display space) accordingly the following day or week. One feature of this type of output is that it is built into the data processing system and produced on a regular basis.

The third type of output is the *special analyses* that are produced for higher level management to answer specific questions that contribute to management decisions. These analyses are therefore not a part of the regular scheduled processing, but usually draw on the same data used to produce action documents or control reports.

We should also define what we mean by a data processing system or information processing system. The term *data processing system* is often used to mean the equipment used in data processing: a computer primarily, but also auxiliary equipment, such as card punches, machines that separate computer-printed output from the carbon paper between the sheets, or other machines that transcribe computer output from magnetic tape onto microfilm or microfiche. We will use the term *information processing system* to mean the set of computer programs, input forms, output report forms, and all the procedures followed in using the equipment, programs, forms, and reports. All these elements *must* form a system in the sense of being systematic and carefully organized to accomplish the objectives of the data processing.

Of course, the objectives are to provide everyone in the organization with the *information* needed to do his or her job. For this reason, what I call an information processing system is often called a management information system. Do the objectives seem impossibly broad? They have often turned out to be so. One attempt at solution has been the development of very complex (and costly) ways of storing data, representing all the interrelationships among the data. Often (older) solutions have been restriction of the objective to segments of the organization's data processing called *applications;* thus we might have an accounts receivable system, an inventory system, a general ledger system, and so on. These systems attempt to provide everyone's needs for accounts receivable information, for inventory information, etc. They are easier to design and implement, but fall short of meeting the information needs at the higher management levels, where diverse bits of information must be related. We will try to think of an overall integrated information processing system, and consider the portions devoted to accounts receivable, inventory, and other areas as subsystems. This is a difficult problem; we will discuss it more in Chapter 11.

1.2 WHY USE A COMPUTER?

Is a computer fun to be around? Not very. Does anybody love a computer? I hope not. We can respect a computer's capabilities, and we can enjoy making the computer do what we want it to; I hope you will come to respect and enjoy computer use as you learn more about it. But we must look further for good reasons for using a computer.

There are three principal reasons for using a computer: timeliness, accuracy, and cost efficiency, not necessarily in that order. Let us consider these three factors, one at a time. A computer can process data much faster than any manual or punched-card process can. The speed can enable a computer to provide information to us significantly earlier than we could get it without using a computer. However, raw speed is only one component of timeliness. The computer processes can help further by catching errors earlier and making it easy to correct errors, thus shortening the processing schedule. However, sometimes the processing schedule of an information processing system makes the system produce some results *later* than from a manual system. Sometimes timeliness is critical; sometimes the faster processing is only helpful; sometimes it is irrelevant.

Accuracy is a major feature of computers. Computers *very* rarely make arithmetic errors. They achieve greater precision of results than we usually get through any other means. They follow their programs consistently, so they do not cause the random handling or logic errors that people are prone to make. We sometimes read about big errors made by (or with the aid of) a computer, and it is true that certain large or systematic errors occur in computer processing that would be too obvious not to be caught in manual processing. But a computer system generally includes *more* checks on the accuracy of data than a manual system can have. These checks should always include tests for *reasonableness;* the instances of payroll checks for $1,000,000 or so, for example, are evidence that a programmer did not include all the appropriate tests in the programs.

Very few information processing systems using a computer cost less than the manual systems they replaced. Yet most are installed primarily for reasons of cost efficiency. Is this because we are terrible estimators? Well, the history of data processing is that we are not good estimators of either time or cost required for a system, but the reasons for the apparent cost overruns are more subtle. When the decision is made to convert an application to a computer, it may well be true that exactly the same functions could be done less expensively by computer. But if we analyze the costs of *operation* of a data processing system, a large portion of the cost is for data entry. Once data are entered, they can be kept on magnetic tape or disk (more about them later) for further use, at rather little additional cost. And, again for a relatively small cost, these data can be used to provide additional reports and analyses, provide better management control over operations, and support other by-products of the originally designed system. Many of these by-products are items that would always have been desirable, but the company could not afford the cost if they had to be done manually. The computer significantly lowers the cost of the by-products, and they become economically justified. The sum of the incremental costs of the by-products brings the total information processing cost above the cost of the former manual system. But the services provided, including the by-products, are far greater than those provided manually.

Another reason that computer systems cost more than their clerical predecessors is business growth. Though a computer system may cost, say, 30 percent more than the previous system did, an increase of 40 percent in the number of transactions processed and a little inflation might easily have raised the cost of the clerical system by 50 percent if it were continued.

1.3 A BRIEF SURVEY OF SOME APPLICATIONS

During the time in which business has used computers and the punched-card data processing machines that preceded computers, our ingenuity has succeeded in the application of computers to an increasing variety of tasks. We will explore several very briefly here, and examine some in greater detail later.

The United States Bureau of the Census

One of the largest data processing tasks anywhere is the processing of census data by the United States Bureau of the Census. The Bureau has been in the forefront of the development of data processing for almost a century, so we will use it as a focus in showing some of that development.

Established in the eighteenth century, the Census Bureau takes a census of the United States population every ten years. During the second half of the nineteenth century, the population was doubling every ten years, and since the 1880 census took seven years to process, there was every expectation that the 1890 census data could not be processed by 1900. Herman Hollerith, who worked for the Census Bureau, developed machines that would punch census data into cards, and sort and count cards. These machines were used to process the 1890 census, and successfully completed the task in only six years. The machines have been vastly improved since then, but we still use the 80-column card designed by Hollerith.

The Census Bureau supported much of the development of punched-card data processing machinery, until the equipment became powerful and flexible enough to be economically feasible in other applications. Then two rival companies formed to continue the development; these companies were the bases for the IBM and Sperry Rand UNIVAC empires of today.

Though some of the ideas fundamental to computers were built into primitive experimental machines in the late 1930s, World War II provided an impetus to computer development. Machines capable of calculating mathematical tables were completed in the mid- to late 1940s, but Remington Rand produced the first commercially available computer, the UNIVAC I, in 1951. The Census Bureau was one of the first customers, since the demand for ever more comprehensive and specialized analyses had outstripped the capabilities of punched-card equipment. The storage of data, as well as its processing, needed improvement, and with the impetus of the Census Bureau, Remington Rand led the development of the use of magnetic tape for computer storage. Now the Census Bureau takes not only the general census of the population every ten years, but also many smaller and more specialized surveys. The data are analyzed by computer and the results are published, but in addition, the Census Bureau is able to copy samples of the data onto magnetic tapes that are made available (under careful controls to ensure our privacy) to other organizations for special analyses and research.

Inventory and Order Processing

A wholesaler or a mail-order retailer fills orders from a warehouse inventory, and must send a packing slip or invoice to the customer giving the status of the order (and the shipment, if they are different). Computer processing helps the operations of filling orders and printing accurate invoices or packing slips.

At the heart is the inventory file, which not only lists each product in inventory, and its models, sizes, and colors, but also keeps count of how many of each are on hand, on order from the supplier, and committed to orders not yet filled. The set of these counts, updated by each order processing event, is called *perpetual inventory*. In processing each order, the computer checks each item for validity, often supplies the price from the file, and checks the quantity on hand. If there are not enough items on hand, the computer keeps track of the *back-order* file, and automatically fills the orders when more items are received into the warehouse. The computer may print a *picking slip* listing items that can be filled in order of their location in the warehouse; this speeds the filling of orders. The computer will also print the packing slip or invoice.

Order processing was one of the earlier tasks to use punched-card data processing equipment. When data on products, customers, and orders were kept on punched cards, the equipment used to process these cards included:

1. Keypunches, at which operators punch data into cards containing, for example, names, addresses, and account numbers of new customers;

2. Card verifiers, at which operators pretend to punch the cards again; the key strokes are compared to the punches in the cards to verify the accuracy of the card punching;

3. Sorters, to sort cards into a specific sequence, such as ascending customer account number;

4. Reproducers, to copy selected data from one card deck into another; for example, product descriptions might be reproduced from a master deck into cards whose data will later print invoices;

5. Tabulators, which print reports, invoices, etc.

Computers made possible tremendous improvements in order processing systems, and many computers in the 1950s were dedicated primarily to tasks like this, mostly in the larger companies. Computers became larger, more powerful, and more expensive in the late 1950s and 1960s, and more flexible too, so that large computers can handle order processing easily as just one of many tasks.

While one segment of the industry was building larger, faster, and ever more complex computers, other segments were applying the same technological advances to production of smaller computers that would provide the benefits of computer use to smaller companies. Small computer development accelerated with the development of minicomputers, especially by Digital Equipment Corporation. There is no clear definition of *minicomputer;* generally, a minicomputer has a sale price in the range of $10,000 to $100,000. The minicomputers at first were extremely limited in capacity and power, and were used primarily in special situations in scientific laboratories and process control environments. Since around 1974 the industry has been using minicomputers in business data processing environments, and extending computer use to thousands of businesses that could not justify the expense of a larger computer.

The most dramatic recent hardware advance is *large-scale integration:* Entire complex circuits can be etched onto a chip smaller than the letter "o" on this page. Large-scale integration made possible the development of the *microprocessor,* which is the entire arithmetic and control sections of a computer in a module about the size of your pencil eraser. A modest amount of main storage is of similar size. The microprocessors are manufactured and marketed for less than $40 each. They are embedded in *microcomputers,* which bring the cost of an entire computer system, including some input and output, to under $700. For business data processing, floppy disks and tape cassettes provide secondary storage, and again bring computing power to a vast new class of potential computer users.

Now a quite small business can use a computer in order processing. Order processing systems are also integrated into more general business systems: Sales and inventory records are available to support accounts receivable statements and processing of payments, accounting journals, purchasing and receiving systems, special sales analyses, and a close and efficient control of inventory.

Forecasting

One of the most helpful functions of computers in assisting management is forecasting. Since the data supporting regular business operations—order processing, payroll, inventory, customer records, etc.—can easily be stored by the computer, those data are available for analysis and forecasting of future trends, demands, resources, production levels, and other components of the planning process. Analysis of the organization and its past operation leads to a model of its behavior in whatever aspects are of current interest. Of course the model may have to include data from outside the organization—for example, costs of materials, interest rates, population. Then it becomes possible to make assumptions on some variables on the basis of the model.

For example, a retail business may keep careful records of sales as related to all the different advertising the business has used. The analysis of these data yields a model of the sales production of each of many dif-

"The computer says its projected forecast shows you will be re-elected, but that it personally wouldn't vote for you."

ferent advertising forms and approaches. With that, the business may project a particular program of advertising for the next year. With some assumptions on the uncertainties of the predictive value of the model, the computer can forecast the inventory (and, therefore, the working capital) required to make the sales generated by the advertising, and make estimates on the likelihood of running out of stock at each of several levels of inventory acquisition. Using these data as a basis, management can make intelligent decisions concerning an advertising strategy and the working capital required to implement the strategy.

Forecasting was one of the most widely publicized early applications of the computer. Though Remington Rand had produced the first commercially available computer in 1951, the company felt overshadowed by IBM, which had a heavy lead in punched-card data processing. Therefore, Remington Rand spent many thousands of dollars during the 1952 presidential election campaign preparing for election night processing. A great deal of election history was boiled down, summarized, and stored on the computer's magnetic tapes, and the UNIVAC I was carefully programmed to make projections based on early returns. The computer performed well that election night, made early and fairly accurate projections, and made a large contribution toward publicizing the potential of computers—and the UNIVAC I.

Banking

Banking was one of the earliest fields to see computer use, and the current volume and complexity of transactions just could not be handled without computers. The central application, of course, is in the maintenance of account records, including the posting of checks and deposits. Savings accounts, loans, and credit card accounts are also maintained in computer files; the computer computes and posts interest and prepares timely statements with little human effort. The status of each account is made available to inquiries very quickly. Beyond these daily, weekly, and monthly activities related to individual accounts, the computer's files support a variety of reports and projections that enable each bank's management to control activities and adjust policies and directions quickly and from accurate and up-to-date knowledge of the state of the business.

Banking is an activity that makes substantial use of on-line computing. The current status of each customer's account is the key piece of data; when a bank's computer can keep these data in storage accessible at any time, it can provide services such as after-hours transactions at a walk-up terminal that would not be feasible otherwise. We will further discuss on-line computer concepts in Chapter 3.

Let us take some time here to define a few terms. First, many computers and systems act in a *batch processing* mode, which means that data are gathered into batches and fed into the computer in batches. For example, all banking transactions for the day might be gathered and posted to customer accounts in one batch after the banking day is finished. *On-line* systems are mentioned with, at times, two different meanings. One is that files are *on-line* to the computer—on disk packs or other direct-access devices (more about those in Chapter 2) available for the computer's use in a fraction of a second. The second meaning, the one we will use, is that a computer *user* is *on-line* to the computer through a terminal of some kind.

In some systems the user supplies input on-line, but does not get direct feedback from the computer. We will talk about on-line systems that implement two-way communication and are thus *interactive* or *conversational* systems. Finally, a *real-time* system is one which provides output quickly enough to control a process. Moon-rocket navigation computers obviously run real-time processes. To the extent that the feed-back to the user at an interactive terminal can be said to control the process, this too is a real-time process. Many systems are a combination of types: A banking system will process checks in a batch-processing mode, but a teller may inquire interactively of an account balance before cashing a large check. A transaction at a walk-up terminal that validates a credit card input and account status and then dispenses cash is obviously on-line, interactive, and real-time processing.

Scheduling

A manufacturing plant that must make a variety of products is a complex operation. A computer can analyze current and projected demand for the various products, taking into account the capabilities of equipment, production lines, and personnel, and the requirements for producing each product, and produce an operating schedule for the plant. Similar programs are used to schedule airplane flight crews, to determine how best to cut logs into lumber, and to schedule activities of a large construction project. Of course, these are highly complex computer programs, which are based on mathematical tools of operations research. The computer is able to apply the operations research tools to a greater mass of detailed data than even the best human scheduler can manage.

General Ledger

All of the business record-keeping applications contribute toward a company's general ledger, which summarizes income, expenses, profit and loss, assets and liabilities. The order processing subsystem reports sales, and furnishes data to the accounts receivable subsystem, which in turn summarizes to the general ledger the receipts in the current period and the accounts receivable assets. Similarly, the inventory subsystem furnishes data at any time on the value of inventory on hand (though periodically this must be reconciled with a physical count). The inventory subsystem also helps to support the activity of ordering goods to restock the inventory, and those orders are a part of the accounts payable subsystem. Normally a business will also maintain an inventory of capital assets—plant, equipment, furniture, and so on—by computer, both to maintain control of and responsibility for those assets and to contribute toward the capital asset portion of general ledger statements.

A general ledger system usually includes a chart of accounts, which essentially catalogs which journal entries are valid and supplies additional information on how they should be posted. Checking accounting transactions against this *chart of accounts* helps to ensure that transactions are properly made and processed.

Insurance

Besides the general accounting and payroll activities that any business must handle, an insurance company must maintain data on both its current policies and the past history of its policies. Current policies must be serviced by premium notices, posting premium receipts, sending policies, notices, and policy updates and riders, and processing claims, redemptions, and nonrenewals. The history is constantly analyzed by the actuaries: What greater or lower risk is associated with certain medical or occupational conditions (for life, disability, and health insurance) or with location, occupancy, or construction conditions (for property insurance), or with automobile type, location, use, and driving history (for automobile insurance). The history of each of these factors is closely monitored for trends, and costs must be projected on the basis of history and anything else that can be brought to bear. The results are used to support changes in premium rates, dividends, terms, discounts on extra charges for certain conditions, programs to urge safe conditions, creation of new policy types and discontinuance of old ones, and even orientation of the business. The data base of current status and past history, accessible to the computer, makes the detailed and continuing analysis possible.

Technical Areas

Many businesses use computers in technical areas that are more or less specialized to particular industries. Manufacturing operations use computers to control machine tools; the specifications for machined parts are analyzed, and the computer provides detailed instructions that control the tools. The parts are manufactured more quickly and with less waste than under direct human control. Engineering calculations of stresses by computer permit complex structures with more economical use of materials than if all calculations had to be done manually.

Highway route analyses minimize construction costs while maximizing the safety factors. Petroleum refineries are almost exclusively operated under computer control: Computers monitor temperatures, rates of flow, pressures, volumes, and composition at each stage in the refining process, and control valves, pumps, heaters, coolers, and addition of reagents to maintain an optimum operating level for production of the products desired at the moment, with close quality control.

Airlines rely on an extensive computer system to service reservations and tickets. Newspapers use computers to assist in editing and typesetting their stories and advertisements, and even to sort the papers into bundles and mark the destination of each bundle.

There are many such applications, and the list grows every month. You should not be surprised to learn that computers are used to assist in the design of computers! This short summary of applications should suffice to give some idea of the breadth of computer use; we now explore one application, payroll processing, in greater detail.

1.4 A CLOSER LOOK AT PAYROLL PROCESSING

Why choose a payroll subsystem for an in-depth discussion? Payroll is one of the simpler applications, and one whose basic function is more readily understood than many other applications. Besides, it is somewhat representative; the components of a payroll subsystem generally include the components that are found in other subsystems as well.

What information is required from a payroll subsystem? What input is necessary to support the output? It may seem strange to start by specifying the outputs from a system, but this is the approach that leads to the most effective design.

The primary objective, of course, is to pay the employees. Everyone is interested in receiving a payroll check, and also insists that it be accurate and on time. The head of the payroll department also needs control reports and a payroll register, which show exactly what was paid to each employee. The payroll register should also show exactly which deductions were made from each employee's earnings. Of course, the employee is also interested in that, so attached to each employee's check is an itemized statement of hours worked, pay rate, gross pay, all deductions, and net pay. Other department heads and the accounting department want summaries of the payroll costs per department. Periodically, the deductions from employees' checks must be applied for their purposes, so itemized and summarized reports must accompany remittances to insurance programs, the Internal Revenue Service, state and perhaps local tax departments, labor unions, United Appeal, and every other agency for whom payroll deductions are made.

The input necessary to support a payroll subsystem can be divided into two categories. First is data that are relatively stable: name, social security number, address, pay rate (hourly wage or salary), department, number of exemptions, choice among insurance plans, deductions authorized, and so on. The second category is data that vary each pay period: number of hours or days worked, days of sick leave or vacation taken.

One of the advantages of computer processing of payroll data is that the relatively stable data can be organized and stored in what we will call the *payroll master file*, ready to be used when the data specific to each pay period are brought in. This contributes to a simplification of data collection each pay period, which is very welcome because of the usually tight time schedule for producing the payroll. The *only* essential inputs each pay period are hours worked, sick leave and vacation pay taken, and social security number. Why the social security number? It is the link from the current input to the stable data on each employee; both the current pay period input and the payroll master file are organized in sequence according to social security number, and associated by matching the social security numbers.

Actually, the *first* step in payroll processing in each pay period is to update the payroll master file. New employees must be added, and exemptions, deductions, pay rates, and so forth, change for old employees. The update to the payroll master file can be done earlier, and on a somewhat more relaxed schedule, than the rest of the processing. In addition to updating the master file, the update produces a *payroll change report*, listing every change made to the file; this report is checked carefully by the payroll clerks to ensure accuracy of the updates.

The time cards (and we will include data on vacations and sick leave taken) are collected in batches, and a total of hours worked computed manually for each batch. The next step is to edit the time card data. The editing has several functions.

1. *Balance the input.* Make sure the hours worked add up to the total manually computed for each batch. This helps to ensure accuracy of the data entry, and guard against leaving out or inserting data.

2. *Check each time card for valid form.* No nonnumeric characters, for example, should stray into hours worked or social security number. Hours worked should also be checked for reasonableness: Perhaps any record of more than 80 hours worked per week would be rejected or at least reported for attention.

3. *Check each time card against the master file.* Report any social security number that is not in the master file. This can and will happen, caused by a variety of errors, and must be corrected.

4. *Associate time card data with master file data.* Both are necessary, used together, in the next step.

The editing produces an edit and error report, and errors must be corrected quickly to prepare for the next step. The combination of editing functions gives us a more accurate set of payroll data than we could possibly have in a manual system; the few errors uncovered are efficiently drawn to the attention of the payroll department for correction.

The next step is the computational one. Gross wages are computed, deductions are taken, sick leave and vacation are accrued or credited, and the results of the computations are stored both for the current pay period and for the year-to-date totals. This step usually also produces the *payroll register,* which lists all the detail of hours worked, gross and net pay, deductions, and sick leave and vacation status for each employee. The payroll department uses the payroll register in answering any questions about the payroll.

Then comes the step when actual checks, with the statement of earnings and deductions, are printed for each employee. The blank check forms are kept under close security, and control totals (primarily of hours worked, but also of gross and net pay) are computed, printed, and matched with the corresponding totals from earlier steps.

Recently, a strong interface has been built between payroll systems and bank systems: Not only can larger companies deposit payroll checks directly to the employees' bank accounts, but they can accomplish it by supplying the data on a magnetic tape rather than on paper checks, saving printing and handling of the checks themselves.

Further steps produce summaries that contribute to the general ledger subsystem and report labor costs by department and other categories. Still further steps periodically report the accumulation of all deductions.

This is still only a skeletal outline of the usual payroll subsystem. There are variations—extra or alternate steps dictated by the special needs of a company. We have glossed over many details; in later chapters we will fill in some of these details to illustrate various points.

1.5 MAIN IDEAS

a. The object of information processing is to distill information for our use from data.

b. Business information processing produces information at three levels: action documents, periodic reports and summaries for managerial control, and special analyses leading to management decisions.

c. An information processing system consists of computer programs, input forms, output reports, and the procedures by which people use them.

d. Computers are used because they produce timely, accurate, and cost-efficient information. But cost efficiency usually means somewhat increased cost for greatly increased services.

e. Computers are heavily used in almost all aspects of business life; the list of applications is long, and still growing.

f. A batch processing system requires input to be collected into a batch, and processes the batch before reporting results to the user. An on-line, interactive system reacts directly to individual pieces of data as they are entered by the user.

g. A payroll subsystem is representative of other subsystems: A master file holds stable and cumulative data; processing steps include master file updates, input editing, computation and printing of a register of detail, and printing of periodic reports.

1.6 QUESTIONS FOR IMAGINATION AND REVIEW

1. Find examples of action documents, managerial control reports, and special analyses leading to management decisions. Include some that are combinations of these functions, since the distinctions are not precise.

2. List interrelationships among the applications outlined in Section 1.3. How would you go about making sure that the data processing of these applications facilitates the interrelationships rather than making them difficult or incompatible?

3. Learn more about one of the applications outlined in Section 1.3, in some organization with which you are familiar.

4. Try to develop more comprehensive lists of:
   a) data elements needed in a payroll master file;
   b) editing steps that should be performed to ensure accuracy of payroll processing;
   c) controls that should be applied to payroll processing to prevent errors or fraud.

5. Find examples of business data processing applications *not* mentioned in this chapter.

6. Classify the applications of computers given in this chapter and others you can think of in the following categories:
   a) work best as batch processes;
   b) require interactive processing;
   c) could be done either way.

Of those in the last category, list what you think might be advantages of batch processing and advantages of interactive processing.

7. This chapter presents a philosophy of information processing. Analyze and criticize the philosophy, drawing especially on judgments you may make on organizations or applications you know that conform to, or violate, this philosophy.

CHAPTER 2
AN INTRODUCTION TO COMPUTER FUNCTIONS AND ORGANIZATION

We now introduce the computer itself. First we discuss the functions that a computer must be able to perform, and then introduce the features of computer organization that enable the computer to perform those functions. In particular, we develop the concept of computer instructions, where they are stored, how they are executed, what they accomplish, and how they combine into programs. We analyze the hardware of computers, especially the different types of input and output devices and why each is used for certain purposes. The chapter concludes with a short summary of the computer languages in which people write programs.

The discussions in this chapter are by no means exhaustive. In fact, they are rather superficial. Still, a broad understanding of how a computer functions, and why things are done the way they are, will enable the student to keep in perspective the whole picture as we concentrate in later chapters on the finer details of computer use. We hope this chapter will contribute toward that broad understanding, especially if the student asks some of the questions that will naturally arise.

2.1 COMPUTER ORGANIZATION

We can list four major functions that any computer must be able to perform. Then we will see how a computer is organized in order to be able to perform those functions.

A computer must be able to do *arithmetic*. It is sufficient that it add, subtract, multiply, and divide; more complex mathematical tasks, like computing square roots, logarithms, and regression coefficients, can be performed by appropriate sequences of additions, subtractions, multiplications, and divisions. Second, a computer must be able to *receive input* from outside itself, and to *send output* to the waiting world. As we shall see later, there are many different input and output devices, with different costs, speeds, and uses. Third, a computer must be able to hold input data and intermediate results in some kind of *internal storage*, and to move data around within that storage. Programs of instructions to the computer are also kept in this storage. Fourth, a computer must be able to *make decisions and exercise control* over the procedure it is following. The decisions to be made are very simple ones:

- Is this number greater than that one?
- Is this number equal to that one?
- Is this string of characters equal to that one?
- Have we read all the data in that file?

The computer must be able to take different courses of action depending on whether the answer to one of these questions is yes or no.

This set of features may not seem like much, but it is sufficient for doing any of the data processing tasks we explored in Chapter 1 and those that we will discuss later. A few more features are needed by the *executive program* (or *monitor* or *operating system*) to manage several concurrent users and input/output devices; these features pertain mostly to timing and to recognizing the status of input/output devices.

How is a computer organized to perform the functions we have described? We will analyze the computer in terms of a main storage section, an arithmetic section, an input/output section, and a control section, connected as shown in Fig. 2.1. Though this diagram, like any other simple one, is a gross oversimplification, it is useful in an introductory explanation.

Main Storage

Let us start with the main storage section. One important feature of the main or internal storage is that any piece of data in it is immediately accessible: In about a *microsecond* (a millionth of a second) a piece of

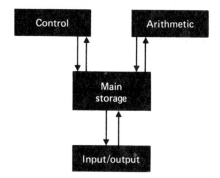

Figure 2.1 Organization of a computer.

data can be retrieved from main storage and used, or placed in main storage. This feature is important to both the flexibility and the speed of any computer.

We need a method of specifying which pieces of data are to be used in an operation. Computers provide this facility by dividing the main storage into words or bytes, and giving each one an *address*. A *byte* is generally the physical storage needed to store one printable character, though other data may be stored in a byte or a sequence of bytes. A *word* is generally a larger physical unit of storage—enough to hold a number, several characters, or an instruction to the computer. Some computers give each byte an address; the addresses of the bytes in storage would start at 0 and increase by 1 sequentially up to the size of the storage unit. For example, some computers may have 524,288 bytes of storage, and addresses would be 000000 to 524287. Incidentally, this amount of storage would usually be called 512K bytes; K (approximating the Greek prefix *kilo-*) stands for 1024, which is 2^{10}. Other computers give addresses only to words; a computer with storage equivalent to the one mentioned above might contain 128K words, whose addresses would be 000000 to 131071.

Figure 2.2 shows examples of how data may be stored in a computer's main storage. In Fig. 2.2(a), each byte of main storage, which contains one character, has an address. As shown, the eighteen bytes with locations 003540 to 003557 contain a record of an inventory transaction:

Locations	*Content*	*Meaning*
003540–003545	011880	transaction date January 18, 1980
003546	A	type A transaction: transfer to quality control
003547–003548	JP	initials of John Powell, clerk
003549–003552	0004	4 units transferred
003553–003557	J2175	product J2175 transferred

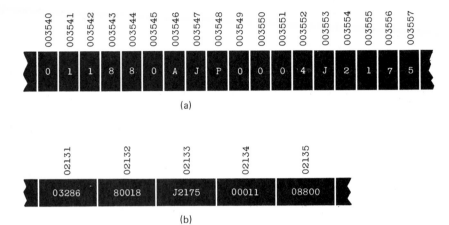

(a)

(b)

Figure 2.2 Data in bytes and words: (a) Each byte has an address; (b) each word has an address.

In Fig. 2.2(b), each word, which can hold five characters, has an address. As shown, the five words with locations 02131 to 02135 contain a portion of a record of a customer order:

Location	Content	Meaning
02131	03286	customer number 03286
02132	80018	date: year 80, day 018 of the year (same date, January 18, as above, but a different representation)
02133	J2175	product number J2175
02134	00011	11 items ordered
02135	08800	$88.00

When we want to store a piece of data, we specify to the computer the address of the word or byte in which we want it stored; we retrieve that piece of data by specifying the same address. For example, we may instruct the computer to add the numbers at locations 002488 and 003940, and put the result in location 002488, replacing the first operand. Similarly, we may instruct the computer to:

- Move the number from location 006584 to location 005408;

- Receive input of a number from device 1 and store it in location 004724;

- Send the number in location 007630 to output device 3.

An important concept to be introduced now is *nondestructive retrieval:* When we retrieve data from main storage in order to use it, the data *remain intact in their original locations.* On the other hand, when we store a number in a given location, the *previous contents* of that location are erased and destroyed.

Arithmetic Section

Many computers are able to store numbers in several different representations. Some representations express the number in the decimal number system, some in binary. Some express numbers as integers, without any fractional part; others express numbers in what we call *floating-point* form. In floating-point arithmetic, the most significant digits of a number are kept, along with an indication of where the decimal point should be. We often see numbers in pocket calculators expressed in floating-point form. Figure 2.3 shows several representations, and examples of each.

A computer that stores numbers in different representations will perform arithmetic operations on numbers in any of those forms. It will also convert numbers from one form into another; the conversions, as well as additions, subtractions, multiplications, and divisions, are done by the arithmetic section. Most computers *cannot* do arithmetic directly on the *character* representations of numbers—the representation that is printable and in which most input comes to the computer. So conversions of input from character form to one of the other representations, and of output back to character form, are essential.

	Number	Expressed as	
Decimal integer	347	000347	Usually a fixed number of digits is
	−28	000028−	used for each number—here we use 6 digits for illustration.
Decimal floating point	347	347000 + 03	$= 0.347000 \times 10^{03} = .347 \times 1000$
	6823.657	682366 + 04	Number is rounded to six digits.
	0.0875	875000 − 01	$= 0.875000 \times 10^{-1} = .875 \times 0.1$
Binary integer	27	0—011011	

$$
\begin{aligned}
1 \times 2^0 &= 1 \\
1 \times 2^1 &= 2 \\
0 \times 2^2 &= 0 \\
1 \times 2^3 &= 8 \\
1 \times 2^4 &= 16 \\
0 \times \ldots &= \underline{0} \\
& 27
\end{aligned}
$$

	Number	Expressed as	
Binary floating point	27	$110110—0 + 00101 = 0.11011 \times 2^5 = 11011.$	

Figure 2.3 Number representations.

Input/Output Section

Most computers have several input and output devices attached to them. Some, like teletypes, accept input directly from people, or, like teletypes or higher-speed printers, send output for people to read directly. As we shall see in Section 2.3, others are one stage further removed from people. There are still other devices, which are called secondary storage devices; output sent to these devices is not directed to people at all, but is stored for later use by a (usually the same) computer. These devices are usually magnetic disk or tape; they hold large quantities of data, and can be written and read at high speed, though access is not nearly so fast as access to main storage is. The advantage of these devices over main storage is the extremely low cost. Because any computer needs *some* form of secondary storage, the use of secondary storage is one of the major themes developed in this text.

When input to a computer is needed, the computer does an input operation; the instruction must specify:

1. which device to read from, and

2. where in main storage to put the data.

Some other functions, like specifying where on a secondary storage device to take the data from, or specifying how much data to read, are usually handled by other instructions prior to the actual input instruction. When the computer wants to send data to an output device, it must specify similarly:

1. where in main storage to take the data from, and

2. which output device to send the data to.

So in input and output operations, data move between the input or output devices and main storage.

Control Section

The control section directs all the others; it tells them what to do, and when, and with what data. How it instructs them, and where it gets its own instructions, are the topics of Section 2.2.

2.2 INSTRUCTIONS AND PROGRAMS

The unit of control in a computer is the *instruction*. From now on, we will use the word instruction in a technical sense; up to now we have been using it somewhat informally. An instruction consists of an *operation code*, and designations of one or two *operands*, or sometimes modifiers to the operation codes. An instruction usually occupies a word in main storage, although in some computers an instruction may occupy half a word, one and a half words, or even two words. An instruction will direct the computer to do one of the elementary functions we listed in Section 2.1:

- Add one number to another.

- Subtract one number from another.

- Multiply one number by another.

- Divide one number by another.

- Convert a number from one representation to another.

- Input from a device into main storage.

- Output from main storage to an output device.

We will discuss the instructions that make and implement decisions later.

Each operand for an instruction is designated by its main storage address. Figure 2.4 shows some instructions as they might be coded for a hypothetical but representative computer. Each instruction includes an operation code and the addresses of two operands. In the input and output instructions, more specifications are usually necessary; for example, something must tell how many pieces of data are to be input or output

Oper. code	Operands		
	Op. 1	Op. 2	
21	05030	06220 (21 = Add)	Add the number at location 06220 to the number at 05030; the result is stored at location 05030.
22	07764	03284 (22 = Subtract)	Subtract the number at location 03284 from the number at 07764; the result is stored at location 07764.
69	12450	04898 (69 = Move)	Move the number at location 04898 to location 12450. The number at 04898 is still intact, but the previous number at 12450 is destroyed.
71	04200	00001 (71 = Input)	Input data from device 1 to locations 04200 and those following, as necessary.
72	10624	00003 (72 = Output)	Output data from locations 10624 and those following, to device 3.

Figure 2.4 Instruction formats.

by this operation. This is often done in a special control word in main storage dedicated to holding just such information.

Instructions are kept in main storage. The control section directs the activities of the computer by pulling instructions, one at a time, from main storage. When an instruction reaches the control section, it is segregated into its components: The operation code tells the control section what kind of elementary operation is to be performed, and then the control section determines from the operand addresses in the instruction where to go for the operands. These steps of retrieving an instruction from main storage and decoding its operation code and operand addresses are called the *instruction cycle* of the execution of an instruction. The instruction cycle is followed by the *execution cycle*, and then the instruction cycle for the next instruction.

During the execution cycle, the control section activates the other sections to get them to perform the specified operation. First, the operands are retrieved from main storage and sent to the section that can perform the operation. Then the control section directs the appropriate section as to which operation to perform on the operands, and finally sends the results to the location in main storage that is designated by the instruction. Computers' instruction repertoires are often arranged so that the result of an operation replaces the first operand of the instruction; this saves the typical instruction from having to include *three* addresses, without any significant loss of power or flexibility.

How does the control section know where to get its next instruction? Generally, instructions are executed from consecutive locations in main storage. After the control section has fetched and executed the instruction in location 06240, it will fetch and execute the instruction in location 06241, and then the instruction in location 06242. The control section keeps an *instruction counter*, which contains the location of the current instruction. At the end of the execution cycle, the control section adds 1 to the instruction counter, and then uses the counter as the address from which to fetch the next instruction.

If sequential execution of instructions were the limit of a computer's capabilities, very few computers would be used. Suppose that a computer executes a single instruction in about 10 microseconds, which is not fast by current standards. Suppose that this computer has 64K words of main storage, which must hold data as well as instructions. Perhaps 50,000 words at most could hold instructions; these instructions would be executed in half a second, and we would then have to go to the work of preparing and entering the next instructions. As you will see, the work of writing computer instructions is exacting and burdensome, enough so that to perform that work and then execute each instruction once would be absurd.

By making provisions for breaking the sequential execution of instructions we complete the picture of the main features of the computer, and show the power of the computer design. Basically, there are instructions called *branch* or *jump* instructions, which tell the control section to break the sequential execution of instructions, and execute instructions starting at some other location. The mechanism is simple enough: A branch instruction causes the control section to store one of the operand addresses in the instruction counter rather than adding 1 to the contents of the instruction counter. For example, the instruction at location 06254 might be a branch instruction with an operand address of 06240. The execution of this instruction would place 06240 in the instruction counter. Therefore, the next instruction to be executed will be taken from location 06240 instead of from 06255.

This permits what we call a *loop* of instructions; the instructions in locations 06240 to 06254 are executed, and then those same instructions are executed again, and again. We begin to have some power or leverage: We write and enter a set of instructions once, and they can be executed many times. Of course, it doesn't make sense to do exactly the same things over and over again, but to be able to repeat the *same operations* on *different data* is quite useful indeed. Most data processing is, in fact, repetition of a set of operations on different data.

By now you are asking yourself what prevents the computer from being stuck in a loop of instructions forever. This is one of the reasons for the use of a *conditional branch* instruction. A conditional branch instruction tests the state of the computer for some condition, and if the condition is true, causes a branch just the way an unconditional branch does. If the condition is *not* true, the instruction does nothing, and the instruction in the next physical location will be executed. If we can find or manufacture some testable condition that will be true so long as the computer should *continue* looping, but will change from *true* to *false* when we want to exit from a loop, we can use a branch instruction to exit from the loop, as shown in Fig. 2.5(a). If a testable condition will remain *false* so long as the computer should continue looping, but change to *true* when the computer should exit, we can use a conditional branch to control the looping, as shown in Fig. 2.5(b). Each of these structures of loops is explored in more detail in later chapters in the context of BASIC programs.

The conditions that can be tested by a conditional branch are simple ones, such as:

- Has the computer read to the end of an input data file?

- Is a number at some location equal to zero?

06240	First instruction in loop
.	
.	
.	
06254	Conditional branch to 06240, to return to loop if condition is *true*
06255	Instruction to be executed when loop is completed

a. Continue looping as long as condition is true

06240	First instruction in loop
.	
.	
.	
06254	Conditional branch to 06256, to *exit* from loop if condition is *true*
06255	Unconditional branch to 06240, to loop again
06256	Instruction to be executed when loop is completed

b. Continue looping as long as condition is false

Figure 2.5 Use of the conditional branch to control loop exit.

- Is a number at some location greater than zero?

- Is one operand equal to some second operand?

- Is one operand greater than some second operand?

Actually, the conditional branch instruction usually tests only one of a set of special indicators or switches; which indicator to test is specified in the first operand of the conditional branch instruction, and the address to branch to is the second operand, as in the unconditional branch. The indicators themselves are usually set by a previous instruction; it may be an arithmetic instruction that records in an indicator whether the arithmetic result was greater than zero, equal to zero, or negative, or it may be a *compare* instruction that compares two operands and records in an indicator which was larger, or whether the operands were equal.

These modest capabilities are surprisingly powerful; using a little ingenuity and following some standard patterns, we can control loops in quite complex ways. As a simple example, suppose we want to execute a loop exactly 20 times. We set aside a location to be used as a counter, and just before we enter the loop, we put the number 20 in it. As shown in Fig. 2.6, a subtract instruction brings the counter down by 1 each time the loop is executed. The conditional branch instruction returns control to the top of the loop so long as the indicator shows that the result of subtracting 1 is not zero. When the loop has been executed 20 times, the counter becomes zero, the indicator shows that result, and the conditional branch finds that setting of the indicator and passes control beyond the loop, to location 06255.

06239	Move the number 20 to location 14300
06240	First instruction in loop
.	
.	
.	
06252	Last instruction of the major task of the loop
06253	Subtract 1 from number at location 14300, leaving result in 14300 and storing indicators
06254	If indicator shows result *not zero*, branch to 06240
06255	Instruction to be executed when loop is completed

Figure 2.6 Executing a loop twenty times.

The other important use for conditional branch instructions is to provide alternate actions depending on the data. For example, we may have a task to

Compute extended price as quantity ordered times price, but if the quantity ordered is a dozen or more, apply a discount of 10%.

This gives us two forms of the expression for extended price:

1. quantity ordered × price

2. 0.90 × quantity ordered × price

The computer should choose which one to use on the basis of a comparison of quantity ordered with the number 12. The instructions that perform the task could be similar to the following:

08904 Compare quantity ordered and 12

08905 If the first operand was greater, go to 08910

08906 Instructions forming extended price as quantity ordered × price

.
.
.

08909 Unconditional branch to 08914

08910 Instructions forming extended price as 0.90 × quantity ordered × price

.
.
.

08914 Continue with other tasks

This outlined sequence of instructions uses a conditional branch at location 08905; for some orders, the branch to 08910 will be taken; for other orders, it will not be. Note the unconditional branch at location 08909; why is it necessary?

We have shown a simple use of a conditional branch instruction to implement a decision process between two alternate tasks, and we will soon see the same decision and others like it in the context of BASIC programs. More complex tasks and decisions do not use any more complex instructions, but use more of the instructions we have already described. Keeping track of where we are and what we are doing as we plan and implement complex tasks is not easy, and we must use all the help that can reasonably be provided to us, in order to develop programs and systems that run correctly, and develop them in a reasonable time. Among the helps we use are higher level languages, which we will explore in a preliminary way in Section 2.4. Among them also are various organization techniques—for data, programs, and entire projects—most of them beyond the scope of this text. But we *will* use one of the organization techniques for programs, called *structured programming;* this will also be introduced in Chapter 4.

We have now introduced the basic architecture of a computer and the types of instructions that drive the computer. The instructions can be strung together into sequences to perform tasks. Now we can define (loosely) a *program* as a sequence of instructions that performs a task for us. And the activity of *programming* is no more nor less than writing such sequences of instructions.

2.3 HARDWARE AND INPUT/OUTPUT DEVICES

In this section we explore briefly the hardware of a computer, and especially the devices used for input and output. This will help put in perspective the reasons for using particular input, output, and storage arrangements in constructing information processing systems.

The devices most used for computers' secondary storage are magnetic disks. The disk units are manufactured in a variety of forms. Some units handle single disks; others handle two disks, of which one is fixed and one is removable. Still others handle *disk packs;* a disk pack is a stack of disks, usually 6 or 11 disks mounted rigidly on a central spindle (see Fig. 2.7). Both top and bottom surfaces of each disk can be used for recording data, but in fact the top surface of the top disk and the bottom surface of the bottom disk are not used, so there are 10 or 20 surfaces used. Reading and writing heads are mounted on arms and are held very close to the disk surface. Each disk surface is coated with a magnetizable

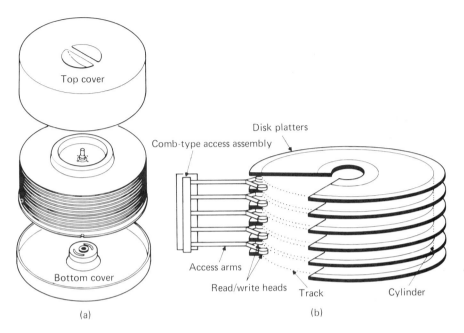

Figure 2.7 Disk packs.

iron oxide, and data are read or written by the heads in much the same way that audio tapes are read or written. The disks spin at a high speed, so when a read/write head is held stationary, it can read or write the data on a circular *track* on the disk. There are 200 or 400 different positions for the read/write heads; hence, there are 200 or 400 tracks on each disk. Each track can hold 5,000 to 20,000 characters, depending on the model, so a disk pack may hold up to 160,000,000 characters. The important feature of magnetic disks is that the computer can direct the drive to reach a particular portion of a particular track on a particular disk, and in less than 250 milliseconds or so, the data from that portion can be read into the computer's main storage. Writing is similar. Because magnetic disks have this feature, they are called *direct-access* storage units. Direct-access devices have advantages for computer secondary storage because the storage is very flexible: Many files can be kept on one disk or disk pack, and space can be reassigned and reused for other files or for up-dated records of the same file.

Let us consider further the implications of the characteristics of magnetic disks. A typical disk pack may hold 50,000,000 characters; the disk pack itself costs about $300 and the disk drive, including the control circuitry that communicates with the computer, costs about $10,000. A

"How much information can it store, say, on the head of a pin?"

disk pack can be removed from the drive and stored, while another pack, containing different files for different applications, is mounted and used. So for each $300 we have long-term storage of up to 50,000,000 characters. To access the data, we must, of course, have the right pack mounted on the drive, and then our computer can access any data in less than 250 milliseconds. That is a substantial waiting time if we need to wait very often. Therefore, we organize files and records so that the physical records (usually called *blocks*) on the disk pack are rather long (600 to 4000 characters), so our waits for disk access can be infrequent.

Let us contrast disk packs with the devices used as a computer's main storage. Many different devices were used in the early days of the computer, but in the 1960s and the first half of the 1970s, almost all main storage was *magnetic cores*, shown in Fig. 2.8. Each core is really an iron

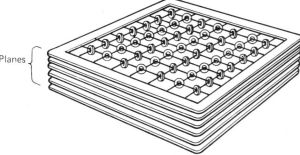

Figure 2.8 Magnetic core storage, and a close-up of magnetic core memory. Each tiny donut-shaped core is about the size of the head of a pin. (Photograph courtesy of IBM Corporation.)

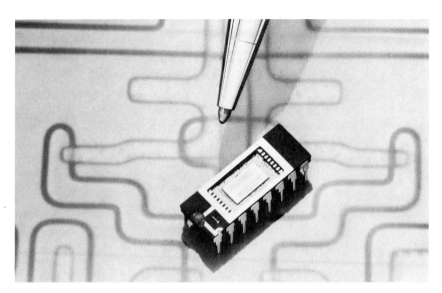

Figure 2.9 A semiconductor storage chip. The tip of a pen points to a Texas Instruments chip containing 65,536 bits. In the background, what appears as abstract drawings is actually a chip section photographically enlarged 1000 times. Courtesy Texas Instruments, Inc.

ring whose magnetic charge is set in either of two orientations by currents passed through wires threaded through the core. Each character is represented by a combination of the orientations of the magnetic charges in eight cores, so a large amount of storage is expensive. A unit of 32,000 character capacity costs about $20,000. Now a variety of semiconductor devices are replacing magnetic core as the major medium of computer main storage. These devices are more compact and less expensive than magnetic core storage; 32,000 characters of semi-conductor storage might cost $5000 (or more or less, depending on the complexity of the control circuitry required). An example is shown in Fig. 2.9.

Main storage speed is one of the primary determinants of a computer's overall internal speed. We need main storage that is able to retrieve for us individual instructions and data items in a microsecond or so. This is a very different requirement from those we place on secondary storage devices; main storage is expensive, so we use it only for the program or programs and data that are *currently being used* by the computer. Other data and programs are kept in secondary storage, which is much less expensive per character but whose access speed is also correspondingly less.

There are other secondary storage devices besides magnetic disks. The main competitor is magnetic tape, which is even less expensive than magnetic disk; a reel of tape may hold 40,000,000 characters, and costs

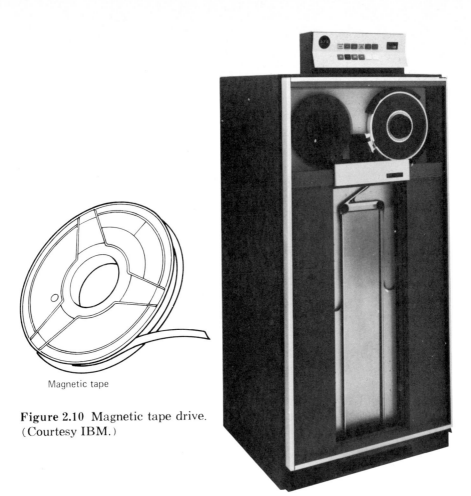

Magnetic tape

Figure 2.10 Magnetic tape drive. (Courtesy IBM.)

$20 or so. A tape drive may cost $5000. Tapes are compact, and will hold data reliably for many years. As with disk packs, the space can be erased and rewritten with new data. The big difference between tapes and disks lies in access; by the physical nature of the tape, access is sequential. The only way to get from one spot on a tape to another is to pass over the tape between the spots. This makes tape very poor at tasks that require jumping from one record to another in a sequence other than the sequence in which they were written. For such tasks we use magnetic disk or other, less common, direct-access devices. We use magnetic tape for *sequential* access applications; if we want to read records in the same sequence in which they were written, tape is very efficient. A computer can retrieve the next record from a tape in about 40 milliseconds.† A magnetic tape drive is shown in Fig. 2.10.

† For sequential access, disk packs may match the access speed of magnetic tapes; the 250 milliseconds quoted above are for accesses that require movement of the access arms.

Now let us turn to some other input and output devices. For many years, the primary input medium was punched cards, which are still heavily used. There are two sizes of cards in use now: 80-column cards and 96-column cards. Examples are shown in Fig. 2.11. The cards are prepared by operators at card punch machines; a professional card punch operator can reliably punch about 200 cards per hour. A good, fast card reader now can read cards into a computer at the rate of 1000–1800 per minute. Computers can punch cards as output too, at up to 300 cards per minute. Punching is slower than reading, of course, because it requires

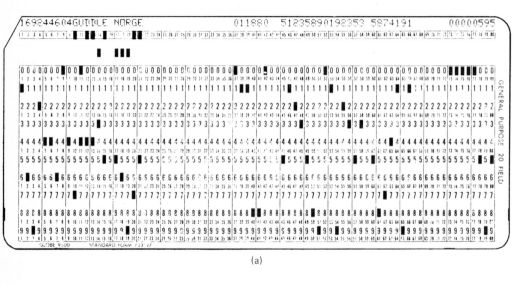

(a)

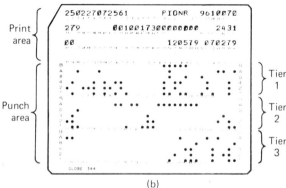

(b)

Figure 2.11 (a) An 80-column card. (b) A 96-column card.

Figure 2.12 A printer. (Courtesy IBM.)

fairly heavy mechanical action; cards are read by a photoelectric process that does not require stopping the card. Data processing systems punch cards to be stored for later rereading. Since magnetic tape and some other devices have become standard, reliable, compact, and inexpensive, systems now punch cards only occasionally.

The main purpose of the output section of a computer is to communicate results to people. The most effective way for a computer to do that is to print the results on paper. Nearly every computer other than the very smallest ones is attached to a printer. These printers are supplied in a variety of speeds and costs, but a common speed for a large computer is 1000 lines per minute; such a printer costs about $100,000. Smaller computers, attempting to handle a smaller volume of work, use slower, less costly printers, which print characters serially across a line as a typewriter does, rather than a line at a time. Figure 2.12 shows a fast printer, and Fig. 2.13 shows an example of printed output.

Some systems require output so voluminous that it would place too great a burden on even 1000-line-a-minute printers. For many of these systems, output lines are formatted as if they were to be printed, but are written to magnetic tape instead. The magnetic tape is then read by another machine, which displays each page of the "printed" output on a screen just long enough for a snapshot to be taken; the snapshots are developed on microfilm or microfiche. This alternative to direct printing is called COM (Computer Output on Microfilm), and it provides at low

```
                              *** INVOICE ***
                           UNIVERSITY OF OREGON
                            COMPUTING CENTER           BILLING CLERK
                                                       PHONE : 686-4394
                           EUGENE OREGON   97403

TO:      STRUBLE                                    INVOICE #:        23364
ADDRESS: CS                                         INVOICE DATE 79-145

PROJECT #:  25364                                   BUS DATA PROC INVEST
***********************************************************************************
CHARGES FOR USE OF COMPUTING CENTER SERVICES AND SUPPLIES DURING MAY,79(04/26-05/25) JULIAN (115 - 145)
***********************************************************************************
MACHINE PROCESSING:

PDP-10 MACHINE CHARGES:
CLASS ACCT PRGRMMR DATE    TTY  JOB  LOG IN    LOG OFF  CONNECT TIME  CPU TIME  K-CORE  L-KCORE  HRG  CHRGS  AMOUNT
  SEQ  NUMBER  (JULIAN) NUMBER NUMBER TIME       TIME    (MINUTES)    (SEC)    SECONDS  (SEC)  UNITS  /100

111  10  000103  79-144   27   35  22:02:46  22:16:00      13          21        61       0     0     74    1.20
111  10  000103  79-144   21   24  22:19:26  22:21:32       2           3        23       0     0     11    0.22
                                                       TOTAL FOR CLASS:                                      1.42

                                         MACHINE PROCESSING:
                                         CHARGES FOR CURRENT MONTH:                                          1.42
                                         CREDITS AGAINST CHARGES:                                            0.00
                                         NET CHARGES FOR CURRENT MONTH:                                      1.42

DISK AND TAPE STORAGE:

PDP-10 DISK STORAGE:
CLASS ACCT PRGRMMR  DATE    DISK BLOCKS                                                                     AMOUNT
  SEQ  NUMBER  (JULIAN)     USED

211  10  000103  79-120        85                                                                           0.55
211  10  000103  79-125        85                                                                           0.55
211  10  000103  79-130        85                                                                           0.55
211  10  000103  79-135        65                                                                           0.55
211  10  000103  79-140        85                                                                           0.55
211  10  000103  79-145        85                                                                           0.55
                                                       TOTAL FOR CLASS:                                      3.30

                                         DISK AND TAPE STORAGE:
                                         CHARGES FOR CURRENT MONTH:                                          3.30
                                         CREDITS AGAINST CHARGES:                                            0.00
                                         NET CHARGES FOR CURRENT MONTH:                                      3.30

PROJECT #:  25364
```

Figure 2.13 Printed output.

cost a compact representation readable by people. It is especially useful for directories, account balances, and so on, for reference, or for audit trails listing all transactions in a system, as mandated by legislation or by financial auditing standards.

Another alternative to printed output for some applications is graphical output. A graph plotter can be directed by a computer to draw line graphs representing data such as business trends, or bar charts or pie charts for visual presentation of budget data, or scattered points and computed regression lines representing statistical data. Computers have preprogrammed packages that make it easy to specify a graph and to label it, and a graph not only takes less paper than a printed report to which it is an alternative, but the message is much more immediately accessible to the user. Figure 2.14 shows an example of a graph produced by a computer. The graph is actually formed by a series of pen movements, each (in most plotters) 0.01 inch in any of the directions (if we think of a map) N, NE, E, SE, S, SW, W, NW. A graph plotter, with its controller, costs about $5000. Graph plotting is not as fast as printing reports, however, and its usefulness is limited.

Sometimes computer printed output is so voluminous that we measure it by the "thick foot." An alternative to such output, and to some uses of COM, is to maintain the data in a computer's direct-access secondary storage and to make small portions available for display at a terminal upon inquiry. There are many different terminals; the greatest distinction is between *hard-copy* terminals, which print on paper, and *CRT* (*cathode-ray tube*) terminals, which can display data faster and which require less maintenance, but do not produce any permanent record for the user. Terminals are used not only for display upon inquiry but also for entry of transactions, thus bypassing the card-punching step. This has more advantages than merely saving wood pulp, as we shall see later. Terminals are also used for entering and running programs, as you will be doing, and generally controlling a computer's activities. They are fairly inexpensive, and their cost is still decreasing generally. A teletype, pictured in Fig. 2.15, may cost $700, and inexpensive CRT terminals (see Fig. 2.16) may cost as little as $800 or so. Terminals with extra features, of course, cost more. One big advantage of terminals is that they can be placed at some distance from the computer they use. Many communicate over telephone wires with computers in other cities, or even by satellite with computers on other continents! Some terminals are made for special purposes, such as recording retail sales, managing airline reservations, or editing news stories.

One of the important features of terminal use is that any terminal does not impose much burden on the computer it uses. Part of the time the communication is at our typing speed, which is rather slow by com-

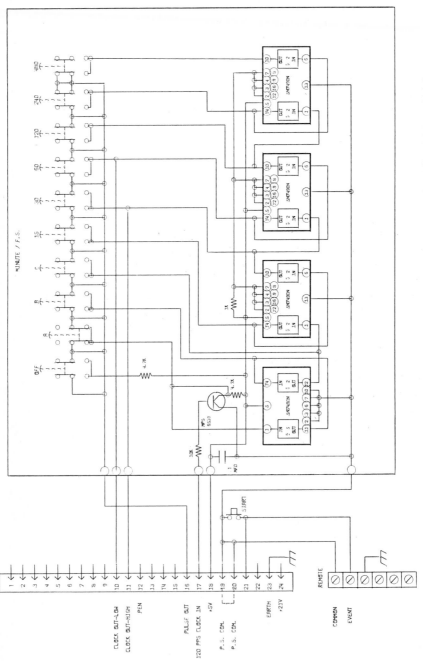

Figure 2.14 A graph drawn by a pen-and-ink plotter.

Figure 2.15 A teletype.
(Courtesy Teletype
Corporation.)

Figure 2.16 A CRT terminal. (Courtesy Hazeltine Corporation.)

puter standards; furthermore, even more time is idle (from the computer's standpoint) while the operator reads what has been displayed and decides what to do next. Since each terminal places demands on only a small fraction of the computer's available time, it is reasonable to ask a computer to serve several terminals simultaneously. Since several terminal users share the computer's time, this kind of use is called *time-sharing*. We will describe the functions a computer must perform in order to manage time-sharing in Chapter 3.

The cost of data entry is one of the largest operating costs in many business data processing systems. Transcribing data from source documents—orders or invoices, payroll forms, inventory transfer forms, time cards, and so on—is expensive, whether the data are punched into cards or tape or directly into the computer from terminals. Not only is data entry expensive, it is also a source of error, and can often be a bottleneck that makes timely output very difficult. Therefore, we look for ways to make original data, in the form of the source document itself, readable to the computer. One device is the magnetic ink character reader. This device reads the specially formatted characters printed in special ink at the bottom of checks and deposit slips. Since the codes on the checks identify quickly and reliably the bank and usually the account within the bank, the opportunity for error is reduced tremendously, and a great deal of hand sorting is also eliminated. The amount of manual data entry required is reduced to the entering of the *amount* of each check or deposit.

Another class of devices read data optically from source documents. Fairly inexpensive devices can *read marks* written by pencil, and the position of each mark in a grid on the form determines which character it represents. Figure 2.17 shows a form used for optical mark reading. More expensive are *optical character readers*, which read and distinguish typed or handwritten characters. The technology for recognizing characters is quite difficult, and is by no means completely accurate. Therefore, optical character readers work in connection with an operator: When the machine cannot clearly decide what a character is, it displays the character to the operator, who makes the decision and keys in the character! If people pay close attention to the quality of their writing, the character reader seldom has to ask for operator decision. Figure 2.18 shows an example of a form used with an optical character reader.

Let us conclude our description of devices by mentioning briefly some other input and output devices. One of the oldest is punched paper tape; paper tape readers and punches cost considerably less than card readers and punches, and the speeds are comparable. Cards are easier to handle, store, and edit, and the use of punched paper tape is decreasing. One of the devices taking the place of paper tape is the magnetic tape cassette.

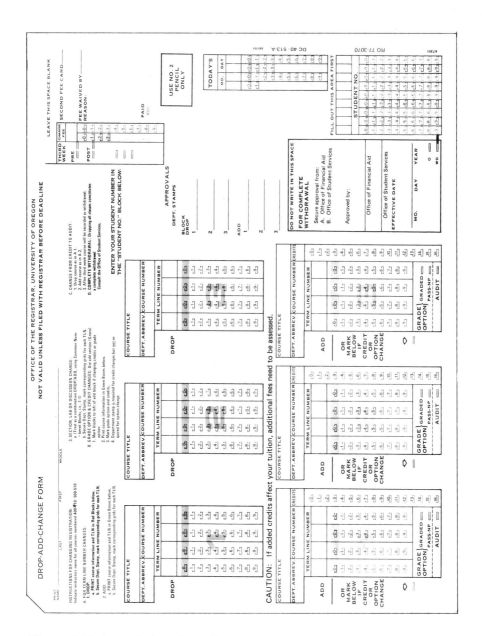

Figure 2.17 An optical mark-reading form.

PRINT NUMBERS CAREFULLY.
USE THE FOLLOWING GUIDE.

0 1 2 3 4 5 6 7 8 9

TO: A BC LUMBER CO.

FROM: SELF

DATE: 12-9-78   SCALED AT CAMP CR.

TRUCKER: C-6   BRAND: ⊕ RP

SCALER NO.

8   4156839

	BUTT DIA.	%	L GROSS D	L DEDUCTS D	GRADE	SPECIES	SPLIT
1	21		4 0 1 7 6		29	02	
2	23		2 8 2 0	2	32		
3	12		2 2 1 0				1
4	14	1	2 0 1 2 4		29		1
5	19		3 6 1 5			1 1	
6	28		1 7 2 6	1	14	02	
7	23		4 0 1 9		20		

TRUCKER

	BUTT DIA.	%	L GROSS D	L DEDUCTS D	GRADE	SPECIES	SPLIT
8	17		1 2 1 6		95		
9	14		3 0 1 1		32	17	
10	08		4 0 0 5		44	02	
11	18		4 0 1 4		29		
12	14		1 2 1 2				
13	25		3 2 2 2 2	1			
14	20	2	2 0 1 8	2	32		
15							9
16							
17							
18							

Figure 2.18 An optical character-reading form.

The cassette technology is taken from the audio cassette industry, and in fact the devices that read and write the data cassettes are usually audio cassette recorders, with some additional control and communications circuitry. Cassette recorders are not fast, and the cassettes do not have a large capacity, but they are inexpensive and very attractive for use with small computers.

Last, we must mention the *diskette*, or "floppy disk," which is a disk about 7 inches in diameter, of flexible Mylar. When inserted into the computer, it is pressed against a rotating surface, so in use it has all the characteristics of magnetic disks but has slower access and smaller capacity. The disk drive costs about $1000, and each disk costs about $7 and holds 250,000 characters or so, so this is a very useful direct-access capability for small computers.

We have presented a catalog of input and output devices, and though we have also discussed the uses of each, the user may still be concerned about how all these things fit together. So we close this section by describing two computer system configurations.

First, Fig. 2.19 diagrams a medium-scale computer used by a manufacturing company in a batch-processing mode. Data are punched into

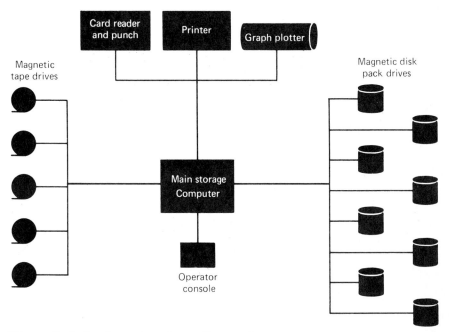

Figure 2.19 Configuration of a medium-scale computer.

cards from the source documents; orders, invoices, time cards, account-ing journal entries, inventory transfers, and cash receipts are the bulk of the input, but there are other, less frequent types of input, too. The major portion of output is printed, though inventory records, sales rec-ords, and accounting journals are also written on magnetic tapes, which are sent to a service bureau for transfer to microfilm and microfiche for compact storage readable by people. The main files—inventory, person-nel, vendor file, customer file—are kept on disk packs for quick access. Some more minor files are kept on disk, too, and still others, which are accessed seldom and always sequentially, are kept on magnetic tape. The disk files are also copied onto magnetic tape every two days for security and backup. The company does engineering calculations on this com-puter, and it is mostly their results that use the graph plotter. Just to give some idea of the size of the operation, we must add that the com-pany has annual sales of $30,000,000, the computer leases for about $30,000 per month, and the entire budget of the data processing depart-ment is $80,000 per month.

The second configuration, shown in Fig. 2.20, is much smaller; it in-

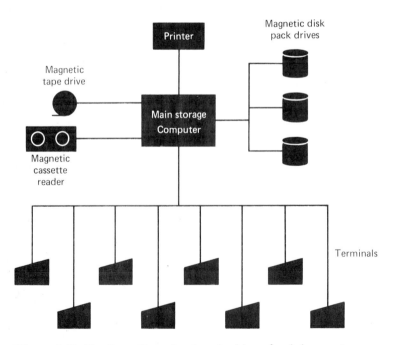

Figure 2.20 Configuration of a terminal-based minicomputer sys-tem.

cludes a minicomputer used mainly in conjunction with terminals. The company is a fairly small mail-order company, but it has two local stores as outlets also. The main files are orders in progress, inventory, and the customer mailing list; all files are kept on disk, and the single (slow) tape drive is used almost entirely to copy files for backup. Almost all input is by terminal: One terminal is in the warehouse, two are in the accounting department (these are also used for management inquiries), one is in the special service department, one is in the computer room for development, and the remaining three do the bulk of the input, especially of orders and new names for the mailing list. Each of the stores has a cash register that records the day's transactions on a tape cassette; the cassettes are brought to the computer daily and entered through the computer's cassette reader. Much of the output of the computer is in response to inquiries at terminals; the printer can print 250 lines per minute, and prints primarily the invoices sent to customers. The computer was purchased for $80,000, and the information processing operating budget is $8,000 per month.

2.4 COMPUTER LANGUAGES

We have explored the capabilities of computers and the instructions by which we direct them to do tasks for us. It is possible to write programs of instructions in what we call *machine language*, including numeric operation codes, numeric operand addresses, and so forth, as shown in Fig. 2.4, and some of us still remember years when that was the only way to write a program. However, since the computer exists to help relieve us of clerical burdens, we have defined languages that we call computer languages, and then written translator programs to enable the computer to translate a program written in a computer language into the machine language. The computer languages help us express our directions to the computer in a similar manner to the way we think out the procedures by which a computer could do a task.

One category of computer language is called *assembly language*. Each line in an assembly language program generally is translated into one machine language instruction. We write operation codes, but symbolically, and also use symbols that have some meaning to our task as operands; the translator keeps track of and assigns numerical locations. Writing in assembly language, we have the full power and flexibility of the computer at our command, but the writing is still tedious and detailed, with much opportunity for error. Also, each computer model has a different machine language and, therefore, its own assembly language, and an assembly language program does not transfer easily to another model. Figure 2.21 shows a segment of an assembly language program that corresponds to the skeleton of Fig. 2.6.

Other computer languages are called *higher-level languages*, because they are closer to our own modes of thinking conceptually about our task and the procedures to accomplish it, and further from machine languages. The language BASIC is one of these higher-level languages, and we will use BASIC as our vehicle for teaching you how to program a computer. BASIC is almost always used in a time-sharing environment, and is the major language used in programming for time-sharing minicomputers and microcomputers. Because of this, BASIC is being used more heavily for business information processing than it was before, say, 1975. Figure 2.22(a) shows a segment of a BASIC program that does the same task as the assembly language segment shown in Fig. 2.21, except that the 20 numbers are input from a user at a terminal rather than from cards.

The language most used in larger computers for business data processing is COBOL (*COmmon Business-Oriented Language*). COBOL has been in use since the early 1960s, and is much less heavily used in time-sharing environments than in card-and-tape-oriented environments. COBOL is a very useful computer language to learn after you have studied programming in BASIC, but BASIC is a better vehicle, I believe, for a first course. Figure 2.22(b) shows a COBOL segment that attempts the same task as that shown in Fig. 2.22(a), with input from cards. The segment is not complete; definition of data areas, among other things, is needed.

There are three languages most important for scientific programming tasks. The first is Fortran (Formula Translation). The oldest of all higher-level languages, Fortran was introduced in the mid-1950s, and its capabilities have been enhanced greatly since then. Like BASIC and COBOL, a Fortran program can be run on another computer with at

```
         LA    2,0        LOAD ZERO INTO REGISTER 2
         LA    3,20       PUT THE NUMBER 20 IN REG. 3
LOOP     GET   IN,CARD    READ THE CONTENTS OF A CARD
         A     2,CARD     ADD NUMBER FROM CARD TO REGISTER 2
         S     3,ONE      SUBTRACT 1
         BNZ   LOOP       IF RESULT IS NOT ZERO, BRANCH TO LOOP
         ST    2,SUM      STORE SUM OF 20 NUMBERS
```

Figure 2.21 Segment of a program in assembly language.

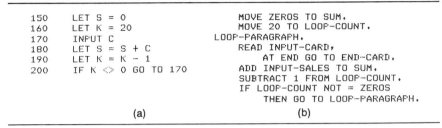

```
150      LET S = 0                      MOVE ZEROS TO SUM.
160      LET K = 20                     MOVE 20 TO LOOP-COUNT.
170      INPUT C                LOOP-PARAGRAPH.
180      LET S = S + C                  READ INPUT-CARD,
190      LET K = K - 1                     AT END GO TO END-CARD.
200      IF K <> 0 GO TO 170            ADD INPUT-SALES TO SUM.
                                        SUBTRACT 1 FROM LOOP-COUNT.
                                        IF LOOP-COUNT NOT = ZEROS
                                           THEN GO TO LOOP-PARAGRAPH.
              (a)                               (b)
```

Figure 2.22 (a) Segment of a program in BASIC. (b) Segment of a program in COBOL.

most minor changes. ALGOL (Algorithmic Language), with many advanced features, was designed by computer scientists in the late 1950s. It is used most in Europe, but provides a very useful vehicle for the study and interchange of computing techniques and advanced ideas in computer science. The language PL/1 (Programming Language 1) was introduced by IBM Corporation for the IBM 360 series in the mid-1960s, and is a combination of features of several higher-level languages. It is used in some data processing installations, but its use is restricted mainly to the IBM 360 and 370 series.

We close this section with a brief introduction to RPG (Report Program Generator). This language was designed in the 1950s for data processing users who were converting from punched-card data processing to the use of small computers. This language, like the others, has been enhanced over the years, but it is still used primarily in small computers implementing relatively simple applications. As the name implies, its main strength is in the easy generation of programs that produce reports.

2.5 MAIN IDEAS

a.   A computer must be able to do arithmetic, accept input, send output, hold data, results, and programs in internal storage, and make decisions. Each operation is implemented by an instruction that is executed by the computer.

b.   A computer's main storage is organized in bytes or words, each with an address. The operands of instructions are specified by their addresses.

c.   A computer program is composed of instructions. Instructions are executed from main storage locations in sequential order, except when directed by a conditional branch or an unconditional branch. The branch instructions provide for the use of loops and decision making within programs.

d.   Main storage devices must access any byte or word in at most a few microseconds; secondary storage devices hold more data, and access the data in milliseconds but in larger blocks. The major secondary storage devices are magnetic disk for direct access, and magnetic tape for sequential access only.

e.   Input and output devices also include punched cards and paper tape, printers, COM (via magnetic tape), terminals, magnetic tape cassettes, and floppy disks.

f.   Higher-level computer languages make programs easier to write and more transportable to other computers than if they were written directly in machine language; translator programs translate programs from higher-level languages to machine language.

2.6 QUESTIONS FOR IMAGINATION AND REVIEW

1. Find out more about the computer you have access to.
    a) What kind of main storage does it have? How much?
    b) What secondary storage media does it have?
    c) What other input and output units are connected to the computer? How are they used and why?
    d) How are numbers and characters represented in the computer?

2. Think of a function that you would like a computer to perform. Then try to outline how a computer could perform that function through use of the operations we have learned about: arithmetic, input, output, moving data within main storage, and branch operations. This is a preview of the design of procedures for computer solution, which will be the detailed subject of much of this text.

3. Think of tasks that you think a computer would *not* be able to perform because they cannot be done by the operations that you know a computer can do.

4. For some business enterprise, list the data that you think the business should keep in a computer's secondary storage. Then for each set of data, decide what secondary storage medium would be most appropriate.

5. If you are using branch instructions that can each test one condition, how would you construct a program segment that branches to location 06468 if $A > B$ *or* $C = 16$ (or both; we will use *or* to mean the *inclusive or*: either one or the other or both)?

6. Similarly, how would a program segment branch to location 07403 if $A > B$ *and* $C = 16$?

CHAPTER 3
USING A COMPUTER

In this chapter we explore how a user actually gets a task done by a computer. There is a big difference between working with a batch processing system and interacting with a time-sharing system. Most of this text concerns using a time-sharing system, but we present the batch processing system for contrast. We show transcripts of two student sessions using BASIC; in one the student calls and runs a program from a library, while in the second, the student types in and runs a complete program. We follow the processes involved in these two sessions, and contrast the student sessions with use of a formatted screen for data entry in an actual business data processing system. We also explore more of the environment and the supporting services required by time-sharing users, including file space and libraries on disk and an operating system that remains in the computer's main storage at all times and controls operation of the computer for the benefit of all users.

3.1 A BATCH RUN

In order to show how a typical run is made in a batch processing computer system, we take as our example the program in a payroll system that captures from cards and edits time card data. The functions of this program were listed in Section 1.4; the data consist of time card and vacation and sick leave reports, with a batch control card for each department. Each batch control card contains the total number of hours worked, and vacation and sick leave taken for a department; checking these totals against the detailed data helps to safeguard the accuracy and integrity of the data and the entire payroll operation.

Figure 3.1 shows a few data cards that could be input to the program. Each card contains a worker's social security number in columns 1–9, except that batch control cards contain CTRL instead. Other fields are as follows:

Department	Columns 10–12
Date (end of week)	Columns 13–18
Hours worked Saturday	Columns 21–25 (Hours and tenths)
Hours worked Sunday	Columns 26–30
.	
.	
.	
Hours worked Friday	Columns 51–55
Hours sick leave taken	Columns 56–60
Hours vacation taken	Columns 61–65

Thus, the data card after the first control card records 8 hours worked each day Monday through Friday for the employee whose social security number is 111222333, from department 011 for the week ending January 18, 1980. The first department has only two employees, and you can verify that its data balance to the batch control card.

Around the data cards in Fig. 3.1 are four additional *job control* cards that are required by the system. These cards establish entry to the system, designate the procedure to be run, and mark off the data cards as separate from the job control cards.

There are two outputs from this program. One is the edit report, which lists all cards that are found to be invalid in any way; the second is a file, either on magnetic disk or magnetic tape, of the *valid* cards. Possible reasons for flagging a card as invalid are:

- Social security number is not nine digits;

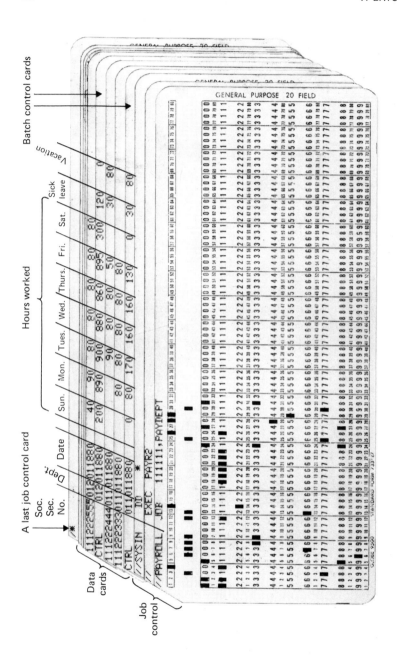

Figure 3.1 Card deck for payroll system input.

- Social security number does not match any record in the payroll master file;

- Department of a time card does not match the department from the last batch control card;

- Invalid date;

- Form of hours worked (or sick or vacation leave) is invalid;

- Hours worked for an employee is not within an allowable range;

- Department totals do not balance to the batch control card.

Depending on the seriousness of the errors, the cards are usually corrected and the program is rerun, since no employee will be satisfied to hear "There was a mistake in punching your card for the computer, so you will have to wait until next week to be paid." If the computer system permits, the correction process may be done by an on-line procedure correcting the file captured on disk, since time is always short for correcting the payroll input and getting on to the rest of the payroll system.

The sequence of events that occur in running this program is as follows:

1. The data cards are punched and verified, and the job control cards supplied.

2. The cards are taken to the computer room and placed in the card reader.

3. The card reader reads the cards into a queue of jobs on disk waiting to be processed.

4. A normal job waits in the queue until the scheduler, a piece of the computer's operating system, gets around to it. In this case, computer operators enter on the control terminal a high priority for this job so that it is the very next one executed.

5. The job scheduler finds the procedure PAYR2 and the program that it calls. The scheduler loads the program from a library on disk into main storage, finds the payroll master file, and space for the output file of valid payroll data.

6. The program itself runs: Data are read from the job queue, treated by the program, and written to either the valid data file or the edit report.

Generally, this kind of procedure is followed for every run in a batch processing system. The data cards are collected into a batch and entered into the computer system. When the program is completed, the resulting report is returned to the user for further action.

3.2 INTERACTIVE USE: A STUDENT SESSION

Now we turn to examples of interactive computer use, showing BASIC facilities as you may have access to them. As a first example, a student in international economics may test an understanding of international monetary and trade policies by running a specially prepared program that simulates a few aspects of a balance of payments problem. The student is asked by the program to make decisions, and the computer reports the simulated results of those decisions. This program repeats the process of decisions and results for a simulated period of four years. A partial transcript of a run of this program is shown in Fig. 3.2. We have circled the input typed by the student; everything else in the figure is typed by the computer. First, the student types the command LOG, followed by, on this system, a *project number* (perhaps shared by the entire class) and a *programmer number* (presumably belonging only to this student). The computer responds with two introductory lines, and then requests the student's password. Under computer control, the printing of the password is inhibited; this helps to protect the privacy of the password. The computer looks up the combination of project number, programmer number, and password in its authorization file, and, if the combination is valid, the computer accepts the student as an interactive user. After some more messages, the computer prints a period as a signal that it is ready to accept a command.

The student types R BASIC to enter the BASIC subsystem. After the command is acknowledged, the student types OLD CS1:BALPAY. In honoring this command, the computer retrieves the program named BALPAY from the library named CS1 on disk, and loads the program into the student's portion of main storage, which we will call the student's *workspace*.

The student types RUN to start the program. The computer reports in a heading line what program is being executed, and when, and then executes the program. The program prints a good deal of explanatory material for the student, especially since the student answered YES when the program asked whether to print directions. We do not reproduce everything, but we do show in Fig. 3.2(b) that the program asks the student for policy decisions for the year 1. After receiving the decisions, the computer calculates the simulated results and prints them.

```
.LOG 25364/103
JOB 19 UO DECSYSTEM-10 603A.03 TTY37
Password:
1640    15-Jun-79      Fri

.R BASIC


READY, FOR HELP TYPE HELP.
OLD CS1:BALPAY

READY
RUN

CS1:BALPAY    16:40           15-JUN-79




THIS IS A DECISION MAKING GAME.
YOUR PART IN THE GAME IS THAT OF DECISION MAKER
FOR THE COUNTRY.  ASSUME THAT THE COUNTRY IS CURRENTLY
IN A VERY POOR BALANCE OF PAYMENTS POSITION.  YOUR
OBJECTIVE IS TO MAKE DECISIONS THAT WILL GIVE THE
COUNTRY A HEALTHY BALANCE OF PAYMENTS POSITION WITHIN  4  YEARS.
WOULD YOU LIKE DIRECTIONS?(YES OR NO) ?YES
YOU WILL BE ASKED TO ENTER VARIOUS VALUES
TO BRING THE COUNTRY BACK INTO BALANCE.  FIRST YOU WILL
BE ASKED FOR THE PERCENTAGE OF CHANGE IN TAXES ON
INVESTMENTS ABROAD.  A REASONABLE ANSWER LIES SOMEWHERE
BETWEEN 7.9 AND -7.9 .   NEXT YOU WILL BE ASKED FOR THE
CHANGE IN THE TARIFF RATE.  A REASONABLE CHANGE
```

(a)

```
ENTER YOUR POLICY DECISIONS FOR YEAR  1

WHAT PERCENT CHANGE DO YOU WISH
IN TAXES ON INVESTMENTS ABROAD ?5
IN THE TARIFF RATE ?7
IN GOVERNMENT SPENDING ABROAD ?-10
IN THE PRIME INTEREST RATE ?0

BALANCE STATEMENT IN MILLIONS OF DOLLARS FOR YEAR  1


INFLOWS

EXPORTS:  GOODS AND SERVICES        $ 17846      86 %
EXPENDITURES OF FOREIGN TOURISTS    $ 2121       10 %
NET INCOME ON INVESTMENTS           $ 857        4 %
```

(b)

NET SURPLUS OR DEFICIT/NET INFLOW   -0.19

THERE WAS A BIT OF IMPROVEMENT THERE, GOOD JOB!!

THERE HAS BEEN A REVOLUTION IN PERU. THE NEW
GOVERNMENT HAS TAKEN OVER ALL OF THE INDUSTRY CONTROLLED
BY FOREIGN INVESTORS. ALSO HARSH RESTRICTIONS HAVE BEEN
IMPOSED ON IMPORTS FROM YOUR COUNTRY.

ENTER YOUR POLICY DECISIONS FOR YEAR   2

(c)

CONGRATULATIONS. YOU HAVE SUCCEEDED IN RESTORING THE
COUNTRY TO A HEALTHY BALANCE OF PAYMENTS POSITION.

TIME: 5.90 SECS.

READY
BYE
Job 19, User [25364,103] Logged off TTY37   1647 15-Jun-79
Saved all files (90 blocks)
Runtime 8.59 sec   148 kcs
Approx. cost $1.02 (day rate)

(d)

Figure 3.2 A student session using a library program.

Again some have been omitted, but in Fig. 3.2(c) we see a printed "encouragement" to the student before the decisions for year 2 are requested. (We should do as much for our national leaders—perhaps we would if they earned it!) Eventually, as shown in Fig. 3.2(d), the program finishes with congratulations to the student. Then the computer reports how much time the program took (in actual work time, not wall-clock time). The user types BYE and the computer acknowledges the termination of the session.

Let us point out two more aspects of the system. First, after the student has typed each command or response, he or she must hit the *carriage return*. This is the signal to the computer that the student has finished entering the input, and the computer should do something with it. Second, there are two modes of attention by the computer; the first is called *monitor mode*, in which the computer types a period at the beginning of a line to show that it has completed a command and is ready for another. The second mode is *BASIC*, in which the computer types READY every time it has completed a BASIC command. The student may be placed in BASIC mode immediately upon LOGging in, depending on how the system and the project number are set up.

Our second example, shown in Fig. 3.3, presents the procedure for typing in as well as running a program. Suppose a student named Norge Guddle is asked to write a program that will compute the energy savings over a three-year period for a business, assuming that a project will save a percentage of the business's heating and that we can expect some inflation in heating costs each year. The total heating bill, the percentage saved, and the inflation rate are all to be furnished as input to the program; thus, the program can be used several times, testing different businesses, projects, or assumptions. Guddle plans his program before he goes to the terminal. The preliminaries of logging in and entering the BASIC subsystem are the same as those shown in Fig. 3.2. The command NEW SAVS tells the system to clear the workspace for a new program that will be named SAVS. Guddle then types in the entire program and the command RUN.

At this point, the BASIC subsystem attempts to translate the program into machine language, but cannot because a closing quotation mark was omitted from line 120. The error message draws Guddle's attention to line 120, and he corrects the line by retyping the entire line. Upon the second RUN command, the revised program is translated into machine language and executed. During execution of the program, the computer asks Guddle for his expected heating bill this year, and Guddle types 40000. Note that there is no comma in the number 40000; a comma would have divided one number from another number: 40,000 is the number 40 followed by another number 0. Guddle responds to two more questions with 40 and 20, and the computer finishes the program by printing the projection of $58,240 as savings over three years. Presumably, if the cost of the energy-saving project in question is under $50,000 or so, Guddle's business will find it worthwhile to undertake the project.

In Chapter 4 we will introduce the structure of programs and programming. Here we want to bring to your attention several aspects of the general process of using a computer. The outline of the process in each session was:

1. Gain access to the computer system, and BASIC.

2. Get a program into your workspace (main storage).

```
.LOG 25364/103
JOB 19 UO DECSYSTEM-10 603A.03 TTY37
Password:
1649     15-Jun-79      Fri

.R BASIC


READY, FOR HELP TYPE HELP.
NEW SAVS

READY
10    REM COMPUTE 3-YEAR SAVINGS ON HEATING BILL
20    REM NORGE GUDDLE     JUNE 1979
100      PRINT "ENTER YOUR EXPECTED HEATING BILL THIS YEAR";
110      INPUT R
120      PRINT "ENTER PROJECTED PERCENTAGE SAVINGS
130      INPUT P
140      PRINT "ENTER EXPECTED INFLATION RATE ON HEATING COSTS";
150      INPUT I
190      LET S = P/100 * R
200      LET S1 = S + I/100 * S
210      LET S2 = S1 + I/100 * S1
220      LET T = S + S1 + S2
300      PRINT "TOTAL 3-YEAR SAVINGS WOULD BE"; T
970   END
RUN

SAVS           16:59          15-JUN-79


? ILLEGAL FORMAT IN LINE 120


TIME:  0.13 SECS.

READY
120      PRINT "ENTER PROJECTED PERCENTAGE SAVINGS";

RUN

SAVS           17:00          15-JUN-79



ENTER YOUR EXPECTED HEATING BILL THIS YEAR ?40000
ENTER PROJECTED PERCENTAGE SAVINGS ?40
ENTER EXPECTED INFLATION RATE ON HEATING COSTS ?20
TOTAL 3-YEAR SAVINGS WOULD BE 58240



TIME:  0.26 SECS.

READY
BYE
Job 19, User [25364,103]  Logged off TTY37     1700   15-Jun-79
Saved all files (90 blocks)
Runtime 2.45 sec    27 kcs
Approx. cost $0.53 (day rate)
```

Figure 3.3 A student session including program entry.

3. Translate the BASIC program into machine language.

4. Run the program.

5. Close down.

In the first session (Fig. 3.2), we put a program into our workspace by the OLD command with a program name, which brought the program from a library. In the second session (Fig. 3.3), Guddle entered the program through the terminal keyboard. What is the program? In each case, the program contains the full direction to the computer on how to acquire data, process data, and print results. At the time the program is being written or entered, there *do not yet exist* any data actually related to the program. Similarly, during the translation phase there still are no data associated with the program. The data are entered only during the *execution* phase, when the program is run. This is a major reason why some people find programming difficult: The programmer must plan for possible configurations of the data without seeing them.

Figure 3.3 showed Guddle's session at a DECsystem-10. Let us now examine Fig. 3.4, which is Guddle's attempt to do the same job on an H-P 3000 system. There are some differences in the commands and the processing, but the outline of the steps is the same in the two systems.

" . . . so you're the one who's trading reci-
pes with the girl at the Dayton office . . ."

```
:HELLO JAN.SHGH
ACCOUNT PASSWORD (PASS)?

HP3000 / MPE III B.00.02.   THU, MAR 22, 1979,   1:39 PM
:BASIC

HP32101B.00.10(4WD)  BASIC  (C)HEWLETT-PACKARD CO 1978
>10   REM COMPUTE 3-YEAR SAVINGS ON HEATING BILL
>20   REM NORGE GUDDLE    MAR 1979
>100     PRINT "ENTER YOUR EXPECTED HEATING BILL THIS YEAR";
>110     INPUT B
>120     PRINT "ENTERPROJECTED PERCENTAGE SAVINGS
ERROR@43
>120     PRINT "ENTER PROJECTED PERCENTAGE SAVINGS";
>130     INPUT P
>140     PRINT "ENTER EXPECTED INFLATION RATE ON HEATING COSTS";
>150     INPUT R
>190     LET S = P/100 * B
>200     LET S1 = S + R/100 * S1
>210     LET S2 = S1 + R/100 * S1
>220     LET T = S + S1 + S2
>300     PRINT "TOTAL 3-YEAR SAVINGS WOULD BE"; T
>970     END
>RUN
ENTER YOUR EXPECTED HEATING BILL THIS YEAR?40000
ENTER PROJECTED PERCENTAGE SAVINGS?40
ENTER EXPECTED INFLATION RATE ON HEATING COSTS?20

UNDEFINED VALUE IN LINE 200
>200     LET S1 = S + R/100 * S
>RUN
ENTER YOUR EXPECTED HEATING BILL THIS YEAR?40000
ENTER PROJECTED PERCENTAGE SAVINGS?40
ENTER EXPECTED INFLATION RATE ON HEATING COSTS?20
TOTAL 3-YEAR SAVINGS WOULD BE 58240
:EXIT

END OF SUBSYSTEM
:BYE

CPU=3. CONNECT=21. THU, MAR 22, 1979,   1:59 PM
```

Figure 3.4 A student session on the HP-3000.

1. We ask for attention with HELLO rather than LOG.

2. We enter the BASIC subsystem by typing BASIC rather than R BASIC.

3. While in the BASIC subsystem, the computer supplies the character > at the beginning of each line. The DECsystem-10 provides no prompt character when in BASIC, but a period when in monitor mode, while the H-P 3000 uses a colon in monitor mode.

4. In the H-P 3000, one usually gives a name to a program only when saving it in a file for later retrieval.

5. In the H-P 3000, a syntactic or grammatical error is caught immediately after the offending statement is typed. The quote mark omitted in line 120 of Fig. 3.3 is thus reported and corrected before Guddle goes on to another statement.

6. Logical errors, on the other hand, cannot be recognized until encountered during program execution. The second S1 in line 200 of Fig. 3.4 is an example; the statement is perfectly valid until we try to execute it without giving S1 a value first. The error must be corrected by retyping the statement correctly and executing the program from the beginning again. The same would be true on the DECsystem-10 and other computers as well.

7. On the H-P 3000, we log off by first leaving the BASIC subsystem with EXIT, and then signing off with BYE.

Let us review the functions represented by the example student sessions. The particular commands used on different computer systems vary, but the functions performed are the same.

1. Gain access to the computer: LOG or HELLO, with account, project, group, or programmer identification as specified locally.

2. Gain access to the BASIC subsystem: R BASIC or BASIC.

3. Get a program into your workspace: OLD programname in the DECsystem-10 for an existing program. The corresponding command in the H-P 3000 is GET programname (we would use that if trying to duplicate Fig. 3.2 on the H-P 3000). To enter a new program, merely type it in, a line at a time. On the DECsystem-10 we recommend the NEW command first, to clear out a previous program and give a name to the new program.

4. Translate and run the program: RUN in both machines.

5. Close down: BYE or EXIT and BYE.

On other systems the commands may be still different, but they will be similar to these, and the differences we see between the DECsystem-10 and the H-P 3000 are representative of the differences we may expect when moving to other systems.

3.3 BUSINESS DATA PROCESSING AT A TERMINAL

When a program is prepared for a business data processing function that is repeated regularly, we arrange the input of data from a terminal to be as easy, fast, and accurate as possible. A CRT (video) screen terminal is the usual medium for such applications, since it is quiet, flexible in its use, and not subject to frequent mechanical failures, and it permits a high transmission and display speed. It does not generate paper documents when not needed, which is an advantage to businesses (and to trees!). To make input easier and more accurate, a program can control the layout of data on the screen. Figure 3.5 shows a screen formatted for input of catalog sales orders. A form that is similar to the order form submitted by the customer is laid out on the screen. The *cursor* on any CRT screen is set to the location on the screen at which the next input or output will appear; in Fig. 3.5 it shows as a white rectangle at the beginning of a line for a second item ordered. The program controls the cursor movement so that when the program is ready for input of the customer name, the input will be in the SOLD TO box at the upper left of the screen. Similarly, when the program is ready for input of items ordered, the cursor will move from one field to the next with a line for each item.

Figure 3.5 Terminal screen for catalog sales entry. (Courtesy Texas Instruments, Inc.)

The consistency of the format of data on the screen helps the clerk to input data correctly. Many CRT terminals are able to control the cursor in a screen format like the one shown in Fig. 3.5; various terminals have other additional features. The TI 770 terminal shown, more complex than most terminals, includes a printer mechanism for essential data, and two magnetic tape cartridge units.

A CRT screen need not be used under strict control of a formatted screen, though business data processing applications use that feature whenever possible. The students' terminal sessions shown in Figs. 3.2, 3.3, and 3.4 could also have been done on CRT terminals. Most screens show 24 lines. When 24 lines have been displayed, the screen *scrolls:* The contents of each line move up a line, while the top line is lost, which leaves the bottom line ready for the next input or output. The effect is the same as if we held a 24-line window to a teletype transcript. Exactly the same interaction would occur, and each line on the screen would show exactly what a line of teletype output showed.

3.4. FILES AND LIBRARIES

Every user in a time-sharing system has the privilege of keeping data on disk; we call the disk space on which each user keeps files the user's *file space.* We will discuss data files in Chapter 6, but in this section we will show the use of files to hold programs. If Guddle, in the session shown in Fig. 3.3, had wished to use his program again on another day, he could have saved a copy in his file space by giving the command

    SAVE

The command could have been given at any time when the program was complete in his workspace—either before or after he ran the program. The computer would have stored a copy of his program in Guddle's file space, under the name SAVS, since that was the name Guddle gave the workspace contents. Then in another terminal session Guddle could have brought his program back into his workspace by executing the command

    OLD SAVS

Thus, to use the program, Guddle need not think through the construction of the program again nor even type in the program. Programming is enough work so that we are indeed happy to write a program once, test it until we are sure it works correctly, and then save the program for regular use. Business data processing systems get consistent, auditable results, and the repeated use of well-developed programs is a routine in which we can have confidence.

Not only is there a file space for each user, but there are also *libraries*, which hold programs that are purposely made available to many users. The user in Fig. 3.2 called the program BALPAY from a library named CS1. Libraries of programs expand the usefulness of computers considerably; such complex tasks as the more advanced statistical analysis techniques should be written into programs only once, and then made available to anyone who has access to that computer.

3.5 THE OPERATING SYSTEM

How does the computer know what to do when we sit down at a terminal and type LOG? How does it understand such a command as OLD CS1: BALPAY? Every computer has an *operating system*, an integrated set of programs that controls all processing done by the computer. The operating system, or at least part of it, remains in the computer's main storage at all times; it is sometimes called a *monitor*, and in some computers it is divided into components called the *supervisor* and the *job scheduler*. We will discuss four main functions of an operating system, to give you a clearer idea of how you accomplish tasks through your interactions with the computer and the operating system.

One function of the operating system is the management of disk space and accesses to disk storage. The operating system maintains a directory, which records at all times:

- A list of the identifications of the authorized users

- Names of the files stored on disk for each user

- Location of each file for each user

- The disk space that is currently unused and available for new files

When a user asks for retrieval of a file through the OLD command, the operating system searches the user's file directory for the file named and, if the file exists, the directory will give its location. Then the operating system will get the file at that location and load it into the user's workspace. When a user asks to SAVE a program, the operating system finds some unused space, stores the program in that space, creates an entry in the user's file directory so the file can be found again, and removes the space used from the list of available space. Essentially the same operations are carried out on data files, as we shall see in Chapters 6 and 9.

A second function is job management. The operating system must recognize when a user wants to activate a job (with the LOG command)

and check the directory of authorized users. When the operating system validates the user, it must allocate needed resources to the user. The first resource allocated is workspace, the user's portion of the computer's main storage. If the user needs other resources, such as a magnetic tape drive, the operating system will recognize a request and allocate a tape drive if one is available. The operating system must protect that tape drive on behalf of that user, so no other users have access to it until the first user releases it or logs off. The operating system responds to all commands, either at monitor level or within the BASIC subsystem. Think of the BASIC subsystem as a subsidiary portion of the operating system; it performs essentially the same functions as the rest of the operating system, but with a simpler and somewhat more restricted set of commands. Among the responses to commands must be refusal: The operating system should respond to an unrecognizable command, while encouraging the user to try again. Occasionally the system must tell the user that the command is recognized but cannot be carried out, if, for example,

- The user's time limit for the session is exceeded;

- The user's quota of disk space has been exceeded;

- The user has asked for a file that he or she should not have access to;

- The user asks for allocation of an unavailable device.

In such instances, the operating system should politely give the reason for not carrying out the command, and remain receptive to a valid command.

A third function is to run programs for users. BASIC programs must be translated into machine language; the operating system must activate the right translator, and if the program is translated without errors, it runs the program for the user. Under operating system control, the user's program accepts data, does computations, and reports results. The operating system exercises control over input and output, and over the time made available for executing instructions. All of a program's input and output are done by requesting action from the operating system; the operating system checks the availability of the device or the disk space requested, and then itself executes the input or output instructions.

This brings us to the fourth function of an operating system, which is to manage the sharing of computer time among users. There may be 32 or so users, all sitting at terminals, each asking for computer service. The objective of the operating system is to provide the appropriate service for each, protecting each user against actions of the others, and giving each user timely response (which sounds almost like the preamble to the United States Constitution!). This is possible partly because each user spends most of the session looking at the computer's response to one input, and thinking about and then typing the next input. During only a small fraction of the time must the computer really be active for any one user. So there is time available for the computer to serve all its users. The operating system manages the computer's time by cycling through all users to see who is waiting for computer action. Each such user receives a *time slice*, often set at 0.1 second; action on most users' requests is completed well within the assigned time slice. If a particular action takes more than a time slice, it is suspended until that user's turn comes again. Usually, a cycle through all users will uncover three or four who have actions pending, and all but one will be completed within the time slice. The result of cycling through users is that each user gets responses quickly enough to feel that the entire computer is at his or her disposal.

3.6 MAIN IDEAS

a. In a batch processing system, data are gathered—usually punched into cards—and fed to the computer with control cards. After waiting in a job queue, the program that processes the data is run and the results printed.

b. In an interactive student session, the student types commands and data at a terminal and gets immediate validation from the computer. If an input is invalid, the computer reports an error message and provides the opportunity for correct input.

c. The minimal steps in an interactive student session are:
  1. Log on to the computer and enter the BASIC subsystem;
  2. Type in a program or call a program from a library or the student's file space;
  3. Translate the program into machine language;
  4. Run the program, including entry of data;
  5. Log off.

d. An interactive program for a business function usually uses a formatted CRT screen; program control over the cursor permits each kind of input to be always in the same location on the screen. This makes data entry easier and more accurate.

e. Programs may be kept on disk, in each user's own file space or in libraries. The SAVE command in BASIC stores a program in the file space; the OLD command brings one back into the user's workspace.

f. An operating system, always resident in a computer's main storage, controls the computer's operation. Among the operating system's functions are management of disk space and access to it, recognition and validation of users, resource allocation, response to commands, translating and running programs, and providing computer time slices to all active users in turn.

3.7 QUESTIONS FOR IMAGINATION AND REVIEW

1. Batch processing systems as well as time-sharing systems have operating systems. In contrast to a time-sharing operating system, what do you see as the functions performed by a batch processing operating system?

2. Try to run a library program, and type in and run the program in Fig. 3.3 on the system to which you have access.

3. In some systems it is most convenient for an entire class of students to use one file space. Since in any file space there can be only one file with any particular name, what mechanisms, procedures, or conventions would you set up so students' files do not get in each other's way?

4. In some systems a BASIC program is *compiled*, that is, translated into machine language before execution of the program begins. In other systems, BASIC programs are *interpreted: Each statement* is translated essentially into machine language just before it is executed. Try to list some advantages of each approach.

5. Above all, an operating system must retain control over its computer, so that no disaster to one user can affect other users. Think of some of the actions and errors a user could make that would make it difficult for the operating system to maintain the integrity of itself and other users. How could an operating system deal with these situations?

CHAPTER 4
PROCEDURES AND THE STRUCTURE OF PROGRAMS

It is often difficult to think through the overall logic of a computer program and write a syntactically correct program to implement that logic at the same time. The difficulty may be especially great for beginning programmers, but it is a problem for experienced programmers, too. One problem is that the thought process of defining a solution to a problem starts with an overall general strategy that is refined as we work out the details of components of this strategy; writing a program, at least in BASIC, does not follow a top-down solution process.

Therefore, we break the programming process into two parts. The first is definition of a procedure, in a somewhat informal procedure language we will develop, which expresses the logic of a solution to the problem at hand. The second part is transcription of that procedure into BASIC. In this chapter we develop a language for expressing procedures that can be transcribed neatly into programs, and discuss the logical process of building procedures in that language. We also introduce program flowcharts as an alternate mode of expressing procedures, and begin the development of structures for the flow of control in procedures or programs with the WHILE structure, the most common structure for specifying loops.

4.1 WHAT IS A PROCEDURE?

If I have a task to be accomplished or a problem to be solved, I either do it myself or have someone (or something) else do it. If I do not do the entire job myself, I must provide that person (or thing) with a *procedure* to follow. We can define a procedure as:

> A finite set of steps or instructions that can be mechanically interpreted and carried out by some agent.

We are accustomed to giving each other procedures and following procedures that others give us. A recipe for making lasagna is a procedure. The directions on how to get from here to the post office are a procedure. The instructions for filling out income tax forms are a procedure. When we give procedures to each other, we are happy not to have to give such precise directions that they can *really* be carried out mechanically. When we receive directions too, we do not require that level of detail, and we are willing to use some intelligence not only to fill in little gaps but to solve little problems on the way. If we are told to go down this street for three blocks but find it closed at one spot for some reason, we are willing to make a minor detour with confidence that we can still reach the destination.

When we tell a piece of machinery to follow a procedure, the steps of the procedure are usually built into the machinery. A toaster burns a slice of bread by following the procedure built in and set in the darkness lever. A washing machine follows a fairly complex procedure of filling, tumbling, spinning, and draining; the procedure is defined by the timer. But when I drive my car to the computer store, I specify a procedure to the car by my actions on the clutch, brake pedal, steering wheel, and so on; the car follows the procedure mechanically.

A data processing procedure includes the steps of gathering and preparing data, input of the data to the computer to be processed by certain programs, validation of the input, uses of the output from the computer, retention of tape files, and so forth. Within that, each computer program is a procedure.

Every procedure is expressed in some language. We use English and a generous portion of arm waving to express the procedure for getting to the post office. Machines use electrical and mechanical impulses through switches, levers, buttons, or valves. The procedure in a computer program is expressed in BASIC, or COBOL, or machine language, or some other similar language. Because the procedure is to be carried out by machine, it must be quite precise. The procedure must also specify actions to be taken in all possible eventualities.

Since the capabilities of a computer are

- input,
- output,
- moving data within main storage,
- arithmetic, and
- decisions that determine which further actions to take,

any language for expressing a procedure for a computer to follow must be able to specify these actions. In Chapter 2, we saw how machine language instructions perform all these actions, and in Chapter 5, we will show how each of these actions is expressed in BASIC. In this chapter, we will use a less formal language for specifying a computer's actions. We will develop procedures in a subset of English; the elements we choose to include in this subset must meet several criteria:

1. They must permit description of the actions a computer can take;
2. They must be natural enough to use that they do not interfere with our mental processes of thinking through what we want a computer to do;
3. They must enforce some precision in our thinking;
4. They must be capable of being translated fairly easily into BASIC or other computer languages;
5. They must *help* in construction of logical program structures that will *correctly* do what we want.

There are several advantages of using an English-like procedure language for developing procedures to be translated later into computer languages. One is that separation of thinking through the logic of the solution and writing correct machine language instructions or BASIC statements can make both easier. A second reason is that when you move to a different computer and a different computer language, you will be able to use the same procedure language in thinking through programs and need only learn how to transcribe your procedures into the new language. The third and perhaps most important reason is that we can introduce language elements for expressing the control structure (flow of control) of a procedure that accomplishes what is called *structured programming*. These language elements facilitate, express, and even enforce clear logical thought. Computer scientists generally agree that these structured programming language elements are better for this purpose than the conditional and unconditional branches of machine language or the similar branches to line numbers that we will use in BASIC.

4.2 DECOMPOSITION OF PROCEDURES INTO COMPONENTS

One of the most useful techniques in solving problems is to decompose the problem into its component parts. Then we can concentrate on each of the components in turn. In specifying solutions to problems, it helps similarly to separate a solution into several parts, and develop or refine each of the parts. If I have a problem, "Somebody spilled a quart of ice cream on my rug," I can state a solution:

"Get the rug cleaned."

This may not be as simple as it sounds, and I may refine the solution by decomposing it into steps:

1. Get some good steaks to lure Chris over to help,

2. Get Chris to help move all the furniture off the rug,

3. Get Chris to help roll up the rug,

4. Wheedle Pat into taking the rug to the shop in Pat's van,

with similar steps taken to return the rug to its place.

One of the advantages of using a procedure language is that we can express large pieces of a program in very general terms in a procedure, then successfully break down the pieces into smaller, more specific pieces until we reach the level of detail that can be directly transcribed into a computer language. Thus the procedure becomes an aid in the problem-solving process, not just an expression of the solution.

Let us illustrate with a very simple data processing example. Our living room needs to be painted (did the ice cream splatter and stain the walls too?), and we have to buy the paint. Our data processing system can help by following the procedure,

"Find the amount of paint required to paint the room."

The procedure we want the computer to follow can be broken down into four steps:

1. Obtain length, width, height.

2. Compute wall and ceiling area.

3. Divide area by 750 ft²/gallon coverage factor, to get number of gallons.

4. Print the number of gallons required.

The first two steps can be decomposed further, giving us the more detailed procedure shown in Fig. 4.1.

What language elements did we use in the procedure? In the most detailed form, there were the following:

- Obtain some data (from the user at the terminal)

- Compute something (or specify add, subtract, multiply, divide)

- Print something

These are elements that we know can be transcribed into any computer language. They are explicit and precise enough to give us confidence that no significant ambiguities remain, and the procedure is a clear expression of what we want the computer to do.

---

1. Obtain length, width, height:
   1.1 Obtain length
   1.2 Obtain width
   1.3 Obtain height

2. Compute wall and ceiling area:
   2.1 Compute perimeter = 2 × length + 2 × width
   2.2 Compute wall area = perimeter × height
   2.3 Compute ceiling area = length × width
   2.4 Compute total area = wall area + ceiling area

3. Divide total area by 750 ft²/gallon, to get number of gallons

4. Print the number of gallons required

Figure 4.1 Procedure to find amount of paint.

4.3 SIMPLE LOOPS: WHILE

Of the several logical structures of parts of procedures, the simplest is the direct linear sequence: Step 2 follows Step 1. The next simplest, and one of the most important, is a simple loop of repetitions of a step. A loop with no exit is not a valid or useful structure, so we insist on some condition for continuing the repetitions. The structure then is

"So long as *condition x* remains true, keep on doing *action y*."

We will specify this structure in our procedure language using less verbiage, and the key word WHILE:

> WHILE *condition x*
> > *action y*

We indent *action y* to make it clear that it is subordinate to and controlled by the WHILE clause. Of course, *action y* may be broken into a series of more elementary actions.

Let us take an example: I am borrowing some money from a bank, and I will repay the loan in monthly installments. Interest is charged each month on only the unpaid balance of the loan. I wonder how long it will take me to pay off the loan, but the bank would like its computer to show me more than that: for each month, it should print the amount of the loan still due, the amount of interest, and the portion of my payment that reduces the amount owed. The bank's computer could follow a procedure:

1. Obtain loan amount, annual interest rate, and monthly payment.

2. Compute monthly interest rate = annual rate/12.

3. Compute and print the table of interest, reduction of principal, and new balance for each month.

Step 1 of the procedure could be decomposed, as we did the procedure in the last section; if the step is clear enough as written, we may not need to decompose it. Step 2 is quite explicit. Step 3 needs more development; we are not sure yet just how a computer should program Step 3 as stated. Obviously something is to be repeated, and we must specify those actions. We must also figure out what condition should control continuation of the repetitions. This is not too difficult: The computer should continue to forecast what will happen, month after month, until the loan is paid off. That is an obvious time to quit. So we can refine Step 3 of the procedure:

3. WHILE loan amount > 0,
   > 3.1 Compute interest for the month = loan amount × monthly interest rate
   > 3.2 Compute loan reduction = monthly payment − interest for the month
   > 3.3 Print loan amount, interest for the month, and loan reduction
   > 3.4 Compute loan amount = loan amount − loan reduction

We have invoked the WHILE construction, and at the same time broken the action to be repeated into four elementary steps.

Let us be certain that we understand precisely what the procedure does. Steps 3.1 through 3.4 are executed in sequence, then executed again, and again . . . . But before Step 3.1 is begun each time, the current value of the loan amount is compared with zero. So long as the amount is greater than zero, Steps 3.1 through 3.4 will be repeated again. As soon as the loan amount reaches zero or falls below zero, the condition of the WHILE no longer holds and repetition of Steps 3.1 through 3.4 ceases. Execution of the procedure would then continue to Step 4 of the procedure if there were a Step 4.

Suppose we want the headings "loan amount," "interest," and "loan reduction" printed over the columns on the report. A step should be added to the procedure. Where should it be added? Certainly not *inside* the loop, since that would cause the headings to be printed again before each output line. The column headings should also not be printed as Step 1, before obtaining the loan amount, and so forth. The headings should be printed just before entry to the loop, in a new Step 3 of the procedure, so the WHILE loop will become Step 4, as shown in Fig. 4.2.

The procedure as given does not represent a very good program. There is no test for the reasonableness of the input; this can be a problem if the program expects a 9% interest rate to be typed in as .09, but the user misunderstands and enters it as 9.0! This is more serious than the possibility of getting the wrong answers; a misunderstanding like this can prevent the WHILE condition from ever becoming false, so we have a potentially unending procedure. Second, there is no recognition that the last payment may be less than the full regular payment. Third, the procedure does not tell me what I originally wanted to know: How long will it take me to pay off the loan? I can find out by counting the lines printed, but the procedure could do better for me than that. We will work out some improvements to the procedure in Section 4.5.

We finish this section by emphasizing a requirement on the actions to be taken inside the WHILE loop. The actions *must* affect the WHILE condition so that eventually the condition becomes false and terminates

---

1. Obtain loan amount, annual interest rate, and monthly payment
2. Compute monthly interest rate = annual rate/12
3. Print column headings "loan amount", "interest", and "loan reduction"
4. WHILE loan amount > 0,
   4.1 Compute interest for the month = loan amount × monthly interest rate
   4.2 Compute loan reduction = monthly payment − interest for the month
   4.3 Print loan amount, interest for the month, and loan reduction
   4.4 Compute loan amount = loan amount − loan reduction

Figure 4.2 Procedure for loan payoff schedule.

execution of the loop. Our example in Fig. 4.2 accomplishes this in Step 4.4, where the loan amount is reduced (at least, it is reduced if the monthly payment is large enough).

4.4 PROGRAM FLOWCHARTS

The form of procedures, using prose and an outline format, is quite useful in helping us develop procedures to be followed by a computer program

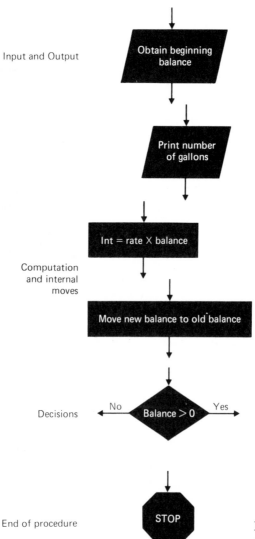

Input and Output

Computation and internal moves

Decisions

End of procedure

Figure 4.3 Program flowchart conventions.

and to document or explain those procedures. Sometimes a graphical form of a procedure is even better, especially in showing explicitly the flow of control. *Program flowcharts*, sometimes called *flow diagrams*, show all the actions in a procedure, but emphasize the flow of control. Because we will use program flowcharts as tools to illustrate flow-of-control structures and some common procedure outlines, we introduce them here.

Conventions followed in program flowcharts are shown in Fig. 4.3. Input and output actions are shown in trapezoids, and computations or internal movements of data are shown in rectangles. Flow of control is represented by arrows; any line connecting two actions must show its direction, so the reader can easily recognize which action follows which. Decisions are represented by diamonds, within which a question is generally shown. The question asks whether a given condition holds; the condition is the one that controls the decision. *Two* lines showing flow of control leave a decision box, representing the choice of paths that are to be followed depending on the given condition. The paths must be labeled so the reader can tell which outcome of the decision follows which path. Only one path *leaves* an input/output or computation box, though several may enter one. We use an ordinary-looking STOP sign to represent the end of a procedure. As a matter of general orderliness, we try to keep the major flow of control going from left to right and from top to bottom.

Figure 4.4 shows a flowchart of a WHILE structure. The flowchart helps make clear the sequence of tests and actions, and, in particular, the fact that if the *condition* is false on the first test, the *action* is not executed even once.

Figure 4.5 is a flowchart representation of the procedure shown in Fig. 4.2 for projecting loan repayments. The content of the flowchart is

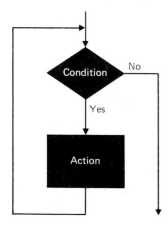

Figure 4.4 Flowchart of a WHILE structure.

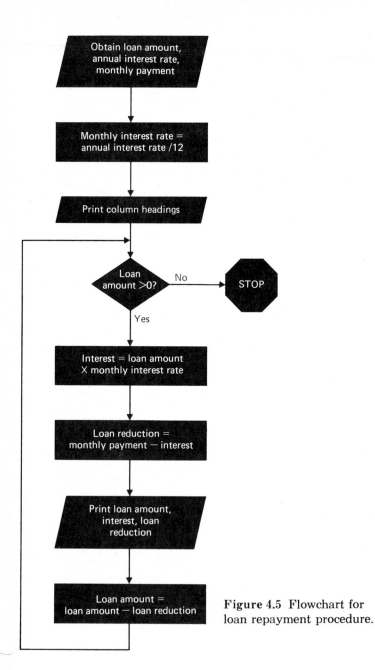

Figure 4.5 Flowchart for loan repayment procedure.

really the same as the procedure; only the form is different. We will use flowcharts from time to time, especially to introduce or illustrate control structures.

Flowcharts have long been used as a tool in planning programs. They have also been used as part of the documentation of finished programs. These are two very different but compatible uses. Recently the industry has been shifting from the use of flowcharts, especially for program planning, and emphasizing instead procedures such as those we introduce in this chapter, written in some *pseudocode*. The procedure elements we have introduced are an example of pseudocode. Among the most important reasons for shifting from flowcharts to pseudocode procedures are that the pseudocode procedures lend themselves more readily to procedure decomposition, also called *top-down programming*, and that pseudocode procedures enforce a program structure that makes the program easier to write correctly, to debug, to understand, and to maintain.

4.5 IF-THEN-ELSE AND IF-THEN STRUCTURES

Suppose we are working on part of a payroll system. Once weekly pay for an employee is calculated, our program must compute the federal income tax that should be withheld. Suppose the formula for tax withheld is

14% of (pay − exemptions × $15).

For example, an employee whose weekly pay is $260 and who has four exemptions should have

14% of (260 − 4 × 15) = $28

withheld from his or her take-home pay. Simple enough? But now suppose that same employee earns only $50 the following week. By the formula, the amount withheld is $−1.40. A negative amount withheld would have to mean that the Internal Revenue Service is giving the employee $1.40 this week, and we do not believe the IRS operates that way! So the rule is not so simple as a single formula. We could say

tax withheld = 0.14 × (pay − exemptions × 15) if
    pay > exemptions × 15,

but we must complete the statement by stating that

tax withheld = 0   if pay ≤ exemptions × 15.

We can put this in a clear logical framework that will help us remember to state both rules explicitly.

IF pay > exemptions × 15
   THEN tax withheld = 0.14 × (pay − exemptions × 15)
   ELSE tax withheld = 0

The IF-THEN-ELSE structure represents alternative actions. *One* will be performed; which action is to be performed will be determined by the test of the IF condition.

For another example, let us return to our loan repayment calculation in Section 4.3. What is the condition that the loan can eventually be repaid? The condition is that repayment can begin, which is to say that the monthly payment exceeds the first month's interest. If this condition holds, some amount will be paid toward the principal, and interest in later months will be lower. We can state the test for this condition as:

IF monthly payment > first month's interest
   THEN produce loan pay-off schedule
   ELSE print "MONTHLY PAYMENT IS INSUFFICIENT"

As in the withholding tax example, one of two actions is to be performed; which one is determined by the outcome of the comparison between monthly payment and the first month's interest. Later we will incorporate this test into the procedure in Fig. 4.2.

In other situations, there is only one action in question, and the choice is *whether or not* to perform that action. Suppose we have quantity ordered and unit price of an item ordered, and that the company's policy is to add a shipping charge of 50 cents if the total ordered is under $15.00. Therefore one of the actions is

Add 50¢ to the total due

The action is performed only if the total ordered (quantity ordered × unit price) is less than $15.00:

IF total ordered < 15
   THEN add .50 to total ordered

This is *not* an IF-THEN-ELSE structure, since there is no alternative action to be taken if the total ordered is greater than or equal to 15. In context, we could have

1. Obtain quantity ordered, unit price
2. Compute total ordered = quantity ordered × unit price
3. IF total ordered < 15
   THEN add .50 to total ordered
4. Print total ordered

The IF-THEN-ELSE and IF-THEN structures are shown in Fig. 4.6 in flowchart form. In each, we see how control passes through a test to an

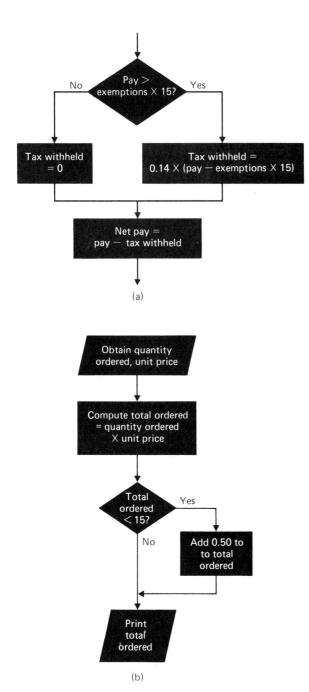

(a)

(b)

Figure 4.6 (a) IF-THEN-ELSE structure.
(b) IF-THEN structure.

---

1. Obtain loan amount, annual interest rate, and monthly payment
2. Compute monthly interest rate = annual rate/12
3. IF monthly payment > monthly interest rate × loan amount
   THEN 3.1 Print column headings "loan amount", "interest", "payment", "loan reduction"
        3.2 WHILE loan amount > 0,
           3.2.1 Compute month's interest = loan amount × monthly interest rate
           3.2.2 IF monthly payment > loan amount + month's interest
               THEN monthly payment = loan amount + month's interest
           3.2.3 Compute loan reduction = monthly payment − month's interest
           3.2.4 Print loan amount, month's interest, monthly payment, loan reduction
           3.2.5 Compute loan amount = loan amount − loan reduction
   ELSE 3.3 Print "insufficient monthly payment"

Figure 4.7 Revised loan payoff schedule procedure.

action controlled by the test, and then to a step beyond the IF-THEN-ELSE or IF-THEN structure.

Let us return to the loan repayment schedule for another example of an IF-THEN structure. Suppose the loan carries interest at 9%, and monthly payments are $50.00. When the loan is almost paid, we may enter the last month with a balance of $20.00. Interest for this month is $0.15, so a full $50.00 payment is not required. The computations should adjust the last payment. This is expressed as an IF-THEN structure:

IF monthly payment > balance + month's interest
   THEN set monthly payment = balance + month's interest

The action to reduce the monthly payment will not be performed when the regular payment is less than the balance plus the month's interest. Figure 4.7 shows how this feature and the test for sufficient monthly payment modify the procedure in Fig. 4.2. Note that the actions of the THEN clause in Step 3 consist of Steps 3.1 and 3.2, down to and including Step 3.2.5. The ELSE clause is the single Step 3.3. The WHILE clause of Step 3.2 consists of Steps 3.2.1 through 3.2.5; Step 3.2.2 is an IF-THEN structure; its THEN clause could be numbered 3.2.2.1 if we wish. The IF test in Step 3.2.2 will be performed every time flow of control passes through the loop (Steps 3.2.1 through 3.2.5), but if we have constructed our procedure correctly, the subsidiary THEN clause will be performed only once.

4.6 MAIN IDEAS

a. A procedure is a finite set of steps or instructions that can be mechanically interpreted and carried out by some agent. The computer is an agent; we specify procedures that can be transcribed into programs that can be carried out by a computer.

b. Use of a procedure language or program flowcharts helps us plan the logic and especially the flow of control in a procedure to be carried out by a computer.

c. A procedure can be expressed in large steps, each of which is refined into more detailed steps; this, too, is a technique helpful in the logical planning process.

d. One simple kind of loop is the WHILE structure:

WHILE condition
   perform an action

e. The IF-THEN-ELSE structure provides a decision between performing two alternative actions. The IF-THEN structure is related, but exercises a choice of whether or not to perform a single action.

4.7 QUESTIONS FOR IMAGINATION AND REVIEW

1. Write a procedure that will help a fare collector on a ferry. The collector should enter the number of people (driver included) in a car; the fare is $2.00 for the car and driver, and 50¢ for each additional person. The sales tax of 6% should be added to the total, and the result printed so the collector will know what fare to collect.

2. Write a procedure that will accept the initial amount of a certificate of deposit, and will print the amount at maturity, given 7% annual interest compounded quarterly for three years.

3. A marketing development man wants a program into which he can feed information on the current population of an area, the annual percentage growth, and a target population. The program should then report the number of years it will take for the area to reach the target population. Write a procedure for this problem, and then transcribe the procedure into flowchart form. (This problem becomes much easier when we learn about *functions* in Chapter 12.)

4. The procedure in Fig. 4.2 or Fig. 4.7 is meant to be used as a projection at the time the loan is initiated. Think about what kind of system would be necessary for the bank to keep track of all of its current loans, crediting payments when they are made and charging interest monthly.

5. Trace the actions followed by the procedure in Fig. 4.7 if the loan amount, annual interest rate, and monthly payment supplied are 1000,

0.09, and 6, respectively. Repeat the procedure if the quantities are 1000, 0.09, and 230.

6. Transcribe the procedure in Fig. 4.7 into flowchart form.

7. Modify the procedure in Fig. 4.7 so it will print at the end of the loan repayment schedule the number of months required for full repayment.

8. Show that the procedure shown by the flowchart in Fig. 4.6(a) can be restated as:

1. tax withheld $= 0$
2. IF pay $>$ exemptions $\times$ 15
   THEN tax withheld $= 0.14 \times$ (pay $-$ exemptions $\times$ 15)
3. net pay $=$ pay $-$ tax withheld

What general statements can you make about conversions from IF-THEN-ELSE structures to IF-THEN structures and vice versa?

9. Write a procedure that will obtain an exam score and print

P if the score $\geqslant$ 70,

N if the score $<$ 70.

10. Modify the procedure of Question 9 to print

H if the score $\geqslant$ 90,

P if 90 $>$ the score $\geqslant$ 70,

N if 70 $>$ the score.

This can be done by two IF-THEN-ELSE structures; the test comparing the score with 70 can be in the THEN or ELSE clause of the IF-THEN-ELSE that compares the score with 90.

11. A sales agent on salary and commission gets a salary of $1200 per month plus a 5% commission on all sales above $20,000. Write a procedure that will obtain the agent's sales for the month, and compute and print the total compensation (salary + commission).

CHAPTER 5

TRANSCRIBING PROCEDURES INTO BASIC PROGRAMS

The development of operating systems for computers in the late 1950s and early 1960s made time-sharing systems possible, and several were developed. By far the most successful early time-sharing system was that developed at Dartmouth College in the early to mid-1960s, mostly by Thomas E. Kurtz under the direction of John G. Kemeny. Their system was built around the BASIC language, which we will be using.

The initials BASIC stand for

Beginner's All-purpose Symbolic Instruction Code.

BASIC systems and several other time-sharing systems are designed primarily for *problem solving*. The emphasis is on ease of writing, entering, and running programs, and while some systems are good for engineering and other advanced computations, BASIC is especially good for beginning students.

BASIC is a relatively simple language for a computer to translate into machine language. For this reason, BASIC was the first language implemented on a number of minicomputers. As minicomputers became more heavily used for business data processing, BASIC was a common language used in business data processing systems on the computers. Often new versions of BASIC were developed with features especially good for business data processing.

In this chapter we introduce the elements of the BASIC language, and show how we can transcribe procedures fairly easily and mechanically into BASIC. With these elements, you will be able to write and run programs that do real tasks. The concepts and naming of variables, the use of line numbers in editing programs and in managing the flow of control, and the construction of arithmetic expressions are topics fundamental to the BASIC language, and a number of other programming languages for that matter. We describe the syntax and function of LET, REM, INPUT, PRINT, GO TO, IF, and END statements, and show how we implement procedure structures using these statements. This chapter ends with a review of commands to the BASIC subsystem and the introduction of new ones.

5.1 THE FORMAT OF A BASIC PROGRAM

A BASIC program consists of a series of *statements*. There is one statement per line on a program listing, and each statement has a *line number*
at the beginning of the line. The line numbers of the statements are up
to five digits long, and are in ascending sequence. Two lines cannot have
the same line number; you will see why when we discuss editing a program.

Every statement begins with a *keyword* after the line number, which
tells the translator immediately what kind of statement is to be translated. The program in Fig. 3.3 shows line numbers from 10 to 970, and
the various statements have keywords REM, PRINT, INPUT, LET,
and END. Other programs include statements with keywords DIM,
FILES, IF, and GO TO, among others.

Every program must end with an END statement; this means the
END statement must have a line number greater than any other line
number in the program. To make sure of this, we recommend the con-
sistent use of a high line number for END; 970 END costs no more than
310 END, and leaves us generally one less thing to remember to watch.
If you use four-digit line numbers, you may use something like 9970
END. Execution of the program stops when flow of control reaches the
END statement.

Most statements are called *executable:* They are translated into
machine language instructions that are executed as the program is run.
LET, PRINT, and INPUT statements are executable; they cause particular actions whenever they are executed. For the sake of simplicity,
we will talk about executing a BASIC statement, but it should be understood that this is merely a short form of talking about executing the
machine language instructions that are translated from the BASIC statement. Some other statements affect the translation process; END is one
of these statements.

The REM statement is still different: REM is short for REMARK,
and REM statements have no effect on translation or execution of a program. They are included in programs as documentation only. We recommend that each program begin with at least two REM statements; the
first gives a title or short description of the purpose of the program, while
the second identifies the programmer and the date on which the program
was written. In more complex programs, we include other REM statements to help explain the structure and operation of the program. You
will note that in Fig. 3.3 all statements except the REM and END statements are indented. Spacing of this sort has no effect on translation or
execution of the statements; the indentation is helpful in distinguishing
REM statements from others at a glance.

5.2 VARIABLES

Any quantities to be used during execution of a program that are changed during execution, or are input by the program from a terminal or from disk, are *variables*. The number of hours worked by an employee during a week is a variable in a program in a payroll system; when each employee is considered by the program, that employee's number of hours worked will be input to the computer, and will *replace in main storage* the previous number of hours worked. One location in main storage—a word or a group of bytes—is set aside to hold the number of hours worked for each employee in turn. The location chosen has an address, but we do not want to have to deal with explicit addresses in a BASIC program, so BASIC permits us to refer to that location and its contents by a name.

For numeric quantities, a name of a variable in BASIC may be a single letter, or a letter followed by a digit. Thus,

A, B, C, K, Q, W, Z, A0, A5, B9, K9, W2

are all valid variable names. The names

AA, 3A, 269, 4*Q, Q*4, W22, 8

are not valid, since they all violate the rule in one way or another.

The BASIC translator must decide from the form of each statement which occurrences of, say, the letter E are references to the variable E and which are parts of keywords END, LET, REM, etc. The translator must be able to make these decisions clearly and quickly; this is the main reason why languages like BASIC are much more restricted in form than English. Whenever the BASIC translator encounters in a program the first reference to any variable (E, for example), it assigns a particular main storage location to that variable; this is the location that will hold the data represented by E during execution of the program. As the translator encounters each reference to E in any statement, it uses the assigned location in the machine language instructions that represent that statement. This is one of the services provided by the translator; we happily leave the clerical task of building and using the table of variable names and corresponding locations to the translator.

Note that during translation E has no value, no contents; the translator has only set up a location to be used during program execution. Values are placed in these locations during program execution, as we shall see later in more detail, by LET statements, which provide a value based on other quantities already inside main storage, and by INPUT statements, which provide a value from the terminal or from disk storage. Values of variables can be *used* in many different kinds of statements, generally any use we would want during program execution.

There are two kinds of variables recognized by BASIC, corresponding to two types of data; the first is numeric, and we have seen the naming conventions for numeric variables. The second type of data is strings of characters, and BASIC provides special variables that can hold character strings. *String variables*, as they are called, are named just as numeric variables are except that a dollar sign $ is attached to the end of the name to make it a string variable name. Therefore, among the valid string variable names are

    A$,   C$,   M$,   B3$,   FO$,   K9$,   Z5$

Any program may contain, for example, both A and A$ as variable names; A has numeric contents, and A$ has a character string as contents; they are assigned separate locations in main storage. The length of a character string permitted as the value of a string variable is limited. Different computers have different limits, from 1 character to 32,767 characters; the DECsystem-10 allows up to 132 characters in a string. The BASIC system must go to more work to store and keep track of string variables; strings of different lengths may be stored successively as the values of a single string variable, and the system must allocate enough main storage and keep track of the length of each string. We can rely on the BASIC system to do this task, while we freely use strings of whatever length and content we wish.

We close this section with advice *not* to use any variable names beginning with the letter O; the O can be confused with a zero. We must be precise when dealing with computers, and a computer cannot tell by context that a zero should be the letter O and accept it as an O. Therefore, we should reduce potential confusion as much as possible, by avoiding the use of any variable names that begin with O.

5.3 PRINT STATEMENTS

Every program needs PRINT statements to report its results to an eager world. A PRINT statement sends data, messages, and results to be displayed at the user's terminal; in Chapter 9 we will introduce another form of the PRINT statement that writes to a file on disk storage. A PRINT statement can print values of numeric or string variables, and constants—numbers and strings (strings are always enclosed in quotation marks) whose values are given directly in the PRINT statement itself. Consider the PRINT statements

```
120   PRINT "YOU WILL SOON MEET A HANDSOME STRANGER"
150   PRINT 46.3
170   PRINT N$
240   PRINT F4
```

If N$ has the value "JOHN PAUL JONES" and F4 has the value 785.91, when the respective PRINT statements are executed, they will print (or display on a CRT) at the user's terminal

```
YOU WILL SOON MEET A HANDSOME STRANGER
 46.3
JOHN PAUL JONES
 785.91
```

Execution of each PRINT statement starts printing at the beginning of a new line. Since PRINT is an executable statement, each PRINT statement will send a new line to the terminal every time the statement is executed; therefore, a PRINT statement in a loop may print many lines at the terminal. If the variable W contains, in successive passes through a loop, the total wages for each employee, the single statement

```
360   PRINT W
```

in the loop will cause the wages of all employees to be printed, one to a line. This kind of task shows, among other things, why the use of variable names is a necessary part of harnessing the power of computers.

We may specify more than one element—string, number, string variable, or numeric variable—to be printed by one PRINT statement. We may control spacing across the line, too. We will describe the spacing control provided by the semicolon and the TAB function, and introduce other ways to control spacing in Chapter 13.

If we want to have an employee's social security number, name, number of hours worked, and wages all to be printed on one line, we can specify so by putting the names of the four variables containing the data in one PRINT statement. Between every two elements in a PRINT statement, there must be a semicolon, and there may be a TAB specification as well. For example, if

S$ has the value "111222333"

N$ has the value "JOHN JONES"

H   has the value 42.5

W   has the value 393.75

the statement

340   PRINT S$; N$; H; W

will direct to the user's terminal

111222333JOHN JONES 42.5   393.75

The semicolon directs one element printed to follow the previous one with no space between, except for a single space *after* a number. If a number is zero or positive, a space will appear before the number as well; this is the space that would be taken by the minus sign if the number were negative.

A PRINT statement may call for printing any combination of numbers, strings, and numeric and string variables, in any order, separated by semicolons. For example, if R$ has the value "KITCHEN" and G has the value 1.82,

410 PRINT "THE ";R$;" WILL TAKE";G;"GALLONS OF PAINT"

will print

THE KITCHEN WILL TAKE 1.82 GALLONS OF PAINT

If a PRINT statement calls for printing more than will fit on one output line, the computer automatically continues printing on a second line, and so on.

The TAB function can be inserted into PRINT statements to cause a skip, somewhat like a tab key on a typewriter, to a designated position on the printed line. Consider the print positions on the line as starting at number 0. A TAB(7) in a PRINT statement will cause a skip to position 7 (the *eighth* position, since numbering started at zero) for printing the next field. That is, it will skip *unless* the printing has *already passed* position 7; if it has already passed position 7, the TAB causes *no action at all*. For example, if V$ has the value "BOLTS" and K$ has the value "A1–34", the statement

160   PRINT V$; TAB(7); K$

will print

BOLTS   A1–34

but if V$ has the value "FIREPLACE TONGS", the same statement will print

FIREPLACE TONGSA1–34

The TAB position is enclosed in parentheses after the word TAB; the TAB function should be separated from other elements of the

PRINT statement by semicolons. TAB functions are useful in printing output in columns or in generally spacing the printing across a line. For example, repeated execution of the statement

```
320  PRINT S$; TAB(12); N$; TAB(38); H; TAB(46); W
```

with different values of the variable could print

```
111222333  JOHN JONES                      42.5    393.75
111222444  CHRIS PATTERSON                 40.2    270.01
111222555  CHRISTOPHER CARTWRIGHT-JONES 38.5   257.95
```

Note that in the third line the name is so long that the variable H is pushed past its usual column, but there is space for the TAB before W to have some effect.

One further useful statement is a PRINT that specifies *nothing* to be printed:

```
310  PRINT
```

This statement will print, naturally enough, a blank line; this can be useful in separating one group of printed results from another group on the page.

Before leaving this section, we must emphasize the role of quotation marks in PRINT statements, and in BASIC generally. Any characters *inside* quotation marks are part of a character string, and mean nothing else to the system. This includes spaces; a space inside a character string is a bona fide character, part of the string. Spaces in BASIC statements *outside* character strings have no role or meaning; we may insert them for readability, at our option. Any other characters outside character strings must have meaning to the BASIC system and must be appropriate in context. Some final examples to illustrate these points:

```
210  PRINT "T"
```

will print the letter T, while

```
220  PRINT T
```

will print the value of the variable named T.

```
230  PRINT "S3; W"
```

will print

```
S3; W
```

while

```
240  PRINT S3; W
```

will print values of the variables S3 and W.

```
250   PRINT "PRINT"
```

will print the word PRINT, but

```
260   PRINT PRINT
```

is invalid because the second word PRINT in the statement does not fulfill any of the rules for valid contents of a PRINT statement.

```
270   PRINT "    VERY GOOD!"
```

will print the message VERY GOOD! starting in print position 4, since the four spaces preceding VERY are part of the string to be printed;

```
280   PRINT        "VERY GOOD!"
```

prints the message VERY GOOD! starting in print position 0, the beginning of the line, since the extra spaces in the statement are not part of the string to be printed.

5.4 LET STATEMENTS AND ARITHMETIC

The LET statement assigns a value to a variable, based on data already in main storage. It is used to assign values to both numeric variables and string variables. The general form of the statement is

line no.   LET *variable = expression*

The expression is evaluated, and the resulting value is stored in the main storage location corresponding to the variable. For example,

```
150   LET B = A + 6
```

will direct the computer to add 6 to the current value of the variable A, and store the result as the new value of the variable B. The variable A in main storage is not changed by the statement; the previous value of B is lost when the new value replaces it.

For string variables, the LET statement may take either of the forms

line no.   LET *variable = quoted string*
line no.   LET *variable = string variable*

The statement

```
160   LET S$ = "ACCOUNTS PAYABLE"
```

will store the string "ACCOUNTS PAYABLE" in the location assigned to S\$. The statement

```
170   LET C$ = P$
```

will reproduce the string currently in P\$, and store the copy in C\$. The value of P\$ is not changed, but the previous value of C\$ is lost. In later chapters we will learn some more operations that can be performed on strings, but for the rest of this section we will concentrate on numeric variables and expressions.

A LET statement can look like an algebraic equation:

```
180   LET X = (B − 3)*C
```

There is a very important difference, however. An algebraic equation is a statement of fact; it may be true or false, but it is a statement of fact. A LET statement in BASIC directs an action; $X = (B − 3)*C$ is neither true nor false, but an action to be accomplished. The action in this case is computation of the value of the expression $(B − 3) \times C$ and storage of the result as the new value of the variable X. We can draw on the Book of Genesis for an analogy; God did not say "There is light," which would have been a simple statement of fact; God said "LET there be light!" which was a command for action. Our powers are more limited, but we use the word LET to remind ourselves that the LET statements cause action. One statement illustrates well the difference between the BASIC statement and an equation:

```
190   LET K = K + 1
```

As an algebraic equation, this is nonsense; K *cannot* be equal to K + 1. As a BASIC statement, it is not only perfectly valid, but useful. The value of K and the number 1 are added to form the value of the expression, and the result is stored as the new value of K. The upshot is that the value of K in main storage is increased by 1.

It is time now to simplify our terminology by taking some small shortcuts. It is cumbersome to say "store the result in the main storage location assigned to the variable A," so we will abbreviate the phrase to "store the result in A." Similarly, instead of referring to the value of the variable A, we will often refer to A. Rather than assume that B has the value 6.29, we will assume that $B = 6.29$. We trust that you have the concepts of variables, main storage locations, and values well enough in hand that these abbreviations of terminology will simplify, rather than confuse. We will also refer to execution of BASIC statements, trusting that you recognize that we really mean execution of the machine language instructions that were translated from the BASIC statements.

The rules for formation of arithmetic expressions, and the corresponding rules for understanding the meaning and the actions taken, are important. An expression is composed of one or more numbers (constants) and variables, connected by operators. Numbers are expressed in ordinary decimal form, with or without a decimal point:

    6.21   4000   .06   0.06   4   87.00

A minus sign can be attached to make the number negative:

   −6.21   −4000   −.06   −0.06   −4   −87.00

Large or small numbers can also be expressed in a scientific notation:

6.21E12 means 6.21×10^{12} or 6,210,000,000,000,

4.17E−4 means 4.17×10^{-4} or 0.000417, and

1E6   means 1 $\times 10^{6}$ or 1,000,000.

Numbers in this form can be used in arithmetic expressions, and can be input from the terminal (looking ahead to Section 5.5). Large or small numbers will also be printed in this form by PRINT statements.

Arithmetic operators available are

> $+$ for addition,
>
> $-$ for subtraction,
>
> $*$ for multiplication,
>
> $/$ for division, and
>
> $**$ or $\uparrow$ for raising a quantity to a power.

Only the last two should need explanation. Division yields a quotient, to approximately six decimal digits, and *not* a remainder. When we study functions in Chapter 12, we will show how to get a remainder of a division when we want one. The expression $X \uparrow 3$ means X cubed: If $X = 2$, $X \uparrow 3 = 8$. BASIC permits fractional powers: $X \uparrow 0.5$ is the square root of X (but only of positive numbers X). Negative powers are also permitted: If $X = 2$, $X \uparrow (-2) = 0.25$. Note that parentheses are necessary; two operators are not permitted together, even if the second is only the sign of a negative number. You will have to check whether $\uparrow$ or $**$ is accepted by your BASIC system; some accept one, some accept the other, and some systems accept both.

In order to write expressions that will mean in BASIC what we want them to mean, we must understand how the BASIC system interprets expressions. This is not trivial, since expressions like

    B $-$ 4/C $*$ D $+$ E $\uparrow$ 2 $*$ F

could conceivably be interpreted in several different ways. There is a precedence of operators that the system applies *within each set of parentheses:*

- First, perform all ↑ or **, from left to right.
- Second, perform all * and /, from left to right.
- Last, perform all + and −, from left to right.

Each expression in parentheses must be evaluated before its results can be used. Applying the precedence rules to the expression above, we find:

1. The first operation performed is E ↑ 2, since that is the only ↑ in the expression;
2. Then 4/C, and the result is multiplied by D;
3. Then the result of E ↑ 2 is multiplied by F;
4. The result of 4/C * D is subtracted from B;
5. The result of E ↑ 2 * F is added to the result of B − 4/C * D.

If this is not what the programmer intended, parentheses can be used to force any desired order of computation. To compute the average of the three quantities B1, B2, and B3, for example, we can write

```
220   LET A  =  (B1 + B2 + B3)/3
```

We introduced arithmetic expressions for their use in LET statements, but we can also use an arithmetic expression in a PRINT statement like

```
360   PRINT "AVERAGE =";  (B1 + B2 + B3)/3
```

without first computing the average and storing it.

We conclude this section with a reminder. The statement

```
470   LET S = W
```

copies the value of W, storing the copy in S. The *second* operand, W, is the source of the data moved to a new location; the *first* operand, S, is the destination of the move. A statement like this is common in programs, and it is common for students to write the statement backwards, which always leads to some kind of disaster in program execution!

5.5 INPUT STATEMENTS

The LET statement assigns values to variables based on data already in main storage; the INPUT statement brings data from the terminal (or from disk storage, as we learn in Chapter 6) and stores the data in variables. An INPUT statement has the simple form

    line no.   INPUT *variable*

The variable may be either a numeric or a string variable. The execution of the statement is in four steps:

1. The computer displays a question mark at the terminal, and waits for input from the terminal.

2. The user types the data, followed by carriage return.

3. The carriage return brings the program to life again; the computer checks the data typed by the user for validity. If the INPUT asked for a numeric variable, the input from the terminal must be a valid form for a number; if the INPUT asked for a string variable, the input must not be longer than the maximum permitted length of a string.

4. If the input is valid, it is stored as the value of the variable listed in the INPUT statement, and execution continues to the next statement; if the input is not valid, an error message is displayed, and the process repeats, starting with Step 1, giving the user another chance to make a valid input.

For example, execution of

    110   INPUT R

could appear at a terminal:

    ?38.2

where the question mark is typed by the computer and 38.2 by the user. The result of execution is that 38.2 is stored in R.

When a program is in execution and it types a question mark to the user, will the user know what to respond with? The user can easily become confused and not know whether to type in a rate, a social security number, or the number of people waiting for a bus at the corner. Therefore, we usually precede the INPUT statement by a PRINT statement that will tell the user, by what we call a *prompt* message, exactly what is expected. Execution of the pair of statements

```
100   PRINT "TYPE SOCIAL SECURITY NUMBER"
110   INPUT S$
```

may appear at a terminal:

```
TYPE SOCIAL SECURITY NUMBER
 ?111222333
```

Here we introduce another feature of PRINT statements. Usually, after executing a PRINT statement the computer does a carriage return. If we *end* a PRINT statement with a semicolon, however, the computer does not do a carriage return. In conjunction with an INPUT statement, this permits the input to be on the same line as the prompt message. Execution of the statements

```
100   PRINT "SOC. SEC. NO."; TAB(14);
110   INPUT S$
120   PRINT "NAME"; TAB(14);
130   INPUT N$
140   PRINT "HOURS WORKED"; TAB(14);
150   INPUT H
160   PRINT "HOURLY PAY"; TAB(14);
170   INPUT R
```

will appear at the terminal as

```
SOC. SEC. NO.   ?111222333
NAME            ?CHRIS JONES
HOURS WORKED    ?42
HOURLY PAY      ?5.80
```

and will result in assigning values

```
"111222333"      to   S$
"CHRIS JONES"    to   N$
42               to   H
5.80             to   R
```

Why did we input social security number into a string variable rather than a numeric variable? The computer keeps numbers in a floating-point representation, in binary in most computers, but decimal in some. Only the most significant six digits are stored, and if we input 111222333 to a numeric variable and then ask for the number to be printed with the program's results, we get back 1.11222E+08, which is hardly acceptable. On the other hand, a string variable accepts all nine digits as characters, and will report back all nine digits faithfully.

It is possible to request input of several variables in one INPUT statement. The user may input the data with a carriage return *or* a comma after each one. For example, execution of

```
230  PRINT "TYPE LENGTH, WIDTH, HEIGHT"
240  INPUT L, W, H
```

may be fulfilled by *either*

```
TYPE LENGTH, WIDTH, HEIGHT
 ?20
 ?3.5
 ?4
```

or

```
TYPE LENGTH, WIDTH, HEIGHT
 ?20, 3.5, 4
```

After each carriage return, the computer checks the input to see whether it has been given enough input. If not, as in the first example above, it asks for more input until satisfied.

Because commas are used to separate pieces of input, we need a special arrangement when we want to type in a string of characters that *contains* a comma as part of the string. What we must do is enclose the entire string in quotation marks. For example, to input a name with the last name first, as JONES, CHRIS, we must respond to the INPUT statement

```
150  PRINT "TYPE NAME, WITH LAST NAME FIRST"
160  INPUT N$
```

with the name in quotation marks:

```
TYPE NAME, WITH LAST NAME FIRST
 ?"JONES, CHRIS"
```

We have now learned enough BASIC to be able to transcribe some simple procedures into BASIC programs. Generally, we transcribe procedure steps as follows.

Obtain ...	into	100	PRINT *"prompt message"*
		110	INPUT ...
Compute ...	into	200	LET ...
Print ...	into	300	PRINT ...

It is fairly simple to transcribe Obtain, Compute, and Print steps in BASIC. Figure 5.1 shows the transcription of the procedure in Fig. 4.1 into BASIC. I have followed two stylistic rules that help any reader relate the program to the procedure:

1. Use variable names that are suggestive of the concepts they represent (such as W for width, G for gallons). With single-letter variable names in BASIC it is not possible to suggest the meanings of variables very well, so we also include in a set of REM statements a table of variable names and their uses.

2. Assign line numbers whose first digit corresponds to the procedure step implemented by each statement.

Following such patterns makes programs easier to write correctly in the first place, easier to correct if there *is* an error, and easier to modify in the future when we need the same task done with minor changes.

```
10   REM   COMPUTE NO. OF GALLONS OF PAINT FOR THE ROOM
20   REM   NORGE GUDDLE      JAN. 1980
40   REM
42   REM  L = LENGTH OF ROOM
44   REM  W = WIDTH OF ROOM
46   REM  H = HEIGHT OF ROOM
48   REM  P = PERIMETER OF ROOM
50   REM  A = WALL AREA OF ROOM
52   REM  C = CEILING AREA
54   REM  T = TOTAL AREA TO BE PAINTED
56   REM  G = NO. OF GALLONS REQUIRED
58   REM
100      PRINT "TYPE LENGTH, IN FEET";
110      INPUT L
120      PRINT "TYPE WIDTH";
130      INPUT W
140      PRINT "TYPE HEIGHT";
150      INPUT H
200      LET P = 2*L + 2*W
210      LET A = P * H
220      LET C = L * W
230      LET T = A + C
300      LET G = T/750
400      PRINT "THIS ROOM REQUIRES"; G; "GALLONS"
970   END
```

Figure 5.1 Program for the amount of paint required.

5.6 GO TO AND IF STATEMENTS

In this chapter we have introduced statements that input and output
data, move data from one location in main storage to another, and perform arithmetic. To complete a minimal set of the essential statements
to do worthwhile programs, we must now introduce GO TO and IF statements, which perform transfers of control within the program.

Every BASIC statement has a line number, and the line numbers determine the physical sequence of statements in the program. Statement
40 precedes statement 50 in the program. The line numbers are also used
in editing programs; we will explore editing in Section 5.8. Still another
use of line numbers is to determine the flow of control—the sequence of
execution of statements. Normally, statements are executed in sequence
of ascending line numbers: statement 100, then statement 110, then
statement 120, and so on, in just the same way that machine language
instructions are executed one after another as they are stored in consecutive locations in main storage. In BASIC, the statements GO TO and IF
operate like machine language branch instructions in breaking the flow
of control, but they specify line numbers, not main storage locations, to
branch to.

The counterpart of the unconditional branch instruction is the GO
TO statement: When execution of statements comes to

```
330   GO TO 120
```

the flow of control branches to statement 120; statement 120, whatever
it is, will be the next statement executed.

The addition of a GO TO statement to the program in Fig. 3.3 gives
a program, shown in Fig. 5.2, that will repeatedly accept a set of input
and report savings. After each problem is completed, the GO TO statement sends control back to the beginning of the program. The trouble is
that the program will repeat the loop forever; the program provides no
way to get out.

Builders of computer systems are not so ignorant as not to give us a
way out! The usual mechanism is *Control C:* Hold down the *Control key*
(just above the left-hand Shift key) and hit C, perhaps twice. This (or
possibly some other signal on your system) will get you out of a program. Remember this escape route; some programming error may one
day get you into a situation in which you need it! Figure 5.3 shows execution of the program in Fig. 5.2, with use of Control C after two problems solved.

Like any programming language, BASIC needs a conditional branch
as well as the unconditional branch implemented in the GO TO state-

```
10    REM   COMPUTE 3-YEAR SAVINGS ON HEATING BILL
20    REM   NORGE GUDDLE    JUNE 1979
40    REM
42    REM   B  = HEATING BILL FOR THE CURRENT YEAR
44    REM   P  = PERCENTAGE SAVINGS EXPECTED TO BE ACHIEVED BY PROJECT
46    REM   R  = PROJECTED INFLATION RATE PER YEAR ON HEATING COSTS
48    REM   S  = DOLLAR SAVINGS EXPECTED IN FIRST YEAR
50    REM   S1 = SAVINGS IN THE SECOND YEAR
52    REM   S2 = SAVINGS IN THE THIRD YEAR
54    REM   T  = TOTAL SAVINGS OVER THE THREE YEARS
100      PRINT "ENTER YOUR EXPECTED HEATING BILL THIS YEAR";
110      INPUT B
120      PRINT "ENTER PROJECTED PERCENTAGE SAVINGS";
130      INPUT P
140      PRINT "ENTER EXPECTED INFLATION RATE ON HEATING COSTS";
150      INPUT R
190      LET S = P/100 * B
200      LET S1 = S + R/100 * S
210      LET S2 = S1 + R/100 * S1
220      LET T = S + S1 + S2
300      PRINT "TOTAL 3-YEAR SAVINGS WOULD BE "; T
310      GO TO 100
970 END
```

Figure 5.2 A loop without an exit.

ment. In BASIC the conditional branch statement is the IF statement. Its general form is

> line no.   IF condition GO TO line no.

The word THEN can be used in place of GO TO. The action of the statement is evaluation of the condition: If the condition is *true*, the computer executes the GO TO clause and branches to the given line number; if the condition is *false*, the computer goes directly to the next statement in sequence.

```
RUN

SAVS          20:51        16-JUN-79


ENTER YOUR EXPECTED HEATING BILL THIS YEAR ?40000
ENTER PROJECTED PERCENTAGE SAVINGS ?40
ENTER EXPECTED INFLATION RATE ON HEATING COSTS ?20
TOTAL 3-YEAR SAVINGS WOULD BE   58240
ENTER YOUR EXPECTED HEATING BILL THIS YEAR ?40000
ENTER PROJECTED PERCENTAGE SAVINGS ?25
ENTER EXPECTED INFLATION RATE ON HEATING COSTS ?15
TOTAL 3-YEAR SAVINGS WOULD BE   34725
ENTER YOUR EXPECTED HEATING BILL THIS YEAR ?^C

READY
```

Figure 5.3 Execution of the program in Fig. 5.2.

Conditions in IF statements may be of the form

expression relation expression

The expressions may be character strings or arithmetic expressions, but, of course, both should be of the same type. We learned in Section 5.4 how arithmetic expressions may be constructed. The allowed relations are

$<$	less than,
$<=$	less than or equal to,
$=$	equal to,
$>=$	greater than or equal to,
$>$	greater than,
$<>$	not equal to,
#	not equal to (in some systems).

Some examples of IF statements are:

```
130   IF R$ = "YES" GO TO 970
160   IF A$ <> "99999" GO TO 540
170   IF K <= 12 GO TO 100
180   IF B ↑ 2 < 4*A*C GO TO 240
220   IF W1 > 17900 GO TO 270
250   IF M*T < 64 GO TO 410
280   IF I = 6 GO TO 360
```

Now let us turn our attention to the transcription of WHILE structures into BASIC. There is no WHILE statement in BASIC, so we must use instead a combination of IF and GO TO statements. The structure

WHILE *condition*
    action

can be transcribed into BASIC as

```
400   IF condition GO TO 420
410   GO TO 500
420   action
  .
  .
  .
490   GO TO 400
500   next step of the procedure
```

Figure 5.4 shows the program transcribed from the loan repayment procedure in Fig. 4.2 or from the flowchart in Fig. 4.5, including the WHILE structure. Pay special attention to the GO TO statements at lines 410 and 490, and the functions they serve. Trace execution of the program as shown and also with either line 410 or line 490 deleted, to see how the flow of control actually works.

We can make one simplification in the BASIC transcription of a WHILE structure. In place of the statements

400   IF *condition* GO TO 420

410   GO TO 500

we can substitute the single statement

400   IF *not condition* GO TO 500

We must construct the logical opposite of the original condition; for example, the logical opposite of

A > 0	is	A <= 0
B = 2	is	B <> 2
C >= B−4*A	is	C < B−4*A
R$ <> "YES"	is	R$ = "YES"

```
10    REM PRINT LOAN REPAYMENT SCHEDULE
20    REM NORGE GUDDLE     JAN 1980
40    REM
42    REM A = AMOUNT OF LOAN OUTSTANDING AT ANY TIME
44    REM R = ANNUAL INTEREST RATE
46    REM I = INTEREST RATE PER MONTH
48    REM P = MONTHLY PAYMENT
50    REM L = LOAN REDUCTION IN CURRENT MONTH
52    REM M = INTEREST AMOUNT FOR THE CURRENT MONTH
60    REM
100       PRINT "TYPE LOAN AMOUNT"
110       INPUT A
120       PRINT "TYPE ANNUAL INTEREST RATE, E.G. .09 FOR 9%"
130       INPUT R
140       PRINT "TYPE MONTHLY PAYMENT"
150       INPUT P
200       LET I = R/12
300       PRINT "LOAN AMOUNT   INTEREST   LOAN REDUCTION"
390 REM   BEGIN WHILE STRUCTURE
400       IF A > 0 GO TO 420
410       GO TO 970
420       LET M = A*I
430       LET L = P - M
440       PRINT A; TAB(15); M; TAB(25); L
450       LET A = A - L
490       GO TO 400
970   END
```

Figure 5.4 Program for loan repayment.

Therefore, in Fig. 5.4 the statements at lines 400 and 410 may be replaced by the single statement

    400   IF A <= 0 GO TO 970

A similar replacement may be made in any program in which an IF statement branches around the next statement, a GO TO statement, to the following statement.

We also use IF and GO TO statements to implement IF-THEN-ELSE structures and IF-THEN structures. Generally, the structure

>   IF *condition*
>   THEN *action 1*
>   ELSE *action 2*

is transcribed into BASIC as

    400   IF *condition* GO TO 460
    410   *action 2*
      .
      .
      .
    450   GO TO 500
    460   *action 1*
      .
      .
      .
    500   *action implementing the next structure*

For example,

>   IF pay > exemptions × 15
>   THEN tax withheld = 0.14 × (pay − exemptions × 15)
>   ELSE tax withheld = 0

is represented as

    400   IF P > E * 15 GO TO 460
    410   LET T = 0
    450   GO TO 500
    460   LET T = .14 * (P − E * 15)
    500   ...

The IF statement tests the condition, and if the condition is true, the GO TO clause sends control to 460 to undertake the action in the THEN clause of the structure. If the condition is false, control falls to the next statement, 410, which therefore undertakes the action in the ELSE clause of the structure. The statement

```
450   GO TO 500
```

is essential to prevent the statements at 460, implementing the THEN clause of the structure, from being executed *as well as* the statements in the ELSE clause. Now: Read that last sentence again; the GO TO statement is easy to overlook, and students do it often. Make a flowchart for the structure with the GO TO statement removed, and see why the GO TO statement is essential and what kinds of erroneous results you will receive if you leave it out.

We can implement an IF-THEN structure such as

IF quantity $\geq$ 12
    THEN multiply price by 0.9

as an IF-THEN-ELSE structure in which there is no action in the ELSE clause:

```
400   IF Q >= 12 GO TO 460
450   GO TO 500
460   LET P = P * .9
```

However, we saw above how we could simplify a sequence in which an IF statement branches around a GO TO statement. We take the logical opposite of the IF condition and combine the IF and GO TO statements:

```
400   IF Q < 12 GO TO 500
460   LET P = P * .9
```

In general, therefore, the structure

IF *condition*
    THEN *action*

can best be transcribed into BASIC as

```
400   IF not condition GO TO 500
410   action
  ·
  ·
  ·
500   action implementing the next structure
```

If the condition as originally stated—for example, quantity ≥ 12—is true, its logical opposite, quantity < 12, will be false, and control drops to statement 410 to perform the THEN action. After that action has been performed, control falls to statement 500 and the next step in the procedure. On the other hand, if the original condition is *not* satisfied, the logical opposite, quantity < 12, is true and the IF statement will send control directly to statement 500, bypassing the statements 410 to 499.

Figure 5.5 shows the BASIC program transcribed from Fig. 4.7. The main structure of Step 3 is an IF-THEN-ELSE; the ELSE clause (Step 3.3) is transcribed into statement 310 and followed by the GO TO statement at 320, which bypasses the THEN clause actions. The THEN clause is transcribed into statements 330–470. Step 3.2 is the WHILE structure, represented by statements 400–470. This step includes an IF-THEN structure in Step 3.2.2, which is transcribed into statements 420–430. Trace the execution of the program if the quantities input are 1000, .09, 6 and again if the quantities are 1000, .09, 230. As you trace the execution, note how the structures of Fig. 4.7 are actually followed.

```
10    REM PRINT LOAN REPAYMENT SCHEDULE
20    REM NORGE GUDDLE    JAN 1980 (REVISED VERSION)
40    REM
42    REM A = AMOUNT OF LOAN OUTSTANDING AT ANY TIME
44    REM R = ANNUAL INTEREST RATE
46    REM I = INTEREST RATE PER MONTH
48    REM P = MONTHLY PAYMENT
50    REM L = LOAN REDUCTION IN CURRENT MONTH
52    REM M = INTEREST AMOUNT FOR THE CURRENT MONTH
60    REM
100      PRINT "TYPE LOAN AMOUNT"
110      INPUT A
120      PRINT "TYPE ANNUAL INTEREST RATE, E.G. .09 FOR 9%"
130      INPUT R
140      PRINT "TYPE MONTHLY PAYMENT"
150      INPUT P
200      LET I = R/12
300      IF P > I * A GO TO 330
310      PRINT "INSUFFICIENT MONTHLY PAYMENT"
320      GO TO 970
330      PRINT "LOAN AMOUNT   INTEREST   PAYMENT   LOAN REDUCTION"
390 REM   BEGIN WHILE STRUCTURE
400      IF A <= 0 GO TO 970
410      LET M = A * I
420      IF P <= A + M GO TO 440
430      LET P = A + M
440      LET L = P - M
450      PRINT A; TAB(14); M; TAB(24); P; TAB(34); L
460      LET A = A - L
470      GO TO 400
970   END
```

Figure 5.5 Program transcribed from the procedure in Fig. 4.7.

5.7 THE LOOP-EXIT STRUCTURE

The WHILE structure represents a loop whose test for continuation or exit precedes all actions taken in the loop. There are loops whose test cannot precede all actions; for example, these loops must first obtain a piece of data, and then test the data for continuation or exit. If the test results in continuation, further actions are taken in the loop. We will represent such a loop in a procedure by

> LOOP
>> *Preliminary actions*
>
>> EXIT WHEN *condition*
>
>> *Further actions*

Figure 5.6 shows in flowchart form the flow of control represented by the LOOP-EXIT structure. The structure is implemented in BASIC by

```
1000   preliminary actions
   ·
   ·
   ·
1500   IF condition GO TO 2000
1510   further actions
   ·
   ·
   ·
1990   GO TO 1000
2000   next step
```

The exit from the loop is upon test of the exit condition in statement 1500. Statement 1990 returns control to the beginning of the loop.

Let us consider an example. We want a program that will help maintain budget accounts. We should be able to type in the account balance at the beginning of the month, and all the transactions—date, description, and amount (positive or negative)—for the month, then have the computer print the ending balance in the account. Obviously, the transactions should be entered in a loop. Let us adopt a convention that when all transactions have been entered, the user at the terminal will type "STOP" rather than another transaction date. Figure 5.7 shows a procedure for this program, using the LOOP-EXIT structure. Figure 5.8 shows the program that follows the procedure. The PRINT statements 120 and 280 are inserted to provide visual separation of transactions on the terminal transcript.

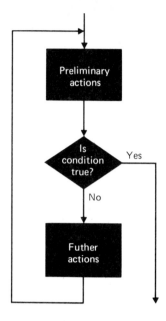

Figure 5.6 Flowchart for LOOP-EXIT structure.

The LOOP-EXIT structure is especially useful in cases like the example we have just considered, where the first input of each set obtained in the loop is tested for some convention to cause exit from the loop that obtains and processes the data from a terminal. In fact, processes that obtain data from a terminal will usually follow the LOOP-EXIT structure.

We have studied the WHILE structure, which tests for exit from a loop at the beginning of the loop, and the LOOP-EXIT structure, whose test is in the middle. The remaining logical possibility is a test at the end. Computer scientists call this a REPEAT-UNTIL structure. A problem that seems naturally to be solved by a loop with a test at the bottom can always be restated with a test at the top of the loop. If we wish, we can

---

1. Obtain beginning balance
2. LOOP
   2.1 Obtain transaction date
   2.2 EXIT WHEN date = "STOP"
   2.3 Obtain description and amount
   2.4 Add amount to balance
3. Print ending balance

Figure 5.7 Procedure for posting transactions to account balance.

```
10   REM   POST TRANSACTIONS TO ACCOUNT BALANCE
20   REM   NORGE GUDDLE    JAN 1980
30   REM
32   REM     B  = ACCOUNT BALANCE
34   REM     D$ = TRANSACTION DATE, OR "STOP"
36   REM     D1$ = DESCRIPTION OF TRANSACTION
38   REM     A  = TRANSACTION AMOUNT
100    PRINT "TYPE BEGINNING BALANCE";
110    INPUT B
120    PRINT
190  REM   LOOP IS STATEMENTS 200 - 290
200    PRINT "TYPE TRANSACTION DATE";
210    INPUT D$
220    IF D$ = "STOP" GO TO 300
230    PRINT "DESCRIPTION";
240    INPUT D1$
250    PRINT "AMOUNT";
260    INPUT A
270    LET B = B + A
280    PRINT
290    GO TO 200
300    PRINT "ENDING BALANCE = "; B
970  END
```

Figure 5.8 Program for posting transactions to account balance.

also call it a special case of the LOOP-EXIT structure in which there happen to be no "further actions." In this text we do not need REPEAT-UNTIL structures, and will not use them.

5.8 ENTERING, EDITING, LISTING, AND RUNNING A PROGRAM

In Chapter 3 we showed an example of a student session at a terminal, entering and running a program, and we introduced some of the BASIC commands. Now we introduce other commands useful to the student, and describe how to edit a program.

A BASIC program must be entered into a user's workspace before it can be edited or run. The workspace is cleared by the command

NEW program name

A program name must begin with a letter; its total length, usually limited to five or six characters, may include letters and digits, but no special characters like + * . , − ;. The user types in each statement with its line number. The BASIC subsystem assumes from the line number that the line contains a statement that is part of the program; anything without a line number is interpreted as a command.

The BASIC subsystem puts the program in sequence by line number. The user may type statements in any order; they will be put into sequence by ascending line number. The program statements entered as

```
140   LET T = 1
170   IF T > S GO TO 210
150   LET S = B*R/100
```

will be placed in the sequence

```
140   LET T = 1
150   LET S = B*R/100
170   IF T > S GO TO 210
```

At any time that a program is in the user's workspace, it may be edited. The user may want to edit the program after seeing a complete listing of it, or after running the program, especially if the run were unsuccessful. In fact, the process of entering the program is part of editing. There are generally three ways in which the user may want to edit the program: add statements, change statements already entered, and delete statements. The user may add a statement to the program merely by typing it in. The line number determines where the statement will be inserted. This is why we generally assign line numbers in multiples of 10; to insert a statement between 110 and 120 we need only type the new statement with a line number of 115, and there will still be room for further insertions if necessary.

To change a statement, we retype the entire statement as we want it, with the same line number. The new statement replaces the old statement. To delete a statement, we type the line number of the statement, and an immediate carriage return. There is also a DELETE command for deleting all statements within a range:

```
DELETE 210-250
```

deletes from the program all statements with numbers 210 to 250, *including* 210 and 250 themselves.

There are two special keys or characters that help us correct errors as we type in statements, commands, and input to programs. First is the *rubout* key, which essentially takes back the last character typed on the current line. Hitting the rubout key three times will delete the last three characters. Some systems use *Control H* for deleting characters; one hits H while holding down the *Control* key. Different systems have different ways of acknowledging the deletion. The second special character is *Control U*. If you hit U while holding down the *Control* key, the entire line being typed is canceled. This is useful when an error is so far back in the line that it is easier to start over than to use one rubout at a time.

At any time we can see a current listing of the contents of the work-space by typing the command

    LIST

The entire program will be listed in line number sequence. We may want to list a program after entering it to check on the accuracy of the entry; or after running it, to decide what editing to perform; or after editing, to check again what the entire program is before running it; or after a successful run, to hand in to the instructor. It is also possible to list a portion of a program:

    LIST 300–380

will list the portion of the program between (and including) line numbers 300 and 380. Figure 5.9 shows the listing of a program, then some editing of the program, and the listing of the program as edited.

If we are through with a program for the current session but want to return to it at another time, we can save the program in our file space with the command

    SAVE

The program will be stored, and our file directory will include its name and location. To recall a program, perhaps the program LAB2, we load it into the workspace by the command

    OLD LAB2

The program is now available for any further editing, listing, and running, but it still exists in the file space. If we wish then to save a *revised version*, the command

    REPLACE

will replace the old version in the file space with the new version; the command SAVE is not accepted if there is already a file of the same name in the file space.

To delete a program LAB2 from the file space, when we no longer need it, we execute

    UNSAVE LAB2

It is a good idea to keep your file space clean and uncluttered by files no longer needed. The command

    CAT

will list for us the names of all files currently in our file space.

```
10   REM   COMPUTE 3-YEAR SAVINGS ON HEATING BILL
20   REM   NORGE GUDDLE    JUNE 1979
40   REM
42   REM   B  = HEATING BILL FOR THE CURRENT YEAR
44   REM   P  = PERCENTAGE SAVINGS EXPECTED TO BE ACHIEVED BY PROJECT
46   REM   R  = PROJECTED INFLATION RATE PER YEAR ON HEATING COSTS
48   REM   S  = DOLLAR SAVINGS EXPECTED IN FIRST YEAR
50   REM   S1 = SAVINGS IN THE SECOND YEAR
52   REM   S2 = SAVINGS IN THE THIRD YEAR
54   REM   T  = TOTAL SAVINGS OVER THE THREE YEARS
100     PRINT "ENTER YOUR EXPECTED HEATING BILL THIS YEAR";
110     INPUT B
120     PRINT "ENTER PROJECTED PERCENTAGE SAVINGS";
130     INPUT P
140     PRINT "ENTER EXPECTED INFLATION RATE ON HEATING COSTS";
150     INPUT R
190     LET S = P/100 * B
200     LET S1 = S + R/100 * S
210     LET S2 = S1 + R/100 * S1
220     LET T = S + S1 + S2
300     PRINT "TOTAL 3-YEAR SAVINGS WOULD BE "; T
310     GO TO 100
970 END

READY
DELETE 140-150

READY
160     LET R = 20
10   REM   COMPUTE 4-YEAR SAVINGS ON HEATING BILL
215     LET S3 = S2 + R/100 * S2
220     LET T = S + S1 + S2 + S3
53   REM   S3 = SAVINGS IN THE FOURTH YEAR
54   REM   T  = TOTAL SAVINGS OVER THE FOUR YEARS
300     PRINT "TOTAL 4-YEAR SAVINGS WOULD BE "; T
LIST
```

```
10   REM   COMPUTE 4-YEAR SAVINGS ON HEATING BILL
20   REM   NORGE GUDDLE    JUNE 1979
40   REM
42   REM   B  = HEATING BILL FOR THE CURRENT YEAR
44   REM   P  = PERCENTAGE SAVINGS EXPECTED TO BE ACHIEVED BY PROJECT
46   REM   R  = PROJECTED INFLATION RATE PER YEAR ON HEATING COSTS
48   REM   S  = DOLLAR SAVINGS EXPECTED IN FIRST YEAR
50   REM   S1 = SAVINGS IN THE SECOND YEAR
52   REM   S2 = SAVINGS IN THE THIRD YEAR
53   REM   S3 = SAVINGS IN THE FOURTH YEAR
54   REM   T  = TOTAL SAVINGS OVER THE FOUR YEARS
100     PRINT "ENTER YOUR EXPECTED HEATING BILL THIS YEAR";
110     INPUT B
120     PRINT "ENTER PROJECTED PERCENTAGE SAVINGS";
130     INPUT P
160     LET R = 20
190     LET S = P/100 * B
200     LET S1 = S + R/100 * S
210     LET S2 = S1 + R/100 * S1
215     LET S3 = S2 + R/100 * S2
220     LET T = S + S1 + S2 + S3
300     PRINT "TOTAL 4-YEAR SAVINGS WOULD BE "; T
310     GO TO 100
970 END
```

Figure 5.9 Editing a program.

5.9 MAIN IDEAS

a. A BASIC program consists of statements, each with a line number, in sequence by line number. Line numbers are used in editing programs, and to indicate destinations of the flow of control in IF and GO TO statements.

b. Variables hold quantities in main storage; numeric variables hold numbers, and string variables hold character strings. They don't mix.

c. The statements introduced in this chapter are:

REM	Remark
END	Physical end of each program
LET	Assigns a value to a variable; the value is obtained by evaluating an expression
INPUT	Assigns a value to a variable; the value is obtained from the user's terminal
PRINT	Prints at the terminal
GO TO	Unconditional transfer of control
IF	Conditional transfer of control

d. Arithmetic expressions are used in LET, IF, and PRINT statements. They are formed from numeric variables, numbers, the operators $+$, $-$, $*$, $/$, $\uparrow$ or $**$, and parentheses.

e. A GO TO statement transfers control to a given line number. An IF statement transfers control if the condition is true. Conditions are specified as relations using the operators $<$, $<=$, $=$, $>=$, $>$, $<>$ or $\#$.

f. When the test for exit from a loop must follow some actions in the loop, we use the LOOP-EXIT structure:

LOOP

preliminary actions

EXIT WHEN *condition*

further actions

g. Procedure steps are transcribed into BASIC statements:

"Obtain a value"	into	PRINT, INPUT pair
"Print"	into	PRINT
"Compute" or "Set"	into	LET
WHILE	into	IF, GO TO structure

IF-THEN-ELSE	into	IF, GO TO structure
IF-THEN	into	IF, GO TO structure
LOOP-EXIT	into	IF, GO TO structure

h. BASIC commands and special keys are summarized in Fig. 5.10.

Command	Action
LOG	Starts timesharing system log-on procedure.
BYE	Logs off the system.
CATALOG or CAT	Lists the names of the files in user file space.
NEW	Erases user workspace.
	Prepares machine to accept name of a new file. The accepted name will be the name of the file currently in user workspace.
OLD	Erases user workspace.
	Prepares machine to accept the name of a file in a program library or the user's file space. The content of the specified file is then copied into user workspace to become the file currently in user workspace.
LIST	Lists the contents of user workspace onto terminal together with its file name.
LIST *m*	Lists line *m* of the content of user workspace onto terminal with its file name.
LIST *m–n*	Lists lines numbered *m* through *n* of the content of user workspace onto terminal together with its file name.
DELETE *m–n*	Deletes lines numbered *m* through *n* from content of user workspace. Single lines can be deleted by typing the line number and then the RETURN key. To insert or replace a line in the content of the user workspace, simply type the line and then press the RETURN key.
RUN	Translates and executes the program currently in user workspace.
SAVE	Places a copy of the user workspace into the user file space. An error message will be returned if SAVE attempts to write over an existing file in the user's file space.
REPLACE	Writes over an existing file in the user's file space with the file by the same name which is in user workspace.
UNSAVE	Deletes specified file from the user's file space, e.g., UNSAVE REPORT.
↑ C (CONTROL C)	A sequence of two or more ↑ C will halt execution of a program.
↑ U (CONTROL U)	Cancels line currently being typed in.
Rubout	Erases the last character of the current input line.

Figure 5.10 BASIC commands.

5.10 QUESTIONS FOR IMAGINATION AND REVIEW

1. How many different valid variable names are there in BASIC?

2. Which of the following are valid numeric variable names in BASIC, which are valid string variable names, and which are invalid for either?

E	E3$	$3	E3.1
EZ	3E3	E10	E.1
E3	$E	E0	3
3E	E$3	E−1	3$
E$	E*	E+1	

3. Which of the following are valid PRINT statements? Which are invalid, and why? If A = 142.87, B9 = −21.4, and F$ = "PEOPLE STRAINING THEIR EYES", what do the valid PRINT statements print?

```
310    PRINT "ON A CLEAR DAY, YOU CAN SEE"; F$
320    PRNT   A,B9
330    PRINT B9 A F$
340    PRINT WAGE =;A
350    PRINT F$, B9, "A"; 2.00
360    "INVOICE AMOUNT";A
PRINT "PLEASE REMIT"; 2.00
380    PRINT "2.00";2.00;A;"A";"F$";"A;F$;2.00"
390    PRINT "(A + B9)/2 = ";(A + B9)/2
```

4. Construct PRINT statements that will print:

   a) A message YOU ARE OVERDRAWN BY the variable W,

   b) The same message, but with a dollar sign preceding the number,

   c) The quantities B, C, D, allowing for each quantity 10 spaces for the number and blank spaces following the number.

5. Which of the following are valid LET statements? Which are invalid, and why? If T = 6.1, and Y = 6, what is the result of each valid LET statement?

```
180    LET K = 1
190    LET T = T−7
200    LET F$ = "YES"
210    LET F$ = "7"
```

```
220    LET F$ = 7
230    LET T = "1"
240    LET X = -4
250    LET Y0 = - Y ↑ 2
260    LET Y1 = Y(S-3)
270    LET Y2 = (Y-2)*(Y-3) ↑ 2
280    LET Y3 = (Y22-7)*22Y
290    LET Y4 = (Y+4)*Y-3)
300    LET Y5 = Y*-2
```

6. Construct LET statements that will compute the following expressions and store each one in X:

a) $\dfrac{-b + \sqrt{b^2 - 4ac}}{2a}$

b) $h \times r + (h - 40)\dfrac{r}{2}$

c) $0.11m$

d) $b + f(i - d)$

7. What are the differences between a REM statement and a PRINT statement?

8. Construct a pair of PRINT and INPUT statements to prompt the user and receive input from the terminal for each of the following:

a) Does the user have more input? Put the response in R$.

b) Ask for city, state, and zip code; put the response in C$.

c) Ask for quantity ordered; put the result in Q.

d) Ask for product number; put the result in P$. Why not P?

9. Which of the following are valid statements? Which are invalid, and why? If Y = 90, B = 4, and Y$ = "NO", what is the result of each of the valid statements?

```
150    IF Y > B-4 GO TO 460
160    IF 8 < Y <= 9 GO TO 460
170    IF Y$ = 8 GO TO 460
180    IF Y$ = YES GO TO 460
190    IF Y$ <> "YES" THEN 460
200    GO TO Y
210    IF Y-8 <= B*6 THEN GO TO 460
220    IF Y-8 < B-4 GO TO 460
```

10. Convince yourself that a GO TO statement followed immediately by the line number that is the destination of the GO TO, as in

```
340   GO TO 350

350   ...
```

can always be eliminated without changing the results of the program.

11. Form the one-statement equivalents of each of the following pairs of statements:

a) 400   IF B > T GO TO 420
   410   GO TO 480

b) 620   IF Y$ = "STOP" GO TO 640
   630   GO TO 350

c) 1050   IF 3*K <= (Q−4) ↑ 2 GO TO 1070
   1060   GO TO 2000

12. Transcribe into BASIC the procedures you wrote for Questions 1, 2, and 3 of Chapter 4.

13. Transcribe the following procedure into BASIC:

1. Set K = 4
2. Set T = 0
3. WHILE K > 0
   3.1 Obtain quantity ordered, price per unit
   3.2 Add quantity × price to T
   3.3 Subtract 1 from K
4. Print the value of T

14. Which of the structures WHILE and LOOP-EXIT can be described as a special case of the other?

15. Tillamook is 157 lovely miles from The Dalles. We want a program that will tell us, for different combinations of miles per gallon and price per gallon, the cost of the gasoline that will get us from Tillamook to The Dalles. The program should accept miles per gallon and price per gallon and print the cost in a loop, with exit from the loop when zero is typed in as miles per gallon. Write a procedure and then the BASIC program to do this task.

16. PRINT statements in BASIC may include commas rather than semicolons, and generally eliminate the use of TABs as well. We may think of the print line as divided into five zones of fourteen spaces each (with an extra two spaces in the last zone). A comma in a PRINT statement is equivalent to a TAB to the beginning of the next zone. Think of advantages of the commas, and convert a program from the use of TABs to commas. Think of disadvantages, too.

17. Following Question 7 of Chapter 4, modify the program in Fig. 5.5 so that it will print at the end of the loan repayment schedule the number of months required for full payment.

18. Transcribe into BASIC the procedures you wrote for Questions 9, 10, and 11 of Chapter 4.

CHAPTER 6
READING AND MANAGING FILES

Every business and every governmental body need data. To be useful at all, the data must be organized; it would be chaos if all data were mixed higglety-pigglety. A business usually organizes data by arranging them in accounting journals, ledgers, file folders, note books, filing cabinets—and computer storage media. The data must be organized within computer storage media, too. In any data organization, in the computer or not, it is helpful to store together data that are similar. In computer storage, we call a collection of similar data stored together a *file*. This chapter is about processing files. First we explore further the definition and structure of a file, and the way in which files are used in business data processing systems. Then we discuss the representation and use of files in BASIC. During the discussion, we show how files are managed and maintained in a data processing system.

We also show how the user may simulate the use of a file through DATA statements in BASIC systems that do not support files. Finally, we introduce the COPY command, which enables the BASIC user to move entire files around within disk storage and copy them onto the user's terminal.

6.1 FILES IN BUSINESS DATA PROCESSING

A file is a collection of similar data that are stored together. The usual reasons for choosing to store certain data in a particular file are:

The file contains all the data in some particular class;

The data in the file will be used later, and this particular collection of data will be handy for those later uses.

Let us give some examples of computer data files:

A file of the current registrations of all students at your college or university;

A file of current account balances for all customers of your local electric utility;

A file of personnel data for all current employees of your local electric utility;

A file of payments made on a bank's credit cards since the last billing;

A file of names and addresses of the customers of a mail-order house;

A file of United States zip codes and the corresponding state abbreviations for each;

A file of inventory data for all products sold by a mail-order house;

A file may contain a computer program, or a set of programs, depending on the system.

We can also describe a file as a collection of data on individual entities in some population. In the first example above, the population is the student body of your college or university, and each student is one of the entities. In these terms, we call the data on *one* of the entities a *record*. So in the examples above the current registration data for one student would be a record, the account balance for one customer of the electric utility would be a record, and so forth.

We are interested in certain data on each entity in the population, so we keep in each record a consistent set of descriptions of the entity. For example, if we keep the name of a customer in a record, we will want *every* record to contain a customer name; the same is true of previous account balance, payments during the month, charges and credits during the month, etc. Each of these descriptions of the entity can be called a *data element* or *data field*, and each record in a particular file will contain the same data fields.

Product number
Size
Color
Model
Description
Quantity on hand
Quantity on back-order (ordered by customer)
Supplier
Quantity on order from supplier
Reorder point
Usual reorder quantity
Price
Cost

Figure 6.1 A record in an inventory file.

Let us give some more specific examples of possible data fields or descriptors in a record. A record in a file of inventory data for products sold by a mail-order company might include the data elements shown in Fig. 6.1. Not all data elements will contain values for every product. For example, some products do not have different colors or sizes or models, but a consistent place in the record is provided for these elements nevertheless. Figure 6.2 shows the possible data fields of records in a personnel (or payroll) file.

Social Security number
Name
Home address
Birth date
Starting employment date
Current position or classification
Work location: plant, dept., etc.
Pay rate
Sex
Dependents claimed
Deductions authorized (union dues, insurance, etc.)
FICA wages for the year to date
Accrued vacation
Accrued sick leave
Deductions made this year to date

Figure 6.2 A record in a personnel file.

Usually we want a program to take the same action on each record in the file, and it is very helpful to be able to expect the arrangement of data fields in all records to be the same. It is most natural to construct our programs to treat each record (therefore, each entity) as a unit. A program will usually include a section that processes a record, thereby taking some action on an entity; this section will be executed repeatedly for each record in the file.

As an example, consider a program that a merchandising company might run weekly to list the products that are on back-order to its customers and the quantity of each that are on order from its suppliers. This program would take its data from the inventory file shown in Fig. 6.1. The task, for each inventory record, is to print a line on the back-order report listing:

- Product number, and size, color, and model,

- Description,

- Quantity on back-order (to customer),

- Quantity on order from supplier,

but to print the line only if the product *is* back-ordered.

The procedure can be written as:

1. WHILE there are records yet to be read from the file
   1.1 Read a record
   1.2 IF back-order quantity > 0
       1.2.1 Print a report line

As we shall see, many programs follow the general outline:

1. WHILE there are records yet to be read from a file
   1.1 Read a record
   1.2 Process the record

6.2 THE SYSTEMS FLOWCHART

The typical business information processing system includes several programs, as well as clerical activities. For example, the payroll system outlined in Section 1.4 requires clerical transcription of updates to the payroll master and of time card data, and programs to update the payroll master, to edit the time card data, to produce the payroll register and add data for the current period to the year-to-date master file totals, and to print checks. It is useful to have a standard method of showing the outline of a business data processing system, including clerical steps, input documents, files, programs, reports and other outputs, and the relationships among all these system components. The systems flowchart is a diagrammatic representation. Figure 6.3 shows a systems flowchart for

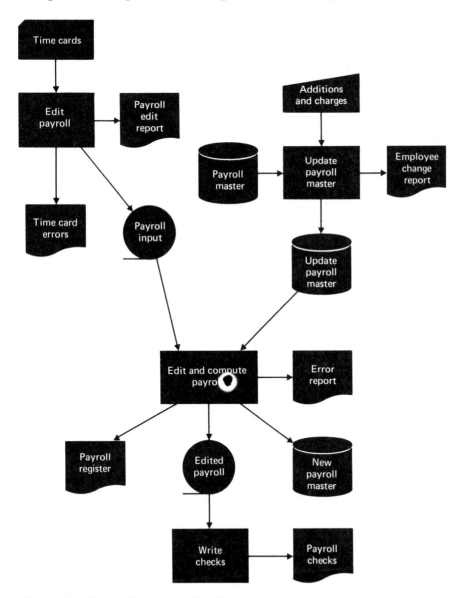

Figure 6.3 A payroll systems flowchart.

a payroll system; it shows all files, the programs that use and update each file, reports produced by each program, and the sequence of operations.

Systems flowcharts are in common use in data processing, so there are fairly standard conventions for them. The most important conventions are described below, and the diagrammatic components are shown in Fig. 6.4.

1. Each program is represented by a rectangle. The name of each program, or a short phrase describing its purpose, should be written in the rectangle.

2. A sequential file is represented by a circle with a horizontal tail, which is meant to look like a reel of magnetic tape. The name of the file should be written in the circle or on the tail.

3. A direct-access file is represented by a cylindrical shape, which is meant to look like a magnetic drum or disk pack. The name of the

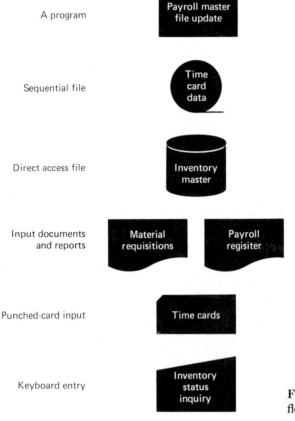

Figure 6.4 Systems flowchart components.

file should be written in the figure. Some people use this shape to represent sequential files as well as direct-access files.

4. Input documents and reports are represented by a shape that looks like a torn sheet of paper. The name of the document or report should be written in the figure.

5. Punched-card input is represented by a rectangle with a triangle cut from the upper left; this is meant to look like a punched card. Many punched cards now are manufactured with rounded corners, but for many years all had straight corners except for the one corner cut.

6. Keyboard entry, as at a teletype or video terminal, is represented by a trapezoid, meant to look like a stylized keyboard.

7. Each file that is input to a program is connected to the program by a directed arrow into the program. Each file that is output from a program is connected to the program by a directed arrow pointing to the file. Generally, input files are arranged above or to the left of their programs, and output files below or to the right of their programs.

6.3 SEQUENTIAL AND DIRECT-ACCESS FILES

The examples of file processing that we have seen until now have involved sequential files. That is, the records in the file are accessed only in the sequence in which they were written into the file. For many applications, sequential file organization is not only the simplest form but is exactly what is needed. When a payroll system is to print checks from data in the payroll master file, it is quite appropriate to process the records of the file in sequence, and print checks only for those employees who worked during the pay period. When an accounts receivable system is to print monthly statements to its customers, it is reasonable to process the records in the customer billing file in sequence, printing a statement for each customer if there has been activity during the month or if there is a nonzero balance in the account.

A sequential file may be stored on any of a number of physical devices. The most obvious is a magnetic tape, since by the very nature of a tape, the file must be accessed sequentially. A sequential file may be stored on punched cards; cards can be processed manually in almost any way imaginable, but a card reader attached to the computer must read the cards sequentially. A magnetic disk can also hold a sequential file, and this is the simplest way to store files on disk.

There are times when a program needs direct access to a particular record in a file, followed by direct access to another record that bears no sequential relationship to the first. For example, a program that processes orders may take sequentially the file of orders, but may need to find the price of each item ordered from a record in a product master file. The accesses needed to records in the product master file will not be in any sequential order or any other order predictable in advance. If a program had to start at the beginning of the product master file and search sequentially for the product needed, for every item of every order, the process would be incredibly slow. We need much more direct access to each product record.

The same order-processing program may need to check inventory quantity available for each product ordered, and to reduce the quantity

"Sorry, but I'll have to check on you. What is your Social Security number?"

available by the amount we presume will be shipped. For this task, the program must not only access records in an inventory file (it may be the same file as the product master file we discussed above) in unpredictable order, but must also update and rewrite the records accessed.

The type of direct access to records that is required for these applications is possible only if the files are stored on magnetic disk or a similar device. The disk access mechanism does permit the computer to move the disk access arm directly to any desired track on a disk and to read a desired record from that track, waiting only for the disk rotation to bring the record under the read-write heads.

A direct-access mechanism is only part of the story. If we want a direct-access file, we also need a way to tell the computer exactly where to go to find each particular record we need. We might have some formula, such as taking the last four digits of the product number as the number of the record in the file: Product number A234567 would be the 4567th record in the file, and the computer could find it directly.

The reader will recognize this as a rather stringent and limiting condition not easily met. There are advanced techniques that help in solving some of the difficulties of working out an appropriate formula, but we will close this section by describing the file organization called *indexed sequential*. The indexed sequential file is ordered on some key contained in each record: product number, social security number, customer or account number, or a similar, unique identifier. The file is stored sequentially, but on magnetic disk. The computer will also maintain an *index*, probably also on disk, which gives the disk location of each of several segments in the file, much as an encyclopedia volume's binding says HAN-IND. The computer can quickly scan the index and determine which segment of the file a desired record is in, and then search sequentially that segment. This is a compromise between sequential access and direct access, but it is effective in a wide number of applications.

6.4 READING SEQUENTIAL FILES IN BASIC

We will restrict our attention now to sequential files, and explore how they can be read by a BASIC program.

The first responsibility in any file processing program is to establish the connection between the file and the program. We must tell the computer's operating system that we want to read a file, and we have to tell *which* file. In BASIC, this is done by the FILES statement. The simple statement

```
70   FILES   PAYR
```

tells the operating system that we want to use the file PAYR in our program. If we want a program to access more than one file, we can declare several files in the same FILES statement:

    70 FILES PAYR, PERSM, PAYREG

This statement causes the operating system to look in the user's file directory for these three files, and make them available to the program.

A data path is established for each file used in a program. The paths are identified and distinguished by a *file access number*. File access numbers are assigned by the system in the same sequence as the files are mentioned in the FILES statement; in the example above,

    PAYR   has file access number 1,

    PERSM   has file access number 2,

    PAYREG   has file access number 3.

The file access number for each file is our means of designating which file to access in all further file-handling statements in a BASIC program. Among other advantages, this gives us flexibility: If we want to rerun a program using a different file or set of files, only the FILES statement need be changed. In some other languages and systems, this kind of flexibility is extended by the provision of a job control statement that associates a file name used internal to the program with the name (and sometimes the location) of the actual file to be used in a particular execution of a program.

Our program can read a record from a file with a version of the INPUT statement. The general form is

    line no. INPUT $\#k$, *list of variables*

where

    k is the file access number of the file to be read

    list of variables is a list of variable names, separated by commas, into which data should be read

As an example,

    110 INPUT #1, S$, A, B

reads a string followed by two numbers, from the file whose access number is 1, and stores

    the string in S$,

    the first number in A,

    the second number in B.

The data fields in the file are read in sequence, and stored as values of the variables. Suppose the file PROD contains

```
P101   "TEGWID, SMALL"   6.25      3
P104   SCUPPER          15.75      2
W128   AXLETREE         49.75      1
```

The statement

```
70  FILES  PROD
```

connects our program to this file, with file access number 1. The first execution of

```
110   INPUT #1, P$, D$, C, Q
```

will read the first record from the file and store

the string "P101"	in P$,
the string "TEGWID, SMALL"	in D$,
the number 6.25	in C,
the number 3	in Q.

The operating system keeps a pointer, which shows how much of the file has been read; further reading starts from that point, and pushes the pointer along. A second execution of the statement at line 110 will read

"P104"	into P$,
"SCUPPER"	into D$,
15.75	into C,
2	into Q,

and a third execution will start by reading "W128".

In some computers and under some computer languages, fields within records to be read from a file are designated by position within the record:

Characters	1–9	Social security number
	10–35	Name
	36–42	Wages paid this year to date
	etc.	

In such records a field such as name occupies 26 character positions, even for very short names, and a really long name of 28 characters cannot be stored and must be shortened. In other computers or other languages, the fields of a record may vary in length, depending on the data themselves, and some character is used as a field separator character to mark the separation between one data field and the next.

BASIC allows fields to vary in length. The comma is accepted as a separator between numbers or strings, and a space is accepted as a separator between strings. Several consecutive spaces are recognized as one separator, and may appear after a comma, too. This rule is sufficient for separating numbers, but not for strings. After all, we would often like to include a space or a comma as characters *within* a string. This problem is solved by having the computer recognize quotation marks around strings. When scanning a record, the computer recognizes a quotation mark as the beginning of a string, then accepts all characters—including any spaces or commas—until the next quotation mark as the value of the string. We saw an example above: "TEGWID, SMALL" is recognized as one string.

One of the disconcerting features of BASIC is that the scan for fields is based entirely on a search for field separators and does not recognize the concept of a record. It is most useful to think of files as composed of records, and construct procedures and, therefore, programs that process records. We will generally represent a record as contained in one line of the contents of the file, and we will see later that a program that creates a file will normally produce a line containing each record. But the BASIC scan in reading fields takes no notice. If an INPUT statement requests values of three variables from a file, the next three fields are read from the file, whether they are found as part of a line, a full line, or even three lines. For example, if the first INPUT from the file PROD above were

```
110   INPUT #1, P$, D$
```

the strings "P101" and "TEGWID, SMALL" would be read into P$ and D$, and the *next* INPUT would start by reading 6.25.

Many programs that read data from sequential files are organized to read records and process each one until there are no more records to be read. Therefore, we need a way to enable a program to recognize that there are no more records to be read. There are at least three ways:

1. Count the records ahead of time, and somehow give the count to the program, so that if there are, say, 263 records, the program may count 263 times through a read-process loop and then leave that loop.

2. Arrange to have a last record in the file that does not contain real data but a "sentinel value," which can be recognized by the program

as a signal that there are no more data. For example, the PROD file
above could contain a last record

```
STOP   0    0    0
```

Just after reading each record from the file, a program would test
whether the product number P$ is "STOP", and if so, jump out of
the loop that reads and processes records.

3. Rely on the operating system to know when the reading of a file has
   reached the end of the file, and allow the program to ask the operating system.

Record counts and sentinel values have their uses, but also their disadvantages. When Method 3 is available, it is usually the best and easiest
way for a program to control looping until the end of the file.
    In BASIC, the operating system is capable of telling a program
whether there are still records to be read in a file. We want a test for the
condition *end of file;* in BASIC the statement that tests conditions is the
IF statement, so the end-of-file test is a form of the IF statement. The
condition specification must include designation of which file to test, so
the file access number must be a part of the statement. The general form
of the statement is

line no. IF END $\#k$ GO TO *line no.*

where

k is the file access number of the file to be tested

line no. at the end of the statement designates where the program
should go if we are in fact at the end of the file.

So the statement

```
100   IF END #1 GO TO 400
```

will jump to statement 400 if there are no more records to be read in the
file whose access number is 1, but will instead pass to the next statement
(110?) if there are more records to read.
    As we translate into a program a procedure

1. WHILE there are records not yet read

   1.1 Read a record

   etc.

it is most natural to construct the pair of statements

```
100   IF END #1 GO TO 200
110   INPUT #1, P$, D$, C, Q
```

Statement 200 would start the representation of Step 2 in the procedure. We will see this pattern many times. Note that the IF END statement precedes the INPUT statement; what would you expect to happen if the order were reversed? Figure 6.5 shows a program flowchart for the WHILE structure.

Let us close this section with an example. Suppose the file PROD contains inventory records; each record contains for one product:

Product number,

Product description,

Cost of each item,

Quantity on hand of the product.

We are asked for a program that will report the total value of inventory: the sum of (cost) × (quantity on hand) for all products. Figure 6.6 shows the procedure that can do the task, and Fig. 6.7 shows a program in BASIC that follows the procedure. Note that the WHILE construction is implemented by the IF END statement, with the loop being closed by the GO TO statement in line 230. The GO TO statement returns control to statement 200, so the end-of-file condition is tested before *each*

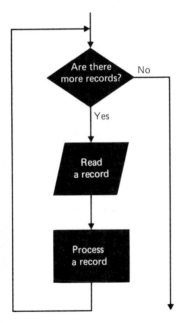

Fig. 6.5 WHILE structure reading a file.

---

1. Set Total value $= 0$
2. WHILE there are records in PROD not yet read
   2.1 Read a record from PROD
   2.2 Add (cost) $\times$ (quantity on hand) to total value
3. Print Total value

Figure 6.6 A file-reading procedure.

```
10    REM    REPORT TOTAL VALUE OF INVENTORY
15    REM      FOLLOWING PROCEDURE OF FIG. 6.6
20    REM    STRUBLE    JAN 1980
30    REM      T   = TOTAL VALUE OF INVENTORY
32    REM      P$  = PRODUCT NUMBER
34    REM      D$  = DESCRIPTION OF PRODUCT
36    REM      C   = COST PER ITEM OF PRODUCT
38    REM      Q   = QUANTITY ON HAND OF PRODUCT
70       FILES PROD
100      LET T = 0
190   REM   LOOP TO READ AND PROCESS RECORDS
200      IF END #1 GO TO 300
210      INPUT #1, P$, D$, C, Q
220      LET T = T + C * Q
230      GO TO 200
290   REM   PRINT TOTAL VALUE
300      PRINT "TOTAL INVENTORY VALUE = "; T
970   END
```

Figure 6.7 A file-reading program.

INPUT. The IF END statement passes control to statement 300 to implement Step 3 of the procedure when all records have been read and processed.   •

6.5 THE DATA AND READ STATEMENTS

Some BASIC systems used in education do not support the use of files by students. The concept of files is central to any study of business data processing, so we recommend that in systems that do not support files, the students do the next best thing and simulate files by using the DATA statement. DATA statements allow the programmer to include a set of data *in the program itself*. The general format of the DATA statement is

line no. DATA *data fields*, separated by commas

The DATA statements are not executable, so their placement in a program is arbitrary; it is best to place them just before the END statement.

For example, a set of DATA statements

```
500   DATA   P101, "TEGWID, SMALL",   6.25,   3
510   DATA   P104, SCUPPER,          15.75,   2
520   DATA   W128, AXLETREE,         49.75,   1
```

in a program could simulate a portion of a product file.

The data in DATA statements are read into variables by the READ statement. The READ statement is just like the INPUT statement reading from a file, with substitution of the word READ for INPUT, and deletion of the file access number. For example,

```
110   READ   P$, D$, C, Q
```

in a program that includes the DATA statements above will read

```
"P101"              into P$,
"TEGWID, SMALL"     into D$,
6.25                into C,
3                   into Q.
```

A second execution of the READ statement will read data from the DATA statement 510.

To complete the simulation of a file by DATA and READ statements, we need an IF END statement to test for the end of the data in the set of DATA statements. The IF END statement *without* a file access number has this meaning:

```
210   IF END GO TO 400
```

jumps to 400 if there are no more data to be read from the DATA statements. Figure 6.8 shows the program in Fig. 6.7 revised to use DATA statements simulating a file. Not all systems include an IF END statement that tests for the end of the data in DATA statements; in such systems, the student will have to use either a similar piece of BASIC provided by the system, or a sentinel record such as

```
980   DATA   STOP, D, 0, 0
```

which can be read and tested.

The DATA statement can be used in programs for purposes other than simulation of files. Values that form a table that is used by a program but changed only rarely may be kept in DATA statements and read as a preliminary part of a program. The usefulness of this feature will become more apparent when we discuss arrays in Chapter 10.

The word READ, with a file access number, can be used to read data from a *file*. Files to be read by READ statements are called *text files*,

```
10   REM   REPORT TOTAL VALUE OF INVENTORY FOLLOWING PROCEDURE OF FIG. 6.6
15   REM   USING DATA STATEMENTS TO SIMULATE THE PROD FILE
20   REM   STRUBLE    JAN 1980
30   REM      T  = TOTAL VALUE OF INVENTORY
32   REM      P$ = PRODUCT NUMBER
34   REM      D$ = DESCRIPTION OF PRODUCT
36   REM      C  = COST PER ITEM OF PRODUCT
100      LET T = 0
190  REM  LOOP TO READ AND PROCESS RECORDS
200      IF END THEN 300
210      READ P$, D$, C, Q
220      LET T = T + C * Q
230      GO TO 200
290  REM  PRINT TOTAL VALUE
300      PRINT "TOTAL INVENTORY VALUE = "; T
490  REM  DATA STATEMENTS SIMULATING PROD FILE
500      DATA P101, "TEGWID, SMALL", 6.25, 3
510      DATA P104, SCUPPER,       15.75, 2
520      DATA W128, AXLETREE,      49.75, 1
970  END
```

Figure 6.8 A program reading DATA statements.

and each line in such a file has a line number. The line numbers themselves are bypassed during READ statements; otherwise, the action of READ statements is exactly like that of INPUT statements. Text files have an advantage in that they can be loaded into a user's workspace and edited like programs. That is a dangerous notion in connection with files used in business systems, since we want to ensure the integrity of files by treating them only with well-developed and tested programs; therefore, we stay away from text files for data.

6.6 THE COPY COMMAND

The COPY command copies an entire file from one location on disk to another. The general form of the command is

COPY *source* > *destination*

The greater-than sign (>) is used because it looks like the head of an arrow. The source of a file to be copied may be either

    library:filename   to copy a file from a library

or filename   to copy a file from the user's file space

The destination of the COPY may be either

    filename   to copy a file into the user's file space

or TTY: to copy the file onto the user's terminal

Note the colon (:) in the specific destination TTY:. The colon clarifies to the operating system that the destination is the *device* TTY: rather than a filename TTY in the user's file space.

Let us show several uses of the COPY command. First, a data file to be used by a laboratory exercise program may be copied from a library, where the master version remains intact, to the student's workspace, where it must be in order to be read by a student's program. For example,

```
COPY   CS2:DSALE > DSALE
```

copies the file DSALE from the CS2 library into the user's file space, where it also has the name DSALE.

```
COPY   CS2:PAYR > EMPL
```

copies the file PAYR from the CS2 library into the user's file space, but gives the name EMPL to the copy in the user's file space.

Second, the user may obtain a copy of the file at the user's terminal. The command

```
COPY   CS2:DSALE > TTY:
```

copies the file DSALE from the CS2 library to the user's terminal. When a student is about to run, or has already run, a program that takes data from a file, it is essential for the student to know the contents of the file in order to know whether the program is doing the correct thing.

```
COPY   ULAB2 > TTY:
```

copies the file ULAB2, either a program or a data file, to the user's terminal.

Finally,

```
COPY   DT37 > DT38
UNSAVE DT37
```

effectively renames the file DT37 in the user's file space, giving it the new name DT38. This is done in two steps: The first, using COPY, makes a copy of the file, giving the new name DT38 to the copy; the second step, UNSAVE DT37, removes the copy of the file with the old name.

Three points should be stressed:

1. COPY is a command, *not* a statement that can be included *in* a BASIC program.

2. COPY never harms, deletes, or changes in any way the original copy of the file being copied.

3. COPY has *no* effect on the user's workspace. The user may have a program in the workspace, and execute any COPY command without affecting the contents of the workspace in any way.

6.7 MAIN IDEAS

a. Data stored in a computer system are organized into *files*. A file contains data on some group of entities; the data about one of these entities is a *record*. A record contains *data fields*; each field is a string or a number.

b. A *sequential file* permits access to records only in the sequence in which the records were written. A *direct-access file* permits access directly to any record desired, regardless of which record in the file was last accessed. An *indexed sequential file* provides a table of segments of a file; the system determines from the table which segment contains the record desired, and the record is finally located by sequential access within the segment.

c. An information processing system includes files, programs that use and maintain files, and operational procedures. A *systems flowchart* shows the relationships and flow of control in such a system.

d. Each file to be used in a BASIC program is declared in a FILES statement, which establishes a *file access number* for each file. All other file references in the program are in terms of the file access number.

e. Fields in a file (usually a record) are read by an INPUT statement that includes the file access number. The system reads fields in the file sequentially.

f. A form of the IF statement allows a program to test whether it has read to the end of a file. This statement is used to implement WHILE loops that continue until end-of-file.

g. DATA statements define a block of data within a program that can be read by READ statements. It is not reasonable to keep the data for a program in the program itself, but where necessary, DATA statements can simulate a file.

h. The COPY command copies an entire file from a library or the user's file space to the user's file space or the user's terminal.

6.8 QUESTIONS FOR IMAGINATION AND REVIEW

1. A file CUST contains, for each customer of a mail-order company:

   Customer number,

   Name,

   Address,

   City, State, Zip (in one string),

   Total purchases,

   Date of last purchase.

Write a program that will print, for each customer in the file:

   Name,

   Address,

   City, State, Zip,

followed by two blank lines. Can you modify the program to print *two* names and addresses across the page?

2. Think of several situations in which some form of direct-access file, rather than a sequential file, would be needed. In each case, how might the file be organized?

3. The file EQUIP contains a record for every item of capital equipment owned by a company. The record contains:

   Property control number,

   Description,

   Serial number,

   Year purchased (last two digits only),

   Original value,

   Number of years of useful life.

The company uses a straight-line depreciation method: The depreciation of each item each year is the original value/the useful life. Write a procedure and then a program to calculate:

   Total original value of the equipment,

   Depreciation charged in 1980,

   Total depreciated value in 1980.

Make sure that no item is depreciated below a value of zero.

4. Usually, a program reads a file and is finished with it. In BASIC, it is possible for a program to reread a file. The statement that resets the pointer into the file to the beginning of the file to prepare for rereading is

     line no. RESTORE $\#k$

where k is the file access number. The RESTORE statement can reset the pointer for rereading of data from DATA statements as well. Use the RESTORE statement and read the file RESLT twice in a program. The file RESLT contains a record for each division or profit center of a company. Each record contains

     Name of the division,

     Gross revenue for the quarter,

     Profit for the quarter.

In one reading of the file, a program can compute the total revenue and total profit for the company, and the percentage return (profit/revenue). In a *second* reading, the program should print for each division or profit center:

     Name of the division,

     Gross revenue for the quarter,

     Profit for the quarter,

     Percentage return for the division,

     Difference between percentage returns for the division and for the whole company.

5. Change the program in Fig. 6.8 to use a sentinel record to mark the end of the file. This requires a change from a WHILE structure to a LOOP-EXIT structure for the processing loop.

6. Explain the difference between the actions of the pair of commands

```
OLD HYPE
LIST
```

and the command COPY HYPE > TTY: In what circumstances are the OLD and LIST sequence not satisfactory?

7. Suppose the user's workspace contains a program named ZZZZ, and the user's file space contains files AAAA, BBBB, and CCCC. What will be the result, in workspace, file space, and terminal listing, of each of the following commands (independently, each from the above conditions):

a) NEW LAB8

b) NEW CCCC

c) SAVE

d) COPY BBBB > TTY

e) COPY BBBB > TTY:

f) COPY ZZZZ > TTY:

g) RENAME CCCC

h) RENAME CCCC
   SAVE

i) OLD   AAAA
   RENAME   DRAW
   SAVE

j) COPY AAAA > DRAW

CHAPTER 7
PROCEDURE STRUCTURES

In earlier chapters we have established the elements of the BASIC language, a few simple programming structures, and the importance and use of files. We are now ready to discuss a series of logical program structures and computing techniques that will enable you to write programs of some complexity for real tasks. We introduce no new structures to use in a computer procedure language; we develop computing techniques common to many computing tasks, using the structures we already have. The emphasis on recognizing and using each logical structure and technique should enable you to break up a complex task into its logical components, then program each one and fit the pieces into a working program.

7.1 COMPOUND CONDITIONS IN IF-THEN-ELSE STRUCTURES

Often the choice of which of two actions to perform depends on a compound condition:

> IF condition x *and* condition y
>
>   THEN ...

or   IF condition x *or* condition y

>   THEN ...

Following the rules of logic, the compound condition

> condition x *and* condition y

is considered true if *both* condition x and condition y are true; otherwise, the compound condition is false. Similarly, the compound condition

> condition x *or* condition y

is considered true if *either* condition x or condition y *or both* are true, and false only if both condition x and condition y are false. This is called the *inclusive or*. A payroll program may have two formulas for computing gross weekly pay. One formula pays time and a half for any hours worked over 40:

> pay = hours $\times$ wage + .5 $\times$ (hours $-$ 40) $\times$ wage;

and the other formula does not:

> pay = hours $\times$ wage.

The second formula must be used for employees who worked fewer than 40 hours. (Show that the first formula would give such employees a *lower* gross pay.) The second formula must also be used for certain employees declared "exempt" (actually, in many places such employees are exempt from the burden of receiving all overtime pay, not just the time-and-a-half factor). Therefore, computation of gross pay follows the procedure

> IF hours worked $\leq$ 40 *or* employee is exempt
>
>   THEN gross pay = hours $\times$ wage
>
>   ELSE gross pay = hours $\times$ wage + .5 $\times$ (hours $-$ 40) $\times$ wage

Some computer languages allow compound conditions directly in IF statements; in most versions of BASIC, we must use separate IF statements. If the number of hours worked is the variable H, the hourly wage is W, and the variable E\$ has the value "EXEMPT" for exempt employees, the procedure above can be implemented:

```
300   IF H <= 40 GO TO 340
310   IF E$ = "EXEMPT" GO TO 340
320   LET G = H * W + .5 * (H - 40) * W
330   GO TO 350
340   LET G = H * W
350   next step
```

If the number of hours worked is less than or equal to 40, the first IF statement sends control immediately to statement 340; under the terms of the procedure, it matters not whether such an employee is exempt. If the number of hours worked is greater than 40, control passes to statement 310, since the exempt status of this employee determines which formula is to be used.

Consider another part of an order processing example. Suppose the total amount of an order has been calculated, and the policy of the company is to give an additional discount of 2% on the total order if

the order amount is \$300.00 or more

and there is no past-due balance in the customer's account; otherwise, a handling charge of \$5.00 is to be added to the order. The procedure, therefore, is

IF order total ≥ \$300 *and* past-due balance ≤ 0

    THEN reduce order by 2%

    ELSE add \$5.00 to the order

If T is the order total and P9 is the past-due balance, this procedure can be transcribed into BASIC as

```
400   IF T >= 300 GO TO 420
410   GO TO 430
420   IF P9 <= 0 GO TO 450
430   LET T = T + 5
440   GO TO 460
450   LET T = .98 * T
460   next step
```

If the first condition, T >= 300, is true, control must pass to the second test, since both conditions must be true in order for the order to receive

the discount. On the other hand, if the first condition is false $(T < 300)$, we know immediately that the compound condition is also false, so at 410 control can pass immediately to addition of the handling charge.

We can simplify the programming by applying one of the rules of logic and taking the logical opposite of the compound condition. The procedure

    IF condition *x and* condition *y*

        THEN action A

        ELSE action B

is logically equivalent to

    IF *not* (condition *x* *and* condition *y*)
        THEN action B
        ELSE action A

And by a principle of logic known as DeMorgan's rule, this is in turn equivalent to

    IF (*not* condition *x*) *or* (*not* condition *y*)
        THEN action B
        ELSE action A

Note that the *not* applied to the compound condition can be distributed to the individual conditions, but that the *and* changes to *or* in the process. Applying this to our order processing example, we have

    IF order total < \$300 *or* past-due balance > 0
        THEN add \$5.00 to the order
        ELSE reduce order by 2%

which can be transcribed into BASIC as

```
400   IF T < 300 GO TO 440
410   IF P9 > 0 GO TO 440
420   LET T = .98 * T
430   GO TO 450
440   LET T = T + 5
450   next step
```

One of the most common compound conditions to be tested is whether some value is *within a specified range*. We may wish a program to print a warning message if the hourly wage is not within the range of, say, 2.75 to 25.00. This requires *two* tests, one against the lower limit and one against the upper limit of the range. The test

    wage is not within 2.75 to 25.00

can also be written as

    wage < 2.75 *or* wage > 25.00,

which is a form we can handle. The procedure step

    IF wage < 2.75 *or* wage > 25.00
        THEN print warning message

can be transcribed into BASIC as

```
300   IF W < 2.75 GO TO 330
310   IF W > 25.00 GO TO 330
320   GO TO 340
330   PRINT "WARNING! WAGE RATE OF ";W;" FOR ";S$
340   next step
```

or shortened slightly to

```
300   IF W < 2.75 GO TO 330
310   IF W <= 25.00 GO TO 340
330   PRINT "WARNING! WAGE RATE OF ";W;" FOR ";S$
340   next step
```

This discussion does not exhaust the possibilities: There are conditions such as IF END that cannot be transformed into their logical opposites in BASIC; working with an IF-THEN structure may or may not be simpler; some compound conditions are still more complex; the *exclusive or* logical connective requires more programming. Another level of complexity, choosing among more than two alternative actions, is introduced in Section 7.4.

7.2 CONTROLLING A LOOP BY COUNTING

There are many instances in which the action in the loop is to be performed a given number of times. Suppose we are considering a savings plan, in which we make a deposit D at the beginning of each month. Interest is compounded monthly (for simplicity) at a rate of I per year. After ten years (120 payments), how much money will be in the fund? We can represent as actions in the loop the activity of one month in the savings plan: A deposit D is added to the fund at the beginning of the month, and interest is credited at the end of the month. Before the first month begins, the fund holds a balance of zero; the actions of deposit and interest calculation are to be performed 120 times.

To control a loop so that these actions are performed exactly 120 times, we set up a counter. We set the counter to an initial value of 1, representing the fact that we are about to perform the actions of the loop for the first time. Each time we perform these actions, we must also add 1 to the counter, so that the counter contains 2 as we are about to perform the loop actions for the second time, contains 3 for the third performance, and so on. The control of the loop should, therefore, be a WHILE structure: WHILE the value of the counter is less than or equal to 120, we have not yet performed the loop actions 120 times, so we must continue performing the loop. This is expressed by the following procedure:

1. Obtain the values of D and I
2. Set the accumulated value V to zero
3. Set the counter K to 1
4. WHILE K $\leq$ 120
   4.1 Add D to V
   4.2 Multiply V by $(1 + I/12)$
   4.3 Add 1 to K
5. Print the value of V

In the general case, if some action is to be done a given number of times, say N times, the repetition can be controlled by:

1. Set a counter K to 1
2. WHILE K $\leq$ N
   2.1 Action
   2.2 Add 1 to K

Figure 7.1 shows a flowchart representing the procedure for computing the value of the savings plan. In both procedure and flowchart, I prefer the more informal verb "Set" to the word LET by which the action will be implemented in BASIC. However, any language that is informative, natural, and unambiguous will do perfectly well.

Figure 7.2 shows a BASIC program that implements this logic. The variable K is used as the counter. It is initialized to 1 by statement 300, and increased by 1 in statement 430 so that each time control reaches statement 400, the counter represents which time the loop actions (statements 410 and 420) are about to be performed. When K contains 2, the computer is about to perform the loop actions for the second time, and so on. The WHILE structure is thus represented by the IF statement at line 400 and the GO TO statement in line 440, which closes the loop.

Controlling a loop by counting is such a common operation that a special pair of statements is provided in BASIC. The statements use the keywords FOR and NEXT; they serve as slices of bread for a sandwich, and the actions to be repeated in the loop constitute the filling.

1. Set counter K to 1
2. WHILE K $\leq$ *limit*
   2.1 Loop actions
   2.2 Add 1 to K

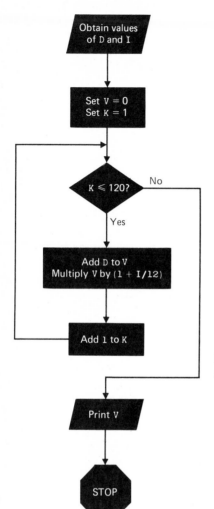

Figure 7.1 Flowchart for the value of a savings plan.

is implemented by

    100   FOR K = 1 TO *limit*
    110   loop actions
       •
       •
       •
    190   NEXT K

```
10   REM   COMPUTE VALUE IN SAVINGS PLAN AFTER 10 YEARS
15   REM   OF MONTHLY DEPOSITS EACH OF AMOUNT D
20   REM   G STRUBLE     JAN 1980
30   REM     V = ACCUMULATED AMOUNT IN SAVINGS PLAN
32   REM     D = AMOUNT OF MONTHLY DEPOSIT
34   REM     I = ANNUAL INTEREST RATE
36   REM     K = COUNTER OF MONTHS
100     PRINT "TYPE VALUE OF THE MONTHLY DEPOSIT"; TAB(34);
110     INPUT D
120     PRINT "TYPE ANNUAL INTEREST RATE"; TAB(34);
130     INPUT I
200     LET V = 0
300     LET K = 1
400     IF K > 120 GO TO 500
410     LET V = V + D
420     LET V = V * (1 + I/12)
430     LET K = K + 1
440     GO TO 400
500     PRINT "VALUE AFTER 10 YEARS = $"; V
970   END
```

Figure 7.2 Program for the value of a savings plan.

Any numeric variable may be used as a counter in a FOR loop, and though its value may be *used* in computations inside the loop, the statements in the loop should not *change* its value. The NEXT statement must name the same variable specified as the counter in the FOR statement. The *limit* specified may be any numeric expression; the most usual cases are a constant or a simple variable; no variables in the expression should be changed inside the loop. Essentially, the statement

    100   FOR K = 1 TO *limit*

replaces the statements

    100   LET K = 1
    101   IF K > *limit* GO TO *line no.*

where *line no.* is the line number of the statement immediately following the NEXT statement, hence representing the exit from the loop to the next step. Similarly,

    190   NEXT K

replaces the statements

    190   LET K = K + 1
    191   GO TO 101

where 101 is the IF statement above, which tests for exit from the loop. Thus in Fig. 7.4, statements 300, 400, 430, and 440 can be replaced by

    400   FOR K = 1 TO 120
    440   NEXT K

A general form of the FOR statement allows an initial value of the counter to be any expression, and an increment (called STEP), which may be any number, such as 2 or .05, or an expression. Thus a portion of a procedure

1. Set K to *initial value*
2. WHILE K ≤ *limit*
    2.1 loop actions
    2.2 Add *increment* to K

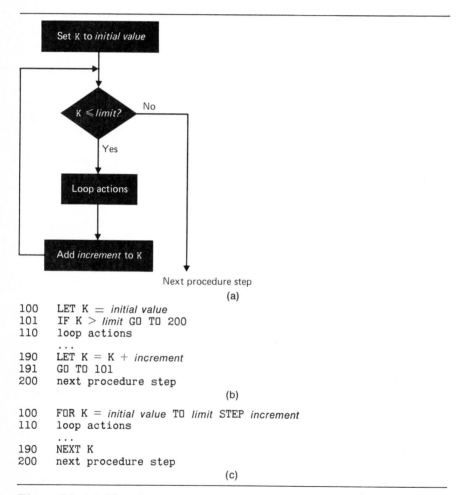

```
100    LET K = initial value
101    IF K > limit GO TO 200
110    loop actions
       . . .
190    LET K = K + increment
191    GO TO 101
200    next procedure step
```
(b)

```
100    FOR K = initial value TO limit STEP increment
110    loop actions
       . . .
190    NEXT K
200    next procedure step
```
(c)

Figure 7.3 (a) Flowchart. (b) BASIC using LET, IF, GO TO. (c) BASIC using FOR, NEXT.

shown in flowchart form in Fig. 7.3(a) and implemented in BASIC in
Fig. 7.3(b) using LET, IF, and GO TO statements to transcribe the
WHILE structure directly, can be written more simply using FOR and
NEXT statements as shown in Fig. 7.3(c). Assuming that the *increment*
is positive, each of these representations is absolutely equivalent.

As an example, suppose we want a table showing the value of $100
compounded quarterly for 5, 10, and 15 years at a variety of interest
rates. The interest rates to be used are annual rates 3%, 3.25%, 3.50%,
..., 12%, that is, each rate from 3% to 12% in steps of 0.25%. A procedure can be stated simply as

1. Print headings
2. Set I = 3.0
3. WHILE I ≤ 12.0
   3.1 Compute values after 5, 10, 15 years
   3.2 Print the values
   3.3 Increase I by 0.25

Using the FOR and NEXT statements, the program is also simple, as
shown in Fig. 7.4. Note that the PRINT statements 100–120 print headings for the table. Placed where they are, these statements print the
headings *once, before* any table values are printed. Those of you with
sharp eyes have also noticed that the limit given in the FOR statement
is 0.121, though we wish the table to go to 12%. This is not a misprint.
Just as the number 1/3 cannot be represented exactly by a finite number

```
10    REM   PRINT TABLE OF VALUES OF $100
15    REM   COMPOUNDED QUARTERLY FOR 5, 10, 15 YEARS
20    REM   AT INTEREST RATES 3%, 3.25%, ..., 12%
25    REM   G STRUBLE     JAN 1980
40    REM       I  = ANNUAL INTEREST RATE
42    REM       V1 = VALUE AFTER 5 YEARS AT INTEREST RATE I
44    REM       V2 = VALUE AFTER 10 YEARS
46    REM       V3 = VALUE AFTER 15 YEARS
100      PRINT TAB(12); "TABLE OF VALUES OF $100"
110      PRINT " RATE"; TAB(14); "5 YEARS"; TAB(27); "10 YEARS";
120      PRINT TAB(40); "15 YEARS"
200      FOR I = .03 TO .121 STEP .0025
210      LET V1 = 100 * (1 + I/4)^20
220      LET V2 = 100 * (1 + I/4)^40
230      LET V3 = 100 * (1 + I/4)^60
240      PRINT I; TAB(12); V1; TAB(25); V2; TAB(38); V3
250      NEXT I
970   END

READY
```

Figure 7.4 Program to print a table of values at compound interest.

of decimal digits, the numbers 0.03, 0.0025, and 0.12 cannot be represented exactly by a finite number of *binary* digits, and most of our computers do their arithmetic on the binary representations of numbers. The
computer uses *approximations* to 0.03, 0.0025, and 0.12. When 36 approximations to 0.0025 are added to 0.03, will the resulting approximation to 0.12 be greater or less than the direct approximation to 0.12?
I would prefer not to guess. However, I am confident that the approximations are good enough so that $0.03 + 36 \times 0.0025$ will be less than 0.121,
and that $0.03 + 37 \times 0.0025$ will be greater than 0.121. Therefore, I use
0.121 as a limit in the FOR statement. You should look carefully at how
the test for exit is carried out, to convince yourself that the computer
really does exit from the loop at the appropriate time.

Because of this behavior, use of fractional increments in FOR statements is not common. No such difficulties arise for integer increments,
which are used much more often. We will find a great deal of use for FOR
and NEXT statements in Chapter 10.

7.3 ACCUMULATING SUMS

If I must tell someone how to get the sum of a group of numbers using
my trusty pocket calculator, I would provide the following procedure:

1. Make sure the power is on
2. Clear the display
3. WHILE there are still numbers to be added
   3.1 Find the next number
   3.2 Add it to the number currently displayed
4. Announce the result

The procedure to be used by a computer is quite similar. We designate
some variable to hold the sum, substituting for the display of the pocket
calculator. That variable should be cleared or initialized to zero before
we start adding numbers. The numbers can be added to that variable,
one at a time, the way we enter and add numbers one at a time using the
pocket calculator. When all numbers have been added, the designated
variable holds the sum, and can be used in further arithmetic or printed.
In general terms then, a procedure for the computer could be:

1. Set the sum to zero
2. WHILE there are numbers left
   2.1 Find the next number
   2.2 Add the number to the sum
3. Print or use the sum

The loop could be controlled by counting up to a specific limit, as we did in Section 7.2, or by testing whether there are still records in a file. Loop control, of course, depends on how we get the next number, which might be from a file, from the user at the terminal, or from further computation.

For an example, let us return to some parts of a payroll processing program that we encountered in Section 7.1. To put the problem in context, albeit still oversimplified, suppose that each record in a file PAYR contains data on one employee:

Social security number,

Name,

Department (a two-digit number),

Hours worked this week,

Hourly wage,

Overtime code: "EXEMPT" or "OV",

Number of income tax exemptions,

Wages this year to date.

A program is to read each record and compute the employee's total wage. As we saw in Section 7.1, the employee is to be paid time and a half for overtime hours only if he or she is not "exempt." Federal income tax is to be withheld, at 14% of (pay $-$ exemptions $\times$ 15) but not less than zero. Our program should print, for each employee, the social security number, name, hours, wage rate, gross pay, tax withheld, and net pay. At the end of the report, we want totals over all employees of gross pay, tax withheld, and net pay.

Figure 7.5 shows a procedure for this task, which is little more than a restatement of the program specifications. Figure 7.6 shows a program

---

1. Set totals of gross pay, tax withheld, and net pay to zero
2. WHILE there are records left
   2.1 Read a record
   2.2 Compute gross pay
      2.2.1 IF hours worked $\leq$ 40 *or* employee is exempt
            THEN gross pay = hours $\times$ wage
            ELSE gross pay = hours $\times$ wage $+$ 0.5 $\times$ (hours $-$ 40) $\times$ wage
   2.3 Compute tax withheld
      2.3.1 IF gross pay $>$ exemptions $\times$ 15
            THEN Tax = 0.14 $\times$ (gross pay $-$ exemptions $\times$ 15)
            ELSE Tax = 0
   2.4 Compute net pay = gross pay $-$ tax withheld
   2.5 Print employee data
   2.6 Add gross pay, tax withheld, and net pay to totals
3. Print totals

Figure 7.5 Procedure for payroll register.

that follows the procedure. This program combines many of the structures we have been discussing: WHILE, IF-THEN-ELSE, a compound condition for an IF-THEN-ELSE structure, and accumulation of totals. There are three totals, but three are clearly no more difficult to provide than one is. The procedure is almost a necessity as a step toward writing a program of this length; we can set an overall strategy, and follow it, refining each step within that strategy as necessary.

```
10   REM   PAYROLL REGISTER
20   REM   G STRUBLE    JAN 1980
30   REM       T1 = TOTAL OF GROSS PAY
32   REM       T2 = TOTAL OF TAXES WITHHELD
34   REM       T3 = TOTAL OF NET PAY
36   REM       S$ = SOCIAL SECURITY NUMBER
38   REM       N$ = EMPLOYEE NAME
40   REM       D  = EMPLOYEE'S DEPARTMENT
42   REM       H  = HOURS WORKED BY THE EMPLOYEE
44   REM       W  = EMPLOYEE'S HOURLY WAGE
46   REM       E$ = EXEMPTION CODE: "EXEMPT" = NO OVERTIME PAID,
48   REM                           "OV" = ELIGIBLE FOR OVERTIME PAY
50   REM       E  = NUMBER OF PERSONAL EXEMPTIONS
52   REM       Y  = WAGES PAID YEAR-TO-DATE SUBJECT TO FICA TAX
70       FILES PAYR
100      LET T1 = 0
110      LET T2 = 0
120      LET T3 = 0
200      IF END #1 GO TO 400
210      INPUT #1, S$, N$, D, H, W, E$, E, Y
218  REM   COMPUTE GROSS PAY
220      IF H <= 40 GO TO 260
230      IF E$ = "EXEMPT" GO TO 260
240      LET G = H * W + .5 * (H-40) * W
250      GO TO 270
260      LET G = H * W
268  REM   COMPUTE TAX WITHHELD
270      IF G > E * 15 GO TO 300
280      LET T = 0
290      GO TO 310
300      LET T = .14 * (G - E*15)
308  REM   COMPUTE NET PAY, PRINT, AND ADD TO TOTALS
310      LET N = G - T
320      PRINT S$; TAB(11); N$; TAB(36); H; TAB(41); W;
330      PRINT TAB(47); G; TAB(55); T; TAB(63); N
340      LET T1 = T1 + G
350      LET T2 = T2 + T
360      LET T3 = T3 + N
370      GO TO 200
400      PRINT
410      PRINT TAB(20); "TOTALS"; TAB(47); T1; TAB(55); T2;
420      PRINT TAB(63); T3
970      END
```

Figure 7.6 Program for payroll register.

7.4 THE CASE STRUCTURE

In Section 4.5 we studied the IF-THEN-ELSE structure as a way for the computer to determine which of two alternative actions to perform. Sometimes there are more than two alternatives, and in this section we examine some ways of organizing such situations.

One way of handling three alternatives is to combine two IF-THEN-ELSE structures:

IF condition 1
    THEN action 1
    ELSE IF condition 2
              THEN action 2
              ELSE action 3

The second IF-THEN-ELSE structure is the action of the ELSE clause of the first IF-THEN-ELSE construction. Still more alternative actions can be organized into nested IF-THEN-ELSE structures like this, but it becomes difficult to keep track of them. As a simplification of this structure, we present a structure that pairs a criterion for each case with the action to be taken in that case, with as many cases as are necessary. The last condition may be stated "ELSE" by convention to mean that if none of the preceding cases were true, this last action is to be performed. We will represent the structure as

1. Case 1: condition 1: DO action 1
   Case 2: condition 2: DO action 2
   Case 3: condition 3: DO action 3
   etc.

Let us take the withholding of FICA (social security) tax from an employee's pay as an example. This tax is 6.13% of the employee's gross pay, but only the first $22,800 of pay in each year is taxed. This means there are three different formulas to be included in the program:

1. If year-to-date wages (not including the current week) are already $22,800 or more, tax = 0.

2. If the current week's wages bring the total over $22,800, only a portion of the week's wages (22800 − year-to-date wages) is taxed.

3. Otherwise, the entire week's wages are taxed.

This can be restated in a case structure as follows:

1. Case 1: Year-to-date wages > 22800: DO F = 0
   Case 2: Year-to-date wages + gross pay > 22800:
           DO F = .0613 × (22800 − Year-to-date wages)
   Case 3: ELSE DO F = .0613 × gross pay

   Let us clarify the logic of the case structure by referring to the flow-chart in Fig. 7.7, which shows a case structure with three cases. The conditions are tested in turn until one of them is found to be satisfied; when that happens, the corresponding action is performed. It is clear that *only one* of the actions is performed. If, for example, condition 1 is found to be satisfied, action 1 is performed and control passes immediately to the next step; conditions 2 and 3 are not tested on that particular pass through the structure. Note that if none of the conditions is satisfied, none of the actions will be taken.

   There are several ways in which to implement a case structure in BASIC. One of the simplest is shown in Fig. 7.8. Each of the tests is performed, and if one of the conditions is satisfied, the IF statement sends control to a section of the program that performs the corresponding action. The GO TO statement at 1090 is necessary to send control to the next step if none of the conditions is satisfied. The GO TOs at 1190 and 1290 send control to the next step after performing one of the actions.

   Let us return to our FICA tax example and suppose that gross pay

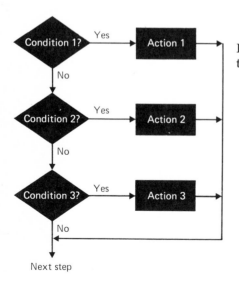

Figure 7.7 Flowchart of a case structure.

```
1000    IF condition 1 GO TO 1100
1010    IF condition 2 GO TO 1200
1020    IF condition 3 GO TO 1300
1090    GO TO 2000
1100    perform action 1
        . . .
1190    GO TO 2000
1200    perform action 2
        . . .
1290    GO TO 2000
1300    perform action 3
        . . .
2000    next procedure step
```

Figure 7.8 Program scheme for a case structure.

```
308 REM   COMPUTE FICA TAX F
309 REM      F9 = LIMIT OF FICA TAXABLE INCOME; WHEN IT CHANGES, CHANGE F9
310     LET F9 = 22800
311 REM      P9 = FICA TAX PERCENTAGE; WHEN RATE CHANGES, CHANGE P9
312     LET P9 = .0613
315     IF Y > F9 GO TO 340
320     IF Y + G > F9 GO TO 360
330     GO TO 380
340     LET F = 0
350     GO TO 390
360     LET F = P9 * (F9 - Y)
370     GO TO 390
380     LET F = P9 * G
390
```

Figure 7.9 FICA tax computation.

for the week has been computed as G, and year-to-date wages is Y. Figure 7.9 shows a program segment following the procedure above and the scheme in Fig. 7.8. Since condition 3 in this procedure is "ELSE", statement 330 is a simple GO TO statement leading to action 3.

7.5 SEARCHING

Now and then we must ask a program to search a file for a particular record. We may think of the file as a table, and we are looking for some data in the table. There are essentially two different kinds of criteria we use to determine which record we want from a file. The first criterion is a direct match of some given piece of data with some field in the desired record in the file. For example, in a student registration file, we may wish to find the name and number of credits of the student with some given social security number. In a product file, we may wish to find the quantity on hand of a given product number. In a file of data on the 50 states, we may wish to find the population of Kentucky.

The second criterion is a search for the most or the least of something, like the employee with the largest total year-to-date wages, or the inventory item with lowest quantity-on-hand. Sometimes we search for the optimum within some restricted category, like the employee with the largest total year-to-date wages among those not "exempt." We will treat the two kinds of criteria separately, since they lead to quite different strategies, procedures, and, therefore, programs.

If we are to search for a record that matches some given piece of data, we call that piece of data the *search key*. The field within each record that is the candidate for matching with the search key is called the *data key*. For example, if we are searching a product file for the record for product number P1215, the search key is "P1215"; the data key is the product number field in each record, and, by extension, the variable into which the product number will be read is also called the data key. We want to set up a search loop for the computer; each time through the loop the computer should read and examine another record. There are *two* criteria for leaving the loop:

1. The desired record has been found;

2. The file has been exhausted without matching the search key.

After the flow of control has left the loop because one of these criteria has been satisfied, the next step of the procedure must test whether the search was successful and must take action accordingly.

Figure 7.10 shows a procedure that accomplishes the search. The search loop has only one action: Read a record. The WHILE clause expresses the two criteria for leaving the loop. To prepare for the search loop, we must give the data key an initial value; that value may be anything that does not match the search key, so it does not cause a false

---

1. Obtain search key
2. Set data key to a value $\neq$ search key
3. WHILE search key $\neq$ data key *and* there are records left
   3.1 Read a record
4. IF search key $=$ data key
   THEN print record found
   ELSE print message that search has failed

Figure 7.10 Procedure to search for a match.

conclusion that a match has been found. The fourth step in the program takes an action that uses the matching record or reports that no match was found. In other situations, the actions taken on success or failure of the search will be different.

The programming of this procedure is fairly straightforward, since all the procedure elements used have been discussed earlier. Suppose we want a program that will print for us the name, wage rate, and year-to-date wages of an employee in the file PAYR (see Section 7.3), given the social security number of the employee. Since the compound condition for continuation of the loop involves the *and* connective, we take the logical opposite of each condition and use an *or* connective for *exit* from the loop, and the programming proceeds nicely, as shown in Fig. 7.11. The program follows the procedure, and once the program is written, it can be shortened slightly. If the search is successful, the test for match is performed in two successsive statements, 300 and 400; it would be possible to change line 300 to

```
300   IF K$ = S$ GO TO 430
```

Then the IF test in statement 400 can be eliminated, and statement 310 changed to

```
310   IF END #1 GO TO 410
```

```
10    REM     FIND NAME, WAGE RATE, AND WAGES YEAR-TO-DATE
15    REM     OF EMPLOYEE, WHEN SOC. SEC. NO. IS TYPED IN
20    REM     G STRUBLE      JAN. 1980
30    REM        K$ = SOCIAL SECURITY NUMBER FROM TERMINAL (SEARCH KEY)
36    REM        S$ = SOCIAL SECURITY NUMBER FROM FILE (DATA KEY)
38    REM        N$ = EMPLOYEE NAME
40    REM        D  = EMPLOYEE'S DEPARTMENT
42    REM        H  = HOURS WORKED BY THE EMPLOYEE
44    REM        W  = EMPLOYEE'S HOURLY WAGE
46    REM        E$ = EXEMPTION CODE
50    REM        E  = NUMBER OF PERSONAL EXEMPTIONS
52    REM        Y  = WAGES PAID YEAR-TO-DATE SUBJECT TO FICA TAX
70        FILES PAYR
100       PRINT "TYPE SOC. SEC. NO.";
110       INPUT K$
200       LET S$ = "N"
202   REM  "N" SHOULD BE DIFFERENT FROM ANY ACTUAL SOC. SEC. NO.
300       IF K$ = S$ GO TO 400
310       IF END #1 GO TO 400
320       INPUT #1, S$, N$, D, H, W, E$, E, Y
350       GO TO 300
400       IF K$ = S$ GO TO 430
410       PRINT "EMPLOYEE NOT ON FILE.   SORRY"
420       GO TO 970
430       PRINT N$; TAB(30); W; Y
970   END
```

Figure 7.11 Program to search for a match.

Programmers often have a choice to make between a program that follows a logical procedure and is thus easy to maintain or change to meet changed requirements, and one that is shorter and perhaps makes more efficient use of computer time. In most situations the easy-to-follow, easy-to-understand, easy-to-modify (*correctly*) program is the better choice.

When we search for the optimal record, in some sense, from a file, we need a very different strategy. If I go to the store determined to buy the very best melon there, I systematically examine all melons. After I have looked at even the first two melons, I have made a choice of which is the best one I have found so far, and I keep that one with me to compare with the next melon. Any time I find a better melon than the one I am guarding, I release that one and guard the better one instead. So at all times I am holding on to the best melon I have found so far. When I have examined all melons, the one I hold at that time must be the very best in the store, so that is the one I buy.

We use the same kind of strategy when instructing the computer to search a file for the best record. At any time, we have the computer hold the data in the best record found so far; this record is the one to be compared with the next record, and whatever record occupies that place when the program runs out of records will be the one reported as best. When we ask for the best from a *restricted* category of records, the first test of each new record read must be whether it is in the desired category, and only if it is may the program compare it with the best record so far. When the grocer hands me a calabash, I look at it first to determine whether it is a melon or not; if I can tell the difference (and if not, I'm not the melon connoisseur I think I am) I will not bother to compare the calabash with the melon I am holding.

In the computer procedure we must hold some value in the "best so far" status as the perusal of records begins. The best thing to keep in the "best" position initially is a value so bad (in whatever sense) that *any* record in the category desired will be better. This would be like keeping the address of the ice cream store in hand until I hold the first melon.

Figure 7.12 shows a procedure that follows the strategy described above. Figure 7.13 shows a program that follows the procedure to find the name and social security number of the employee among the non-exempt employees who has the highest year-to-date wage. The "best" that we must keep track of is, therefore, a set of year-to-date wages, name, and social security number. Since those data in the current record are in variables Y, N\$, and S\$, we use the parallel names Y1, N1\$, and S1\$ to help avoid confusion or error. Only Y1 need be initialized; we set the value to −9999, which is surely lower than the year-to-date wages

---

1. Set "best" to "very bad"
2. WHILE there are records
   2.1 Read a record
   2.2 IF record is within category desired
       THEN 2.2.1 IF record is better than "best"
                  THEN Replace "best" by current record
3. IF "best" $\neq$ "very bad"
   THEN report "best"
   ELSE report that no records were found in the category

Figure 7.12 Procedure for finding the best record.

for any employee! When we find that the current record is for a non-exempt employee with higher year-to-date wage (Y) than the current value of Y1, statements 240–260 replace all data about that previous best by the values Y, S$, N$ of the current and better record.

It is perhaps still not obvious how this program works. Make up for yourself, on paper, a small file PAYR, and simulate on paper the actions

---

```
10    REM   FIND NON-EXEMPT EMPLOYEE WITH HIGHEST WAGE YEAR-TO-DATE
20    REM   G STRUBLE     JAN 1980
34    REM FROM CURRENT RECORD:
36    REM      S$ = SOCIAL SECURITY NUMBER
38    REM      N$ = EMPLOYEE NAME
40    REM      D  = EMPLOYEE'S DEPARTMENT
42    REM      H  = HOURS WORKED BY EMPLOYEE
44    REM      W  = EMPLOYEE'S HOURLY WAGE
46    REM      E$ = EXEMPTION CODE: "EXEMPT" = NO OVERTIME PAID,
48    REM                          "OV" = ELIGIBLE FOR OVERTIME PAY
50    REM      E  = NUMBER OF PERSONAL EXEMPTIONS
52    REM      Y  = WAGES PAID YEAR-TO-DATE SUBJECT TO FICA TAX
54    REM FROM BEST RECORD FOUND SO FAR:
56    REM      Y1  = FICA WAGES PAID YEAR-TO-DATE
58    REM      S1$ = SOCIAL SECURITY NUMBER
60    REM      N1$ = EMPLOYEE NAME
70        FILES PAYR
100       LET Y1 = -9999
200       IF END #1 GO TO 300
210       INPUT #1, S$, N$, D, H, W, E$, E, Y
220       IF E$ = "EXEMPT" GO TO 270
230       IF Y <= Y1 GO TO 270
238 REM   REPLACE BEST RECORD FOUND SO FAR
240       LET Y1 = Y
250       LET S1$ = S$
260       LET N1$ = N$
270       GO TO 200
300       IF Y1 <> -9999 GO TO 330
310       PRINT "NO NON-EXEMPT EMPLOYEES ON FILE"
320       GO TO 970
330       PRINT S1$; TAB(12); N1$; TAB(39); Y1
970   END
```

Figure 7.13 Program for finding the employee with the highest year-to-date wages.

of the computer in executing the program. This is a good way to see how a program does its job, and is also a good way to test your own programs and eliminate most of their errors before you take them to the computer. We will discuss this at greater length in Chapter 8.

7.6 MAIN IDEAS

a. Compound conditions using the logical connectives *or* and *and* are implemented by more than one IF statement in BASIC. Rules of logic help in the transformation of some compound conditions to others more easily implemented.

b. When there are three or more alternative actions, we can express the flow of control in a case structure.

c. Repeated execution of an action a specific number of times is accomplished by establishing, incrementing, and testing a counter. The BASIC language provides FOR and NEXT statements to simplify the programming.

d. The structure of a search for equality between a given search key and a data element in a file is facilitated by a compound WHILE condition and the initialization of the data key before the search loop.

e. A search for an optimal record in a file requires holding the "best" record found so far; the variables that hold that record should be initialized to values *worse* than any real records.

f. The solution to a programming problem can be constructed as a series of subtasks. The subtasks can be resolved into structures and strategies such as WHILE and IF-THEN-ELSE structures, and the components transcribed into BASIC.

7.7 QUESTIONS FOR IMAGINATION AND REVIEW

1. Transcribe the structure

    IF condition a *exclusive or* condition b
        THEN action 1
        ELSE action 2

to BASIC. The structure specifies that if *one* of the two conditions is true, action 1 is to be performed; if *neither* or *both* are true, action 2 is to be performed. The BASIC equivalent can be done several ways using three IF statements; can it be done using two? As an example, we might want to print data on each product for which quantity on hand is below the reorder point *or* for which additional stock is on order, but not if both or neither condition holds.

2. Write a procedure and then a program that will print name and hourly wage of all employees in the file PAYR whose wage is between 8.00 and 12.00.

3. In the program in Fig. 7.2, the arithmetic of statements 410 and 420 can be combined into one statement. Write that statement.

4. Compound conditions can become more complex. Transcribe into BASIC each of these procedure steps.

1. IF B > C *and* E = F *and* G ≤ 12
    THEN add 1 to K
    ELSE add 1 to P
2. IF B = 12 *or* G > F *or* M$ <> "UNCLE"
    THEN add E to T
    ELSE subtract E from T
3. IF R ≤ Q < S *or* P$ = "M"
    THEN add Q × C to T
4. IF (F < 6 *or* G = 4) *and* N$ = "PLEASE"
    THEN print "I GIVE UP"
    ELSE print "NUTS TO YOU"

5. If a file SMPL contains records, each containing
    Census tract number (a string),
    Population, and
    Number of households,
write a procedure and then a program that will read the first 50 records and print for each one the fields in the records plus the average number of inhabitants per household. Then:

a) Modify the program to print the first record and then every third record; still print 50 records.

b) Modify the program further to print at the end of the report the total population, the total number of households in the 50 records printed, and the average number of inhabitants per household in the entire 50 tracts. Is this the same as the average of the 50 averages printed?

c) Safeguard the program so that if the file is exhausted before 50 records are printed, the program still prints its totals and averages.

6. The discussion of the FOR statement dealt with only positive values of the increment. The increment (STEP) is also permitted to be negative; the loop should then count down the variable that controls the looping.

```
100   FOR K = 10 TO 1 STEP −1
```

should result in repetition of the loop actions ten times. Make appropriate modifications to the flowchart and BASIC of Figs. 7.3(a) and 7.3(b) for the case of a negative increment.

7. How many times will the loop actions be repeated if the loop is controlled by each of the following FOR statements?

a) 200 FOR K = 0 TO 6

b) 200 FOR K = 1 TO 7 STEP 2

c) 200 FOR K = 1 TO 8 STEP 2

d) 200 FOR K = .5 TO 6

e) 200 FOR K = 1 TO 0

f) 200 FOR K = 1 TO 0 STEP −1

g) 200 FOR K = 2 TO 2 STEP 1

h) 200 FOR K = 2 TO 2 STEP −1

8. Simulate the program in Fig. 7.6 and show what is printed if the file PAYR contains the three records

```
111222333, "JOE BLOW", 11, 20, 3, "OV", 5, 1200
111222444, "SUE QUEUE", 11, 50, 4, "OV", 2, 18000
111222555, "PAT MULLALEY", 12, 50, 5.80, "EXEMPT", 3,
    17500
```

9. Modify the program in Fig. 7.6 to print two additional totals at the end of the register:

a) Total of all regular wages (earned on up to 40 hours by each employee);

b) Total of wages earned on hours worked over 40.

10. Modify the program in Fig. 7.6 to include the FICA computation of Fig. 7.9. The FICA tax should also be printed and should be subtracted from G in computing net pay.

11. Write a procedure and a segment of a program that will compute federal tax withheld according to the following table:

If wage $\leq$ 33,	tax = 0;
33 < wage $\leq$ 76,	tax = 16% of (wage − 33);
76 < wage $\leq$ 143,	tax = 6.88 + 18% of (wage − 76);
143 < wage $\leq$ 182,	tax = 18.94 + 22% of (wage − 143);
182 < wage,	tax = 27.52 + 24% of (wage − 182).

Then $14.40 for each exemption is deducted from the resulting tax (but of course the net tax must not be negative).

12. Compare the procedure

1. IF A < 6

      THEN add 1 to T1

2. IF B < 7

      THEN add 1 to T2

3. IF C < 8

      THEN add 1 to T3

with a case structure. Make a flowchart for the above procedure to show how it differs from a case structure. Also write a program segment following the procedure and compare it with the program scheme for a case structure.

13. In Step 4 of Fig. 7.10, the search key is compared with the data key to determine whether the search was successful. Could an end-of-file test be used instead?

14. How do the strategy, procedure, and program of a search for equality change if we are to search for and print *all* records that match the search key?

15. Show that the program in Fig. 7.13 will report the *first* of several records that might be tied for "best." What change in the program would make the program report the *last* of tied records? What kind of change would have to be made to report *all* records tied for best?

16. An equipment file EQUIP contains in each record the data on one piece of equipment:

Serial number,

Description,

Location,

Original price,

Age in years,

Useful life.

Assuming that each item depreciates on a straight-line basis to zero residual value, write a procedure and then a program that will:

   a) Print serial number, description, location, and current depreciated value of every item.

   b) At the end of the report, print the serial number and description of the item with the largest current depreciated value.

17. Show that in a search for an optimum record in which *all* records are candidates, not only those meeting some restrictive criteria, the "best record so far" can be initialized by reading the *first record* directly into the variables that hold "best record found so far." In what situations would this improve a program, and in what situations not? How about the program for Question 16 above, for example?

18. A file STU contains for each student currently registered:

Social security number,

Name,

Class standing (0, 1, 2, 3, 4, 5),

Number of credits enrolled this term.

A full-time student is one enrolled for 12 or more credits. Write a procedure and then a program that will print the number of full-time students with each class standing.

19. Write a procedure and then a program to accept from the terminal the serial number of a piece of equipment, and then, searching the file EQUIP of Question 16, print the description, location, age, and current value of the item with the given serial number. Print an appropriate message if the item cannot be found.

CHAPTER 8
TESTING AND DEBUGGING

Up to now we have concentrated on the logic of correct programs, and various program structures to do the tasks. We paid little attention to the problems of arriving at a correct program and making sure it *was* correct. Since we have been discussing quite simple programs, the process of finding and correcting errors has been also reasonably simple. Even so, you probably ran into some problems that were vexing and frustrating.

Most "real-world" programs are much longer and more complex than any with which you have dealt. Some skills in finding and correcting errors, and some techniques to guide the testing toward an ultimate conclusion that there are no more errors are an absolute necessity. These skills and techniques will be useful to you, too, at this stage, so they are the business of this chapter.

8.1 WHAT ARE TESTING AND DEBUGGING?

Errors in computer programs have been called *bugs* ever since there were computer programs. Thus, the process of cleaning out these bugs is called *debugging*. The usual procedure in debugging is to run the program repeatedly, with well-chosen test data, until the program gives correct results on the test data. Our ultimate goal is confidence that our resulting program will give correct results on all data; we want to be able to state with assurance that the program is bug-free. Yet testing shows only the presence of bugs, not their absence. The difficulty of ensuring a correct program is underscored by the examples of bugs that are discovered in production programs that have been in heavy use for months or even years.

Therefore, we suggest a methodology aimed at producing correct programs. First, we should prevent bugs whenever possible. Programmers often spend more time debugging programs than they spend writing them in the first place; more attention paid to the need for testing and some care in *preventing* errors can significantly reduce the debugging time. We have placed our emphasis on design of procedures using well-formulated logical structures primarily with the objective of preventing errors, especially errors of logic. There are other benefits too, as we will see.

Errors can be classified into three types according to how they appear. First are errors in syntax, in which programs violate the grammatical rules of the programming language being used. The translator trips over these errors, and we cannot even run a program until these errors are eliminated. Second is a class of errors that violate rules of the computer during execution of the program. The computer trips over these when trying to execute the program, and usually halts with an error message. Section 8.2 will deal with these first two classes of errors.

The third class is more subtle logical errors. The program is translated and it runs, but it does not produce correct results. Depending on where these errors are, it may be very obvious that something is wrong, or discovery of the bug may require a test of a very special case and a careful calculation of what the results *should* be. We will explore techniques for ensuring the absence of logical errors in Section 8.3.

Generally, we will learn how to design a small but sufficient set of test data from the procedure. A *desk check* of a program, in which we *simulate* the execution of the program (or at least portions of the program) before trying to run it, helps us find and correct logical errors. The desk check can be particularly efficient: Since early in the debugging of a program each error is so serious that its effects invalidate everything else, each computer run can, therefore, find only one such error. The desk check, however, can correct several such errors. Also effective is a *structured walk-through*, in which we explain to someone else how the program works. Not only can someone else see some of my errors more quickly than I can, but the activity of explaining the program requires me to sharpen my perception and I often detect my errors as I explain.

Another stage in the methodology of producing correct programs is *program verification*. Again we return to the procedure, and try to make statements about the state of the computer—its contents and the interpretation given to these contents—at the end of each procedure step. We can examine the program to see whether it really accomplishes the proper transformations from each state to the next. We will show an example of a program verification in Section 8.3.

A final stage is the comparison between the results of the program and the requirements that the program was meant to fulfill. We can correct a program that does not follow the procedure, but we must also make a final check on whether the program (*and* procedure) solve the original problem. After all, "What is the use of running, if you are on the wrong road?"

Programmers sometimes get lazy. More often, they are pushed for time. This job must be done *today;* that one *tomorrow.* Testing is tedious and time-consuming, and it is easy to think "I wrote it carefully, and it works on two cases, so it's finished." It is truly amazing how often there is not time to do it right, but unfortunately we must find the time to do it over! Please try to do better. And when you deal with professional programmers, expect and require them to do better.

8.2 WHEN THE COMPUTER TRIPS OVER A BUG

In the first attempts to test a computer program, we usually need not search for the subtle logic errors that undermine our program's structure like termites. The first bugs seek us out like mosquitoes. These are the errors in syntax that prevent successful translation and the bugs that "blow up" the program during execution.

The translator expects our program to follow certain syntactical or grammatical rules; if it does, the translator can generate an equivalent machine language program. There may be errors in it, but they will be our errors of logic. If there are syntax errors, the translator will point them out to us, and identify the type of each error and the statement that the error is in. Some translators are smart enough to detect a variety of suspicious things in our programs; they are not *necessarily* errors, and the translator can and will translate them, but they are *possibly* errors, so the translator will identify the suspicious event and label it with a *warning.* We should pay attention to such warnings, and look over each one to determine whether it does indeed represent an error.

Of course, the translator looks at the program from its own point of view, which often does not coincide with ours. For example, a translator will report that

```
150   IF A = 4
```

has an error

```
?ILLEGAL FORMAT WHERE THE WORDS THEN OR GO TO WERE
EXPECTED IN LINE 150
```

This is how the translator must look at the statement, since it saw that it was dealing with an IF statement. However, my error *really* had nothing to do with a THEN clause; I simply wrote IF where I meant to use LET.

Once translation of the program is completed, execution begins, during which an entirely different set of rules is brought into play. If one of the rules is violated, the system can take one of several actions:

1. Print an error message and stop execution.

2. Provide some indication of the error that the program can test, permitting some remedial action and continuation of the program.

3. Print an error message, but take some automatic action (like setting an offending variable to zero) and continue.

Many BASIC systems designed for student use take action 1 and stop execution in all such situations; systems designed for use in business data processing must include provision for continuation in at least some of these situations, especially those that arise from problems with the input data. (More about those in Section 8.4.)

What are some of the problems that arise during execution? One class of errors arises from operations with files:

- The program attempts to read from or write to a file that does not exist or has not been declared.

- The program attempts to read data (from a file or from DATA statements) beyond the actual data available.

- The program attempts to read a number but finds a character string that cannot be converted to a number.

There are also errors dealing with arrays (see Chapter 10) and functions (see Chapter 12), and a few miscellaneous conditions:

- Exceeding maximum size of a number or length of a string,

- Attempted division by zero,

- Raising zero to a negative power,

- Raising a negative number to a fractional power,

- Exceeding the time limit assigned during execution of the program,

- Attempted use of a value of a variable that has not been initialized.

A BASIC system will identify for us the nature of the error, *and* the statement being executed when the error arose. Finding the *cause* of the error usually requires returning to other statements in the program to see what was done incorrectly or omitted. Therefore, it is *imperative* to have an absolutely current listing of the program. Often it is the typing in of the program that generates the error; we could look all day at an original pencil copy of the program and not find the error because *that* copy does not contain the error! It may also be necessary to review the specifications of the BASIC language statements and their actions, since the error may be caused by a misinterpretation of a statement.

Exceeding a time limit is a special case. Some systems provide a mechanism for establishing a time limit, and, unfortunately, some do not. If your system does, you should use it. It is a very rare programmer who has not at some time (and most of us many times) tried to execute a program that contains an unending (or infinite) loop. I want any such program of mine (and my students) to be thrown off the machine after a reasonable time limit has been exceeded. An unending loop is easy to write. Figure 8.1 contains one; can you find it?

```
10   REM   FIND VALUE OF $1000 AFTER 6 YEARS
15   REM   WITH INTEREST 6% UNTIL $1250, THEN 5%
20   REM   NORGE GUDDLE      JAN. 1980
90       LET V = 1000
100      LET K = 1
110      IF K > 6 THEN 900
120      IF V < 1250 GO TO 150
130      LET V = V * 1.05
140      GO TO 170
150      LET V = V * 1.06
160      LET K = K + 1
170      GO TO 110
900      PRINT K; TAB(9); V
970   END
```

Figure 8.1 Program with an unending loop.

Failure to initialize variables to the desired values is a frequent error. First, what do we mean by initialization? Initialization is the setting of a variable to a value before the program attempts to use a value of that variable. There are two ways in BASIC to give a value to a variable:

LET variable = value

INPUT (from terminal or file) variable

Most variables are naturally assigned values before the program tries to use them. In the payroll register program in Fig. 7.6, the variables G, T, and N are all assigned values by LET statements before the program tries to use those values. Variables H, W, E$, E, S$, and N$ are all assigned values by the INPUT statement before the program attempts to use them. Only the totals T1, T2, and T3 need explicit initialization in statements 100–120; if those statements were omitted, statements 340–360 would attempt to use values before values had been assigned. In Fig. 7.2, the value of the counter K must be initialized in statement 300.

Some computer systems automatically initialize all numeric variables to zero and all string variables to null strings before program execution begins. Others let whatever values are left in the main storage locations remain as values of variables. You can imagine what weird results we can get when we use those values rather than initializing to the values we want! Still other systems initialize all variables to special values that are essentially indicators that the variables have not been assigned values and cannot be used yet. None of these actions, however, helps your program run correctly. The first action, setting values to zero and null strings, is the most dangerous, since zeroes are *sometimes* the desired initial values and this may encourage programmers to forget initialization.

Sometimes we have a difficult time understanding what the computer did, or by what path it got to a particular statement or section, or what intermediate results led to the final results printed. Techniques discussed in the following section will help, but sometimes we need more help. One technique is to insert extra PRINT statements in the program. These statements may display during execution:

■ The fact that the flow of control went through a particular point or section;

■ Intermediate computational results.

For example, we might insert in the program in Fig. 7.13 a statement

```
265  PRINT Y1; TAB(10); S1$; TAB(22); N1$
```

which would report each "best so far" record encountered and help us check the progress of the search. Depending on what kind of problem we were having with the program, we might also insert

```
225  PRINT "NON-EXEMPT CONSIDERED:"; S$; Y
```

When inserting such statements, we must take care not to *change* the flow of control, structure, or computation of the regular parts of the program. When the problems that prompted such statements are solved, we must make one more test run after the statements are removed, to ensure that we have left the regular program intact.

8.3 TESTING AND VERIFYING A PROGRAM

Eventually, enough bugs are squashed so that the program runs to completion, and gives reasonable results. On what data should we test the program, and how much and what kind of testing and analyzing are sufficient to give us confidence that the program is correct?

One requirement of an acceptable set of test data is that it force the program to execute every statement at least once. One might try to send the program through all possible *paths*, but this gets out of hand rapidly. If five successive steps in a program are IF-THEN-ELSE structures, there are 32 possible paths through those steps, while it may take only two well-chosen sets of data to exercise each THEN and each ELSE once. To test all paths should not be necessary, especially if the program follows a logical structure and if we have done some verification analysis (which we will explain later).

We can decide most easily what test data we need by referring to the procedure. For every IF-THEN, IF-THEN-ELSE, or CASE structure we should generate test data that will fall on each side of each IF test. We should also generate one set of test data that will yield equality on each IF test. For example, if a step is

IF distance $\geq$ 150 miles
    THEN ...
    ELSE ...

we should generate a set of test data whose distance will be less than 150 miles, one whose distance is equal to 150 miles, and one whose distance is greater than 150 miles. For each WHILE or LOOP-EXIT structure, we should develop sets of data (perhaps requiring several test runs) that will:

1. Not execute the WHILE actions at all, if that is possible (for example, the data file contains *no* records),

2. Execute the WHILE actions at least twice.

If special actions are taken the first or last time through a loop, test data should be expanded accordingly.

There are requirements for test data for computations, too. Test data that exercise LET statements by adding zeros to something or by multiplying by 1 are not sufficient. We should try to get different values of different variables too, so we avoid the trap of getting the correct result from

```
160   LET B = C * D
```

only because the value of C was the same as the value of G, which was the variable we should have used.

Let us illustrate this using the payroll procedure of Fig. 7.5 and the accompanying program, Fig. 7.6 (see pp. 155–156). Step 2.2 has a compound condition

IF hours worked $\leq$ 40 *or* employee is exempt

This suggests the following test cases:

Exempt,

Nonexempt, hours $<$ 40,

Nonexempt, hours $=$ 40,

Nonexempt, hours $>$ 40.

Step 2.3 contains another IF:

IF gross pay $>$ exemptions $\times$ 15

which requires three cases:

Gross pay $>$ exemptions $\times$ 15,

Gross pay $=$ exemptions $\times$ 15,

Gross pay $<$ exemptions $\times$ 15.

These requirements can be met with the following data.

Hours Worked	Wage	Code	Number of Exemptions
50	3	"EXEMPT"	1
30	3	"OV"	7
40	3	"OV"	8
50	4	"OV"	2

You can quickly verify that these four records fulfill all the requirements on test cases. Two of these test cases have nonzero tax withheld, so all totals are composed of at least two nonzero numbers. Is there concern that the compound IF will do the wrong thing with exempt employees whose number of hours worked is less than 40? A fifth case can be added to the set, and the testing is still not very tedious.

Once a set of test data has been generated, the next step is calculation, based on the *specifications* for the procedure, of what the results should be for these cases. Then we simulate the execution of the program on at least some of the test data. This simulation will usually find more logic errors than all the rest of the debugging and testing combined! *Only then* are you really ready to test your program on the computer, using the test data you have designed.

Another approach to showing that a program is correct is called *program verification*, during which we return to the procedure, and state clearly and precisely the state of the machine—values of all variables— at the beginning and at the end of each step. Then we must analyze the section of the program that implements each procedure step: Can we show that each program section accomplishes the transition we claim from one state to the next? If we have written our program in well-structured segments (this is one reason why some of our programs appear inefficient because one GO TO statement may branch to another), it is usually reasonably simple to verify that each program segment of five statements or so will perform a claimed task. At least, it is reasonably simple and sure after you are sufficiently in command of the language in which you are programming.

Let us consider an example of the payroll register procedure and program shown in Figs. 7.5 and 7.6 (see pp. 155–156).

1. After Step 1 of the procedure, the totals of gross pay (T1), tax withheld (T2), and net pay (T3) are zeroes. Statements 100–120 in the program do achieve this state.

2. At the end of Step 2 of the procedure, all records in the file should be read, and for each one the gross pay, tax withheld, and net pay should

be computed, printed, and added to the three totals. It takes some analysis to show that this is true. First, are all records in the file read and processed (and only once each)?

3. Statements 200 and 210 see to reading records and branching to 400 when there are no more records. After processing a record, do we *always* go back to 200? Examine the statements between 210 and 370 that transfer control. All of them (220, 230, 250, 270, and 290) transfer control *within* the range 220 to 370. Therefore, we can be sure that after each record is read by statement 210, control passes soon, without loops, to 370, whose GO TO closes the loop. We have shown that every record is read, and is processed once. Now: Is the processing correct?

4. Is the record read properly? We refer to the specifications of the file, and check them against the table of variables included in REM statements in the program and against the INPUT statements that read records from the file. It is also useful to take a good look at a portion of the actual file, to make sure that the file specification is accurate and to check on how certain data (such as exemption code) are represented.

5. Is gross pay computed correctly? Statements 220–260 compute gross pay G. What cases should be considered? We can identify the four we listed as we developed test data:
   a) $H < 40$, say $H = 30$. Exemption code is irrelevant.
   b) $H = 40$. Exemption code is irrelevant.
   c) $H > 40$, say $H = 50$, and E$ = "EXEMPT".
   d) $H > 40$, say $H = 50$, and E$ = "OV".

We can show that any other case should be treated like one of these. Tracing statements 220–260 with these four cases can show that gross pay G will be computed correctly.

6. Is tax withheld computed properly? Statements 270–300 perform this computation. Again, we identify the three cases we developed during the test generation. Tracing statements 270–300 for each of these three cases can show that the tax withheld T will be computed correctly.

7. No flow of control at all is involved in the rest of the processing for a record. Net pay is properly computed as the variable N. The appropriate data for each employee are printed. The computed figures G, T, and N are added to the appropriate totals. Therefore, we conclude that yes, each record is read and processed correctly, and the data are printed for each.

8. After all records are processed, do the variables T1, T2, and T3 really contain the totals for all employees of gross pay, tax withheld, and

net pay? Yes, because we showed that those figures are added to those variables for each employee. Statement 410 prints them, and we have verified the entire program.

This kind of verification is made possible by the way in which we wrote the program, implementing each procedure step or substep by a clearly defined set of statements. If the programming does not follow such structures, the arguments, step by step, are much more difficult. One useful technique, looking forward both to debugging and to this type of validation analysis, is to include a REM statement in the program showing each procedure step, included at the beginning of the statements that implement that step. Statements 218, 268, and 308 in Fig. 7.6 are this type of REM statement, but identification of procedure steps can be done more formally.

Program verification cannot be a complete substitute for program testing, and testing without some verification analysis leaves us unsure whether our test data are sufficient. Used together, however, actual testing and verification can give us the desired confidence that we really have a correct, bug-free program.

8.4 LAUNDERING DATA

In order to get correct results from a computer, we need a correct program. We also need correct data, and this means that we must carefully test and launder the data to ensure its correctness. We may be sure that certain data in a file are valid and correct because the program that created the file checked the data carefully and fully. Data input from the terminal must be checked in any and every way we can devise. We will discuss several ways of checking input data.

The first class of tests can be called internal; they involve only tests on the data field itself. If a value should always be within some range, it can be tested, and should be. If a value, including a character string, should have only one of, say, two values, that should be checked. For example, the exemption code in the file PAYR should be either "EXEMPT" or "OV". No program should assume that because the value is not "EXEMPT" it *is* "OV", unless some other program has already laundered that field.

The *first* test to be made on numeric fields should be to determine whether or not the value is in fact numeric. Some versions of BASIC do not provide any reasonable way to make such a test while maintaining control within the program. Such systems may refuse to accept a non-numeric value from a terminal if a numeric value is asked for, and thus permit the user to retype a numeric value. However, a field read as numeric from a file will stop the program if it is not numeric. This is a poor feature in a system designed for actual business data processing. Better systems provide a way to specify, under program control, some action to be taken when a nonnumeric value is entered.

A second class of tests is validation against data in other files. A social security number in a file of time card data can be validated by finding a record with the same social security number in an employee master file. We will learn more about how to implement such tests in Chapter 9.

Internal tests attempt to guarantee the validity of data, but cannot check their accuracy. Validation against other files can help ensure the accuracy of certain fields. A third class of tests, control totals, can help ensure accuracy of other fields. A *control total* is a total generated outside the computer. For example, the total number of hours worked for all employees can be computed from original time card documents for each department. The program that accepts time card data can accept the total for each department as well, and check the control total against a total generated by the program from the time card data entered. If the totals match, we have a fairly good indication of accuracy of the "hours-worked" fields. If they do not match, both totals and the department number should be printed so that the payroll clerks can look for the error.

When a program encounters almost any error in data, it should report the error and attempt to continue processing. Suppose we are processing a file. If the program stops at the first error, it may enable us to find and fix the error, but must we then go through all that again for each of the other (possibly) 39 errors in the file? It would be a great help if a program could identify all 40 errors in one pass through the file, so that we can, in turn, attempt correction of all 40 in one pass through the file.

8.5 MAIN IDEAS

a. Debugging is finding and correcting mistakes in a program; we do testing to show that there are no (more) bugs.

b. The computer identifies for us errors in syntax at translation time, and some other errors at execution time. When the program runs to completion, we must check its results for correctness.

c. A desk check, simulating execution of the program on sample data, catches many programming logic errors.

d. By examining each procedure step, we can develop requirements on the test data necessary to test the section of program that implements that procedure step. Test data must ensure that each statement is executed at least once.

e. Verification of a program is done by referring to the procedure, showing that each procedure step is implemented correctly by the program.

f. Documentation of a program with REM statements can help debugging and testing:

- A table of variables and their uses;
- Statements identifying the program statements implementing each procedure step.

g. Data must be checked or laundered, by internal checks, validation against data in other files, and control totals.

8.6 QUESTIONS FOR IMAGINATION AND REVIEW

1. What symptom of error would you expect if the program in Fig. 7.6 (see p. 156) were changed by each of the following?

a) Statement 200 is changed to

```
200   IF END #1 GO TO 340
```

b) Statements 200 and 210 are interchanged:

```
200   INPUT #1, S$, N$, D, H, W, E$, E, Y
210   IF END #1 GO TO 400
```

c) Statement 220 is changed to

```
220   IF H < 40 GO TO 260
```

d) Statement 240 is changed to

```
240   LET G = 40 * W + (H − 40) * 1.5 * W
```

e) Statement 290 is omitted.

f) Statement 290 is changed to

```
290   GO TO 360
```

g) Statement 210 is changed to any of

```
210   INPUT #1, S$, N$, D, W, H, E$, E, Y
210   INPUT #1, S$, N$, W, H, E$, E, Y
210   INPUT #1, S$, N$, D, H, W, E1$, E, Y
```

2. What symptoms of error would you expect if the program in Fig. 7.2 (see p. 151) were changed by each of the following?

a) Statement 300 is omitted.

b) Statement 430 is omitted.

c) The parentheses are omitted from statement 420.

d) Statement 400 is changed to

```
400   IF K >= 120 GO TO 500
```

e) Statement 410 is changed to

```
410   LET V = V + 0
```

f) Statement 300 is renumbered as

```
405   LET K = 1
```

g) Statement 200 is renumbered as

```
405   LET V = 0
```

3. Make a verification analysis similar to that in Section 8.3 for a program that you have written.

4. In Section 7.5 we noted that Fig. 7.11 could be shortened by eliminating a duplicated list for matching keys. How does a shortening of this sort affect the validation of programs?

5. Make a list of error messages that your BASIC system gave you that did not really describe the actual error. Try to explain why the system gave you the message it did.

6. Design a sufficient set of test data for a program you have written. Explain why each record or set of input is included, and why your set will adequately test the program.

7. Design tests to launder the data in the file PAYR. Change the procedure in Fig. 7.5 accordingly, and implement all you can as modifications to Fig. 7.6.

CHAPTER 9
FILES
OPERATIONS

In Chapter 6, we studied using files generally, and reading files
in particular. We have studied various procedures and techniques used to process data inside a computer's main storage,
and set those procedures and techniques in a context of programs that read data from a file and produce a report. In this
chapter, we extend our study of the use of files to include processes that write data into files. Some of the processes require
the concurrent processing of two input files, and we will pay
special attention to those processes and the merging concept
that they use.

9.1 WRITING A SEQUENTIAL FILE IN BASIC

In Chapter 6, we introduced the FILES statement and its role in establishing a path, identified by the file access number, between the program and a file. If we are to write a file, the FILES statement is used in the same way to establish a path between the program and the file we are about to create. As the FILES statement establishes the data path, it leaves the path in *read mode*, so data can be *read* from the file. If we are to write into the file, we must reverse the mode. Our program sets a path in *write mode* by executing a SCRATCH statement:

line no. SCRATCH #k

where k is the file access number of the file. The pair of statements

    70 FILES NEWAP
    80 SCRATCH #1

establishes a path for the program to write into the file NEWAP.

The SCRATCH statement also acts on the file itself. If the file already exists, the SCRATCH statement deletes its entire contents, so when later statements write records into the file, they write the entire file "from scratch." If the file does not exist, the SCRATCH statement requests the operating system to find space for the file, reserve that space, and enter the file and its location into the user's file directory. From these actions, we conclude that:

1. A program writing a file should *not* include the SCRATCH statement inside the loop that writes records; if SCRATCH is in the loop, each record will be wiped out before the next one is written.

2. A program cannot *add* records to an existing file.

Some other languages do permit a program to add records to a file, though we will see in Section 9.2 that this is poor data processing practice. We will also explain how we can get the same effect as adding records to an existing file.

The statement that actually writes data into a file is a form of the PRINT statement. In fact, the PRINT statement used to write into a file is exactly the PRINT statement that writes to a terminal except for the inclusion of the file access number. To write to a file, the general form is

line no. PRINT #k, *list*

where k is the file access number of the file to be written, and *list* designates the data to be written, and spacing. The format of the list designating data to be written may include anything that may be in such lists in PRINT statements to the terminal—numbers, quoted strings, variable names, expressions, and commas, semicolons, TAB designations as desired for spacing—and the output to the file is exactly as it would be to the terminal. For each computer system there is some limit on the overall length of the data that can be written by one PRINT statement. We will generally think of the data written by one execution of a PRINT statement as a record. When we COPY the file to a terminal, each of these records begins on a new line.

If values of variables are

```
A = 34.9
B = −2.6705
C$ = "SPRINGFIELD"
D$ = "MOUNT PLEASANT"
```

execution of

```
110   PRINT #1,A;B;88.1
```

will write into the file whose file access number is 1

```
34.9 −2.6705   88.1
```

Similarly,

```
120   PRINT #1,C$;TAB(13);A/4
```

will write into the file

```
SPRINGFIELD 8.725
```

and

```
130   PRINT #1,D$;TAB(18);"PENNSYLVANIA"
```

will write

```
MOUNT PLEASANT    PENNSYLVANIA
```

This last example points out a problem. If we have a program write a file, it is because we want a program to be able to read the file back again. We would expect that if one program has written two strings as a record, a program should be able to read the record back as two strings. However, the statement

```
INPUT #1,G$,H$
```

in some program, trying to read the above record, would read

```
"MOUNT" into G$
"PLEASANT" into H$
```

and leave PENNSYLVANIA to be read by the next INPUT #1 statement. The mischief is caused by the space between MOUNT and PLEASANT: The space was just a character inside the string D$, but once written into the file it acts as a separator, so that MOUNT and PLEASANT are recognized as separate strings. We can avoid this unfortunate behavior by executing a QUOTE statement. The statement

line no.   QUOTE #*k*

where *k* is a file access number, sets a switch so that if any string written to the file designated by the file access number contains a space or a comma, the string will be enclosed in quotation marks as it is written to the file. For example, if our program executed

    90   QUOTE #1

in addition to the SCRATCH #1 statement, the records written by statements 110 and 120 above would be the same as described, but

    130   PRINT #1,D$;TAB(18);"PENNSYLVANIA"

would write the record

    "MOUNT PLEASANT"   PENNSYLVANIA

Note that MOUNT PLEASANT is enclosed in quotation marks because it contains a space; because PENNSYLVANIA does not contain a comma or space, it is not enclosed in quotation marks in the output file. A subsequent program can read "MOUNT PLEASANT" back into *one* string variable and PENNSYLVANIA back into a second string variable.

9.2 CREATING A FILE

The first step in any computer process is a program that accepts data from the user and creates a file to be used in further processing. Sometimes this step is combined with others that do the processing, but in a complex system it is usually good practice to construct one program that will capture the data, check them for validity, and write them into a file, leaving the processing of the data to further programs.

A system must check, or "launder," its data before it can dare to use the data. If we permit data that are invalid to go through a data processing system, we will be made keenly aware that the consequences of *garbage in* are *garbage out*, though sometimes we will be lucky and the program will "blow up" rather than run to completion on bad data.

Therefore, we design programs called *data capture and edit*; if such a program is capturing records that consist of three data fields, it could follow the procedure shown in Fig. 9.1. The program needs a criterion for stopping; the procedure presumes that the first field of each record is a string, and that "STOP" is not a valid value for that field, so "STOP" can be used as a convention meaning that there are no more records to be written to the file. Each field, when entered, should be checked for validity in all ways possible, and if an invalid value is entered, the user at the terminal should be required to reenter the value. When the entire record is assembled, it is written into the file.

Let us be more specific and follow through the programming and execution of the program. Suppose we are asked to build a credit authorization file. The fields of the file are:

1. Account number, which should be in the range 1000 to 4999

2. Credit limit, which should be in the range 0 to 10000

3. Name of customer

Figure 9.2 shows a program that follows the procedure in Fig. 9.1 in building this file. The program edits each field for validity as it is entered. Customer name is an exception; it is accepted as entered without editing. Statement 240 may need explanation: LEN is a function that returns the length of the string that is used as the parameter to the function; the effect is to send control to 280 if A$ is not 4 characters. Note that there are two levels of LOOP-EXIT structures: an outside level starting at

---

1. Set file for writing
2. LOOP
   2.1 LOOP
      2.1.1 Obtain value of A$ from terminal
      2.1.2 EXIT WHEN A$ = "STOP" or valid data
      2.1.3 Display error message, ask for retyping of A$
   2.2 EXIT WHEN A$ = "STOP"
   2.3 LOOP
      2.3.1 Obtain value of second field
      2.3.2 EXIT WHEN value is valid
      2.3.3 Display error message, ask for retyping of second field
   2.4 LOOP
      2.4.1 Obtain value of third field
      2.4.2 EXIT WHEN value is valid
      2.4.3 Display error message, ask for retyping of third field
   2.5 Write into the file a record: A$, second field, third field

---

Figure 9.1 Procedure for data capture and edit.

```
10  REM     CREDIT AUTHORIZATION   CAPTURE AND EDIT
20  REM     G STRUBLE     JAN 1980
30  REM     A$ = ACCOUNT NUMBER
32  REM     L  = CREDIT LIMIT
34  REM     C$ = CUSTOMER NAME
70     FILES AUTH
80     SCRATCH #1
90     QUOTE #1
200 REM  OBTAIN ACCOUNT NUMBER
205    PRINT
210    PRINT "ACCT. NO."; TAB(12);
220    INPUT A$
230    IF A$ = "STOP" GO TO 300
235 REM  VALIDATE ACCOUNT NUMBER
240     IF LEN(A$) <> 4 GO TO 280
250     IF A$ < "1000" GO TO 280
260     IF A$ <= "4999" GO TO 300
275 REM  PRINT ERROR MESSAGE AND TRY AGAIN
280     PRINT "ACCT. NO. MUST BE 4 DIGITS, VALUE 1000-4999"
290     GO TO 210
300     IF A$ = "STOP" GO TO 970
395 REM  ACCT. NO. IS OK, SO OBTAIN CREDIT LIMIT
400     PRINT "CREDIT LIMIT";
410     INPUT L
415 REM  VALIDATE CREDIT LIMIT
420     IF L < 0 GO TO 480
430     IF L <= 10000 GO TO 500
475 REM  PRINT ERROR MESSAGE FOR CREDIT LIMIT, TRY AGAIN
480     PRINT "CREDIT LIMIT MUST BE 0 - 10000"
490     GO TO 400
495 REM  OBTAIN CUSTOMER NAME
500     PRINT "CUSTOMER NAME";
510     INPUT C$
595 REM   WRITE RECORD AND GO BACK FOR NEXT RECORD
600     PRINT #1, A$, L, C$
610     GO TO 205
970  END
```

Figure 9.2 Program for data capture and edit: credit authorization.

statement 205, with test for exit at statement 300, and a GO TO statement closing the loop at statement 610. Other entire LOOP-EXIT structures are included among the actions of the outer LOOP-EXIT structure.

Now let us think about this program and the operation it supports.
The program permits an accounting clerk to create a file containing
credit limits for any number of accounts. If the clerk assembles, say, the
records on 337 accounts that should be allowed credit, those 337 can be
entered into the file. But what does the clerk do the following week when
there are six more accounts to be added to the file? Our answer so far is
that the clerk can now use our program to enter all 343 accounts. The
clerk is fully justified in calling that a ridiculous procedure. We need a
method of adding six accounts to the file by entering six accounts. Let
us go back to the drawing boards and get a program that the clerk will
regard as more satisfactory.

The clerk tells us that all we need to do is fix the program so that the new records are written at the end of the already existing file. If we try to design a program to do exactly that, the SCRATCH statement gives us a problem. We cannot write into a file without executing a SCRATCH statement, but if we execute it, it wipes out the previous contents of the file! Our solution then must be to write a program that will create a *new* file; records from the existing file will be copied, one by one, into the new file *and then* new accounts will be accepted from the terminal and written into the new file. Figure 9.3 shows the procedure; note that the procedure is different from that shown in Fig. 9.1 only by insertion of a new Step 2 that copies records from the existing file to the new file. The program that follows the procedure in Fig. 9.3 is shown in Fig. 9.4. The program creates the file NAUTH, which has file access number 2, so the SCRATCH, QUOTE, and PRINT # statements are changed to refer to file #2. The only major change is the insertion of a loop of statements 100–130 that copies the records from AUTH to NAUTH. You may wonder why we do not use the simple COPY command to copy the records from AUTH to NAUTH. The reason is that COPY is a command, not a statement that can be executed within a BASIC program. And if we executed

```
COPY  AUTH > NAUTH
```

before starting execution of our BASIC program, the SCRATCH statement would give us the same problem we outlined above.

Figure 9.5 shows the contents of a file AUTH, the transcript from the terminal of the execution of the program in Fig. 9.4, and the contents of the resulting file NAUTH. You can see that the first four records of

---

1. Set new file for writing
2. WHILE there are records in old file
   2.1 Read a record from old file
   2.2 Write that record into the new file
3. LOOP
   3.1 LOOP
      3.1.1 Obtain A$ from terminal
      3.1.2 EXIT WHEN A$ = "STOP" or valid data
      3.1.3 Display error message, ask for retyping of A$
   3.2 EXIT WHEN A$ = "STOP"
   3.3 Obtain value of second field, checking validity
   3.4 Obtain value of third field, checking validity
   3.5 Write a new record

Figure 9.3 Procedure for adding data to a file.

```
10  REM    ADD CREDIT AUTHORIZATIONS TO A FILE
15  REM    TAKES EXISTING FILE AUTH AND CREATES NEW FILE NAMED NAUTH
20  REM    G STRUBLE    JAN 1980
30  REM      A$ = ACCOUNT NUMBER
32  REM      L  = CREDIT LIMIT
34  REM      C$ = CUSTOMER NAME
70      FILES AUTH, NAUTH
80      SCRATCH #2
90      QUOTE #2
95  REM   COPY RECORDS FROM AUTH TO NAUTH
100     IF END #1 GO TO 200
110     INPUT #1, A$, L, C$
120     PRINT #2, A$, L, C$
130     GO TO 100
200 REM   OBTAIN ACCOUNT NUMBER
205     PRINT
210     PRINT "ACCT. NO."; TAB(12);
220     INPUT A$
230     IF A$ = "STOP" GO TO 300
235 REM   VALIDATE ACCOUNT NUMBER
240     IF LEN(A$) <> 4 GO TO 280
250     IF A$ < "1000" GO TO 280
260     IF A$ <= "4999" GO TO 300
275 REM   PRINT ERROR MESSAGE AND TRY AGAIN
280     PRINT "ACCT. NO. MUST BE 4 DIGITS, VALUE 1000-4999"
290     GO TO 210
300     IF A$ = "STOP" GO TO 970
395 REM   ACCT. NO. IS OK, SO OBTAIN CREDIT LIMIT
400     PRINT "CREDIT LIMIT";
410     INPUT L
415 REM   VALIDATE CREDIT LIMIT
420     IF L < 0 GO TO 480
430     IF L <= 10000 GO TO 500
475 REM   PRINT ERROR MESSAGE FOR CREDIT LIMIT, TRY AGAIN
480     PRINT "CREDIT LIMIT MUST BE 0 - 10000"
490     GO TO 400
495 REM   OBTAIN CUSTOMER NAME
500     PRINT "CUSTOMER NAME";
510     INPUT C$
595 REM   WRITE RECORD AND GO BACK FOR NEXT RECORD
600     PRINT #2, A$, L, C$
610     GO TO 205
970 END
```

Figure 9.4 Program for adding data to a file.

NAUTH are obtained from AUTH. During input of the sixth record, the clerk jumped ahead and attempted to enter the credit limit 750 before the account number; the edit tests are effective at recognizing the input as not valid for account number, and the program asks the user to enter the proper account number.

The entire data processing system that uses the credit authorization file may be set up to refer to the file AUTH in other programs that check orders against the limit in order to validate the extension of further credit. So what do we do with NAUTH? The operational procedure for updating the AUTH file by adding new accounts may be as shown in

```
1001              500              "KERMIT KREY"
1143              200              "BARNEY BLUESTONE"
1151              1000             "CLIFF SWALLOW"
1168              50               "ESTHER KETONE"
```
                                   (a)

```
ACCT. NO.     ?1205
CREDIT LIMIT ?600
CUSTOMER NAME ?"MILES KILOMETRES"

ACCT. NO.     ?750
ACCT. NO. MUST BE 4 DIGITS, VALUE 1000-4999
ACCT. NO.     ?1230
CREDIT LIMIT ?750
CUSTOMER NAME ?"FRED E KATT"

ACCT. NO.     ?STOP
```
                                   (b)

```
1001              500              "KERMIT KREY"
1143              200              "BARNEY BLUESTONE"
1151              1000             "CLIFF SWALLOW"
1168              50               "ESTHER KETONE"
1205              600              "MILES KILOMETRES"
1230              750              "FRED E KATT"
```
                                   (c)

Figure 9.5 Execution of a program to add data to a file: (a) File AUTH; (b) transcript of program execution; (c) file NAUTH resulting from the program.

Fig. 9.6. Steps 4 and 5 of the procedure can be done by the simple commands

```
COPY  AUTH  > BAUTH
COPY  NAUTH > AUTH
```

The *former* backup copy BAUTH is discarded by this procedure, but we always have one previous copy to fall back on in case a problem develops.

1. Assemble and check the forms that authorize additions to the file.
2. Through the program of Fig. 9.4, enter the new accounts.
3. Check the file NAUTH to make sure the file is readable, and includes all the additions accurately. If it does not, return to step 2.
4. Copy the file AUTH to a backup file, perhaps called BAUTH, for use in reconstructing AUTH if necessary.
5. Copy the file NAUTH to AUTH; the new version of the AUTH file contains the added accounts.
6. Delete the file NAUTH. It is no longer needed, and we can release the file space.

Figure 9.6 Operational procedure for adding accounts to AUTH.

The net result is that AUTH is replaced by a new version that includes the new records added at the end. This is what we wanted to accomplish in the first place, but we have constructed a procedure that is much safer to use than a program that would add records directly to the end of an existing file.

This type of backup procedure for files is very common. In a sense, we have generations of files; as we construct the file NAUTH, it is the "son" of AUTH. The sequence BAUTH, AUTH, NAUTH has a grand-father-father-son relationship. Often the file BAUTH is kept on a mag-netic tape at a location removed from the main computer area; it then provides backup against not only minor errors but also major disasters, such as fires or floods. Many organizations would be out of business if their computer files were destroyed; one of the ways to guard against that is to keep files like BAUTH in a secure location removed from the main computer site.

9.3 A READ-WRITE PROCESS

Since Chapter 6 we have worked with procedures whose major outline is

    1. WHILE there are records yet to be read from a file

        1.1 Read a record

        1.2 Process a record

In many production programs the step that processes a record includes writing a record to a new file, as in Step 2.2 of the procedure in Fig. 9.3. We now show another example of such a procedure.

The Biggle-Wiggle Store maintains charge accounts for its customers, and sends monthly billing statements to customers whose accounts either have a nonzero balance or have had some activity during the month. At all times a file BIGWIG contains the current status of the customer accounts, including a summary of the activity in each account for the current month. Figure 9.7 shows the contents of each record in BIGWIG. The file is updated daily; we will explore that update process in Section 9.4. At month-end, the company runs a series of two programs, as shown in Fig. 9.8, to send monthly statements and to reinitialize fields to begin a new month.

We suggest that you outline the program to print customer state-ments, while we turn our attention to the second program. Its task is to take the file that represents the end of, say, February, and produce a file that represents the beginning of March. Figure 9.9 shows how each field of the new file is derived from the old file. The procedure followed by the

Account number (a 4-digit number)
Customer name
Customer address
Customer city, state, zip (all in one string)
Credit limit
Balance at the beginning of the current month
Number of charges made this month
Dollar total of charges made this month
Dollar total of credits allowed this month
Dollar total of payments made this month

Figure 9.7 Contents of the file BIGWIG.

program is very simple, as shown in Fig. 9.10, and the program itself is also short and simple, as you can see in Fig. 9.11. As an example, a record in the file BIGWIG at the end of February could be

```
2370   "MAXIMO WIGGLE" "27 BIGGLE ST."
"EUGENE, OR 97404" 5000   451.25   2   200   15   300
```

This record tells us that Mr. Wiggle had an account balance of $451.25 (he owes) at the beginning of February, that he made two charge transactions in February for a total of $200, and that he was credited $15 and

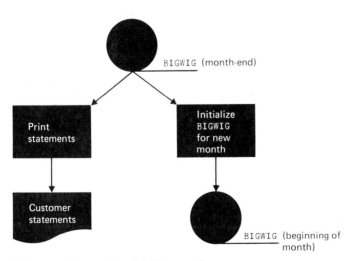

Figure 9.8 Month-end billing cycle.

Account number ⎫
Customer name   ⎪
Customer address ⎬ Copied from old file
Customer city, state, zip ⎪
Credit limit ⎭

Balance at the beginning of current month
 = Balance + Dollar total of charges ⎫
        − Dollar total of credits ⎬ From old file
        − Dollar total of payments ⎭

Number of charges ⎫
Dollar total of charges ⎪
Dollar total of credits ⎬ All set to zero
Dollar total of payments ⎭

Figure 9.9 Derivation of fields for reinitialized BIGWIG.

1. Set NEWWIG for writing
2. WHILE there are records of BIGWIG to be read
   2.1 Read a record from BIGWIG
   2.2 Compute new balance
   2.3 Write a record into NEWWIG

Figure 9.10 Procedure to reinitialize BIGWIG.

```
10   REM PRODUCE FILE NEWWIG FOR BEGINNING OF MONTH
15   REM FROM BIGWIG WHICH REPRESENTS END OF PREVIOUS MONTH
20   REM G STRUBLE   BIGGLE-WIGGLE CO   JAN 1980
30   REM      N  = ACCOUNT NUMBER
32   REM      N$ = CUSTOMER NAME
34   REM      A$ = CUSTOMER ADDRESS
36   REM      C$ = CUSTOMER CITY, STATE, ZIP
38   REM      L  = CREDIT LIMIT
40   REM      B  = BALANCE AT BEGINNING OF CURRENT MONTH
42   REM      C1 = NUMBER OF CHARGES    IN CURRENT MONTH
44   REM      C2 = DOLLAR TOTAL OF CHARGES CURRENT MONTH
46   REM      C3 = DOLLAR TOTAL OF CREDITS CURRENT MONTH
48   REM      P  = DOLLAR TOTAL OF PAYMENTS CURRENT MONTH
50   REM      B1 = BALANCE AT BEGINNING OF THE NEW MONTH
70      FILES BIGWIG, NEWWIG
80      SCRATCH #2
90      QUOTE #2
95   REM   WHILE LOOP CNSTRUCTION
100     IF END #1 GO TO 970
110     INPUT #1, N, N$, A$, C$, L, B, C1, C2, C3, P
120     LET B1 = B + C2 - C3 - P
130     PRINT #2, N; N$; A$
135     PRINT #2, C$; L; B1; 0; 0; 0; 0
140     GO TO 100
970  END
```

Figure 9.11 Program to initialize BIGWIG.

made payments of $300 on his account. The program will write a record into NEWWIG that reflects the account status at the beginning of March:

```
2370   "MAXIMO WIGGLE" "27 BIGGLE ST."
"EUGENE, OR 97404" 5000   336.25   0   0   0   0
```

The balance of $336.25 is the balance at the beginning of March, and the zeroes represent no charges, credits, or payments yet in March.

The operational procedure is similar to that shown in Fig. 9.6, keeping the old BIGWIG file for backup and copying NEWWIG to BIGWIG for further use.

9.4 UPDATING A FILE FROM TRANSACTIONS

Now that we have taken care of Biggle-Wiggle's month-end customer billing, we can turn our attention to the daily process of posting charges, credits, and payments to the customer accounts. This process requires a program to access *two* input files: the BIGWIG file containing information to date on each account, which we will classify as a *master* file, and another file that contains today's charges, credits, and payments, which we will call a *transaction* file. The program must be able to take a transaction—say, a charge of $59.55 on account 1471—find the BIGWIG record for account 1471, add 59.55 to the charges total in that record, add 1 to the number of charges this month in that record, and (if there are no more transactions for 1471) write the updated record to a new file. Records in BIGWIG for which there are no transactions today should be moved intact to the new file, so at the end of the process the new file contains the up-to-date status of all accounts and, therefore, can become the new BIGWIG file.

There are several ways in which such a program could be organized. First, if there are few enough master records that they can all be brought into main storage simultaneously, we could read each transaction in turn and apply it to the proper master record, and write the new master after all transactions have been posted to the records in main storage. To do this we need arrays, which are the subject of Chapter 10. However, the master file for most companies is far too large for this approach to be feasible.

A second approach is to read the first record of the master file, then search the transaction file for all transactions that apply to that account, and write the record, updated by all the transactions found, to the new master file. The process is repeated for the second master file record, the third, etc. Our program would read the entire transaction file once for every account in the master file; this is so slow that it is unthinkable!

What we want is an approach that does not place huge demands on main storage space, and one that runs rapidly. Preferably, each file should be read only once.

If a program is to do this task, the two files must meet some conditions:

1. All transactions for one account (there may be several) must be together in the transaction file. If they are not, our program would apply some of the transactions, write a new master record, and later discover another transaction for the same account. How could we apply that last transaction?

2. If the master file record for account 1271 precedes the record for 1433 in BIGWIG, then the transaction records for 1271 must precede the transaction records for 1433. If the transactions were in the reverse order, we could match the records for one of the accounts, but could not bring together the master and transaction records for the other account without going backward in one file. Try it!

There is one simple way to meet these conditions: Organize *both* files so that the records are in ascending sequence by account number. The update process will naturally produce a new master file that is in sequence, so if we create a master file that is in sequence in the first place, all updates will preserve the sequence. The transaction records will not naturally appear in sequence by account number, but they can be sorted into order before the transaction file is used for updating. In Section 9.8 we will explore the sorting process.

Before we continue developing the procedure for the update program, let us introduce the concept and mechanism of subroutines.

9.5 SUBROUTINES

A subroutine is a more-or-less self-contained section of program that can be executed from some other section of the program, with control returning to that section after the subroutine has been executed. When a program asks for execution of a subroutine, we say that it *calls* the subroutine. A subroutine may be called from several points in a program; therefore, if we have a section of program to do a task that should be done at several different points in the program, we write the section as a subroutine and call it from each of the points at which the task is needed.

A subroutine in BASIC is called by a GOSUB statement, of the form

line no. GOSUB *line no.*

where the second line number is the line number of the beginning of the subroutine. For example,

> 140   GOSUB 800

calls a subroutine that starts at line 800. The action of GOSUB is a transfer of control like a GO TO statement, but with this difference: GOSUB stores the address *of the GOSUB statement* in a special location so that when the subroutine completes execution, control may be returned to the location (line number) just after the GOSUB statement. The effect is that of a GO TO with a rubber band attached; one end of the rubber band stays attached to the GOSUB itself, while the other moves with the GO TO to the subroutine. When the subroutine finishes the task, it "lets go" and the rubber band snaps back to the point in the program at which the subroutine was called. The statement that "lets go" and returns control from the subroutine is

> *line no.*   RETURN

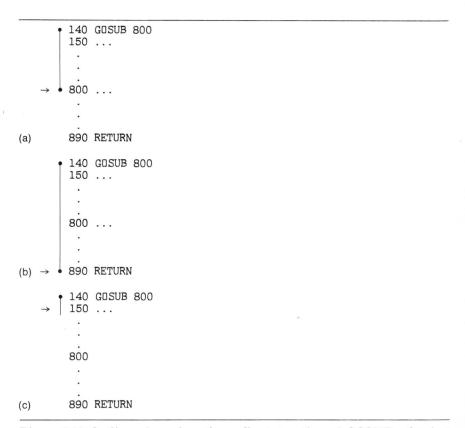

Figure 9.12 Outline of a subroutine call: (a) action of GOSUB; (b) just before RETURN is executed; (c) just after RETURN is executed.

Figure 9.12 shows the execution of a subroutine. The arrow shows at each stage which statement the program is about to execute. First, the GOSUB 800 statement transfers control to 800, but the rubber band connects them. During execution of the subroutine, one end of the rubber band remains fixed at 140, while the other moves with the execution of statements within the subroutine. Eventually, control reaches line 890. The RETURN statement lets go of the rubber band, which carries control back to line 140, and the next statement to be executed will be line 150.

What can be done in a subroutine? Any statements that could be executed anywhere else can be executed in a subroutine. A subroutine may call other subroutines; we may think of a new rubber band stretching to the second subroutine while the first remains connected to mark our place in the first subroutine and the return point from that first subroutine. A subroutine may contain IF-THEN-ELSE constructions and loops. It is bad practice to jump out of a subroutine with a GO TO rather than a RETURN; it can be done, but usually leads to confusion.

Let us examine a more specific example. A payroll program is being written with one section to handle salaried employees, and another to handle workers paid by hourly wage. For each employee, one of these sections is executed. For all employees, a computation of FICA deduction must be made. The computer must recognize that FICA deductions are made only on the first $22,800 of income each year. (What? The figure has risen? Then the program must be changed. The definition of L1 once in the program makes it easier to change than if we had written the program using 22800 directly in several places.) Rather than writing the section of program that computes the FICA deduction in both the salary and wage sections of the program, we write it only once, as a subroutine at 1400, and call the subroutine from the salary or wages section, as shown in Fig. 9.13.

We can also use subroutines to make the structure of a program similar to the way we conceive the procedure that the program follows. When we design a procedure for a complex problem, it is most effective to use top-down design; we design the broadest outline first, and show it in the procedure. Then we can refine each large step of the procedure, perhaps with several levels of greater and greater detail, until we have only elementary tasks that can be programmed quite directly.

Our payroll program could have been organized first with a gross outline in the procedure shown in Fig. 9.14. The overall structure of the program is clear, though very little detail is specified. In later versions we can specify the details. It is helpful to be able to see the overall structure of a program, too. Figure 9.15 shows how the use of subroutines can help show the overall structure. The main part of the program is in statements

```
10   REM   PROGRAM TO COMPUTE PAYROLL DEDUCTIONS
 .
 .
 .
140 REM      Y  = PAID YEAR-TO-DATE SUBJECT TO FICA
150 REM      P  = PAY FOR THE CURRENT PAY PERIOD
160 REM      L9 = LIMIT FOR PAY SUBJECT TO FICA
170    LET L9 = 22800
175 REM      P1 = PAY IN CURRENT PERIOD SUBJECT TO FICA
180 REM      F  = FICA TAX WITHHELD THIS PAY PERIOD
 .
 .
 .
300 REM  SECTION FOR EMPLOYEES ON SALARY
 .
 .
380      GOSUB 1400
 .
 .
 .
600 REM  SECTION FOR EMPLOYEES ON WAGES
 .
 .
 .
690      GOSUB 1400
 .
 .
 .
1390 REM  SUBROUTINE TO COMPUTE FICA WITHHOLDING
1400     IF Y >= L9 GO TO 1440
1410     IF Y + P > L9 GO TO 1460
1420     LET P1 = P
1430     GO TO 1470
1440     LET P1 = 0
1450     GO TO 1470
1460     LET P1 = L9 - Y
1470     LET F = .0613 * P1
1480     LET Y = Y + P1
1490     RETURN
 .
 .
 .
```

Figure 9.13 A subroutine for computing FICA withholding.

1. Initialize variables
2. WHILE there are payroll records to be read,
    2.1 Read a record
    2.2 IF employee is on salary
        THEN Make salary computations
        ELSE Make wages computations
    2.3 Write a record to the payroll register file
    2.4 Add deductions to totals
3. Print totals of deductions

Figure 9.14 Procedure for a payroll program.

```
10     REM   PROGRAM TO COMPUTE PAYROLL DEDUCTIONS
100    REM   SECTION TO INITIALIZE VARIABLES
200        IF END #1 GO TO 1200
210        INPUT #1, S$, N$, I$, W, R, E
220        IF I$ = "SAL" GO TO 250
230        GOSUB 600
240        GO TO 260
250        GOSUB 300
260        GOSUB 900
270        GO TO 200
295    REM   SUBROUTINE FOR EMPLOYEES ON SALARY
300        ...
  .
  .
  .
590        RETURN
595    REM   SUBROUTINE FOR EMPLOYEES ON WAGES
600        ...
  .
  .
  .
890        RETURN
895    REM   SUBROUTINE TO WRITE CHECK REGISTER AND ADD TO TOTALS
900        ...
  .
  .
  .
1190       RETURN
1195   REM   SECTION TO PRINT COMPANY TOTALS
1200       ...
  .
  .
  .
1380       GO TO 9970
1390   REM   SUBROUTINE TO COMPUTE FICA WITHHOLDING
1400       ...
  .
  .
  .
1490       RETURN
9970   END
```

Figure 9.15 Outline of a payroll program.

200 through 270. We may have to look at statement 300 (or the REM
statement that precedes it), for example, to know the function of the
subroutine at line 300, but we see easily the flow of control.

We end this section with two cautions. In some subroutines, there
are several places in which execution of the subroutine is complete; we
may have RETURN statements at each such place. However, we recommend that you have only one RETURN per subroutine, with GO TO
statements leading to that single RETURN as necessary. Figure 9.16
shows both structures. Both yield the same results, but we recommend
the second because the structure and extent of the subroutine are clearer,
and that contributes to nearly error-free programming.

800	IF J = 1 GO TO 840		800	IF J = 1 GO TO 840
810	IF J = 2 GO TO 860		810	IF J = 2 GO TO 860
820	LET A = 2.40 * P		820	LET A = 2.40 * P
830	RETURN		830	GO TO 870
840	LET A = 1.80 * P		840	LET A = 1.80 * P
850	RETURN		850	GO TO 870
860	LET A = 2.20 * P		860	LET A = 2.20 * P
870	RETURN		870	RETURN
	(a)			(b)

Figure 9.16 Exit from a subroutine: (a) multiple RETURN statements; (b) only one RETURN statement.

One common error is to permit control to "fall into" a subroutine. For example, if in Fig. 9.15, statement 1380 were omitted, the program would read and process all records, go to 1200 to print company totals, and then fall into line 1400. Though 1400 is the beginning of a subroutine, there is no fence to keep out intruders, so the statements in subroutine 1400 would all be executed once more. But control reaches statement 1490, and there is nowhere to return to! That is an error, and no good can come of it. So remember to branch around subroutines. It is best to organize a program with all subroutines at the end, so we need remember only one GO TO to branch around all of them to the END statement.

We will see more examples of subroutine use in the next several sections.

9.6 DEVELOPING AN UPDATE PROGRAM

Let us return to the problem of updating the BIGWIG file by the day's transactions, which we introduced in Section 9.4. We discovered that both the master file BIGWIG and the transaction file must be in sequence on the customer's account number. Now we will develop a strategy for the update program and represent the strategy in a procedure.

The essence of an update process is combining a transaction record with a master record. We will, therefore, keep the contents of one master record and one transaction record in main storage at all times during program execution—at least until we exhaust the records in one of the files.

Our objective is to match transaction records with the master records that have the same account number. We can compare the process to a zipper; we match corresponding records (teeth in the zipper). But we need an intelligent zipper, since there may be no transaction, one transaction, or several transactions corresponding to each master record, and there may be transaction records that have no corresponding master record. Therefore, we must manage our progress through both files to guarantee that we recognize all possible matches. Suppose the master file contains records for accounts

  1001,   1003,   1004,   1007,   1009,   1011,

and the transaction file contains records for

  1003,   1003,   1003,   1006,   1007.

As our program considers master record 1001 and the first transaction record 1003, it is clear that 1001 must be disposed of, and 1003 must be held for at least the possibility of finding a master record with the matching account number. After master record 1003 is read, it should be updated by the first transaction 1003. The updated master record must be held so that further transactions for 1003 can also be posted. Our program must, therefore, process and read transaction records until it finds a transaction whose account number does not match the master record currently in main storage. *Then* it can write the updated master record with confidence that all possible updates have been applied. After master records 1003 and 1004 are written, the program finds itself with a master record 1007 and a transaction record 1006. It must hold the master record, since there may be (and are) transactions for 1007 coming later. At this point, the program knows that transaction record 1006 *has no matching master record*. This is an important conclusion, and the program must process the records carefully in order to draw that conclusion.

We can then distinguish among three cases in processing the master and transaction records currently in main storage:

Case 1: Master record has a lower account number: Write the record to the new master file, and read another master record.

Case 2: Master record account number matches the transaction account number: Update the master record from the transaction data and read a new transaction record.

Case 3: Transaction record has a lower account number: Print an error message and read a new transaction record.

After we update a master record in Case 2, we do *not* write the updated master record to the new master file, at least not as a part of the Case 2 processing. There may be a second (and third . . .) transaction record that should update that same master record, so we must keep the master record until we are sure we have applied all updates. When there are no more transactions for that master record, the next transaction has a higher account number, so Case 1 applies and its actions write the now-complete master record, so Case 2 actions have no need to write the record.

Eventually, the program will exhaust the records in one of the files, but it must keep processing the records in the other file as if they had low account numbers. The program must be prepared for *either* file to run out of records first. There are several ways of handling the end-of-file problem; we will follow one that is simple and effective. We choose some number that is guaranteed to be greater than any actual account number. For example, if account numbers are four digits, we may choose 99999. We call this number H9, or *high-values*. When the program finds that a file is exhausted, it sets the account number variable that it would have read to high-values, and continues processing. The records in the other file are processed because their account number is less than high-values. It only remains to set the criterion for stopping the program: *Both* account number variables must be equal to high-values.

We can now gather the various pieces of our strategy into a procedure. Figure 9.17 shows the procedure at a high level. Very little detail is filled in, and therefore the general outline of the strategy is quite visible. Figure 9.18 shows the main portion of a program that follows the procedure. Calls on subroutines are used so that the general outline of our strategy is as clear as in the procedure. Detail not shown in this procedure is left to the subroutines. We will see in the following sections another reason for writing the program of Fig. 9.18 in this way: It can be used with only the most minor changes (file names, H9, K1, K2) for several different tasks, with the subroutines handling the real changes that accomplish the different tasks.

---

1. Initialize
2. Read a master record
3. Read a transaction record
4. WHILE master acct. no. $\neq$ high-values
       or transaction acct. no. $\neq$ high-values
   4.1 Case 1: master acct. no. $<$ transaction acct. no.:
       4.1.1 Write master record to new file
       4.1.2 Read master record
   4.2 Case 2: master acct. no. $=$ transaction acct. no.:
       4.2.1 Update master record from transaction
       4.2.2 Read transaction record
   4.3 Case 3: transaction acct. no. $<$ master acct. no.:
       4.3.1 Print error message
       4.3.2 Read transaction record

Figure 9.17 Procedure to update from transactions.

```
10   REM   PROGRAM TO UPDATE BIGWIG FROM TRANSACTION FILE TRANS
12   REM   PRODUCING UPDATED MASTER FILE EARWIG
14   REM   USING SUBROUTINES:
16   REM     1000 TO READ MASTER RECORD
18   REM     1500 TO READ TRANSACTION RECORD
20   REM     2000 TO WRITE A MASTER RECORD
22   REM     3000 TO UPDATE A MASTER RECORD FROM A TRANSACTION
24   REM     4000 TO PRINT UNMATCHED-TRANSACTION ERROR MESSAGE
30   REM     K1 = RECORD KEY (ACCT NO.) FROM MASTER RECORD
32   REM     K2 = RECORD KEY (ACCT NO.) FROM TRANSACTION RECORD
34   REM     H9 = HIGH-VALUES, LARGER THAN ANY ACTUAL ACCT NO.
50   REM   G STRUBLE   BIGGLE-WIGGLE CORP   JAN 1980
70       FILES BIGWIG, TRANS, EARWIG
80       SCRATCH #3
90       QUOTE #3
100      LET H9 = 99999
110      GOSUB 1000
120      GOSUB 1500
190  REM   BEGINNING OF MAIN PROCESSING LOOP
200      IF K1 <> H9 GO TO 220
210      IF K2  = H9 GO TO 9970
220      IF K1 >= K2 GO TO 260
225  REM   CASE 1: MASTER ACCT. NO. < TRANSACTION ACCT. NO.
230      GOSUB 2000
240      GOSUB 1000
250      GO TO 200
260      IF K1 > K2 GO TO 300
265  REM   CASE 2: ACCOUNT NUMBERS MATCH
270      GOSUB 3000
280      GOSUB 1500
290      GO TO 200
295  REM   CASE 3: TRANSACTION ACCT. NO. < MASTER ACCT. NO.
300      GOSUB 4000
310      GOSUB 1500
320      GO TO 200
9970     END
```

Figure 9.18 Skeleton program to update from transactions.

With the general strategy settled in procedure and even in a program, we can turn our attention to the remaining detail. The first detail is the format of the transaction file TRANS. The essential fields are account number, amount of the transaction, and an indication of the type of transaction. The format shown in Fig. 9.19 also includes the date, which is essential for any follow-up of the transaction. We also include a

Account number
Date
Document number
Type—"CH" for charge, "CR" for credit, "P" for payment
Amount

Figure 9.19 The Biggle-Wiggle transaction file.

document number, in case verification of the computer records against the original documents is necessary. The document number could be the invoice number, credit memo number, or check number, depending on the type of transaction.

The subroutines necessary are shown in Fig. 9.20. These subroutines, combined with the skeleton program in Fig. 9.18, make a complete program. We have adopted the convention of using variable names ending in 1 (or other odd numbers) to represent data from the master file, and

```
965   REM   SUBROUTINE TO READ MASTER RECORD
970   REM        K1  = RECORD KEY (ACCOUNT NUMBER)
972   REM        N1$ = CUSTOMER NAME
974   REM        A1$ = CUSTOMER ADDRESS
976   REM        C1$ = CITY, STATE, ZIP
978   REM        L1$ = CREDIT LIMIT
980   REM        B1  = BALANCE AT BEGINNING OF CURRENT MONTH
982   REM        C1  = NUMBER OF CHARGES IN CURRENT MONTH
984   REM        C3  = TOTAL CHARGES IN CURRENT MONTH
986   REM        C5  = TOTAL CREDITS IN CURRENT MONTH
988   REM        P1  = TOTAL PAYMENTS IN CURRENT MONTH
1000      IF END #1 GO TO 1030
1010      INPUT #1, K1, N1$, A1$, C1$, L1$, B1, C1, C3, C5, P1
1020      GO TO 1040
1030      LET K1=H9
1040      RETURN
1475 REM   SUBROUTINE TO READ TRANSACTION RECORD
1480 REM        K2  = RECORD KEY (ACCOUNT NUMBER)
1482 REM        D2$ = DATE OF TRANSACTION
1484 REM        D4$ = DOCUMENT NUMBER
1486 REM        T2$ = TRANSACTION CODE: "CH" = CHARGE,
1487 REM              "CR" = CREDIT, "P" = PAYMENT
1490 REM        A2  = TRANSACTION AMOUNT
1500      IF END #2 GO TO 1530
1510      INPUT #2, K2, D2$, D4$, T2$, A2
1520      GO TO 1540
1530      LET K2=H9
1540      RETURN
1995 REM   SUBROUTINE TO WRITE A MASTER RECORD
2000      PRINT #3, K1, N1$, A1$, C1$, L1$, B1, C1, C3, C5, P1
2010      RETURN
2995 REM   SUBROUTINE TO UPDATE MASTER RECORD FROM TRANSACTION
3000      IF T2$ <> "CH" GO TO 3040
3010      LET C1 = C1 + 1
3020      LET C3 = C3 + A2
3030      GO TO 3120
3040      IF T2$ <> "CR" GO TO 3070
3050      LET C5 = C5 + A2
3060      GO TO 3120
3070      IF T2$ <> "P" GO TO 3100
3080      LET P1 = P1 + A2
3090      GO TO 3120
3100      PRINT "INVALID TRANSACTION TYPE"; T2$
3110      PRINT K2, D2$, D4$, T2$, A2
3120      RETURN
3995 REM   SUBROUTINE TO PRINT UNMATCHED-TRANSACTION ERROR MESSAGE
4000      PRINT "NO MASTER RECORD FOR TRANSACTION ACCT. NO."; K2
4010      PRINT K2, D2$, D4$, T2$, A2
4020      RETURN
```

Figure 9.20 Subroutines to complete transaction update program.

variable names ending in 2 (or other even numbers) to represent data from the transaction file. This helps readability of the program and its subroutines. The subroutines 1000 and 1500 set account number fields to high-values (H9) if there are no more records to be read from the respective files. The main program, in statements 200 and 210, checks the account numbers for high-values and terminates the program when we have exhausted both files.

This program uses subroutines for both of the reasons suggested in Section 9.5. There are two points in the procedure at which we must read a master record, and three at which we must read a transaction record. We save coding by writing only once for each file the statements that test for end of file, read a record, and set account number to high-values. The other function is simplification of apparent flow of control; we have dramatized that by developing the main part of the program even on a separate page from the subroutines.

9.7 ADD-CHANGE-DELETE UPDATES

There are two kinds of updates to a master file. We were introduced to the first kind in Section 9.6: Transactions add or subtract data from fields in the master file. The second kind maintains the file by:

- Adding new records,

- Deleting records,

- Changing fields by replacing their contents.

New customers must be added to the BIGWIG file; old customers who have moved without a forwarding address, or gone out of business, or refused to pay their bills must be removed from the file. Some fields of records must be replaced, as a customer changes name or address or Biggle-Wiggle changes the customer's credit limit. Add-change-delete maintenance is done by a program different from that used for the update from transactions. It is perhaps not run as often. There are different criteria for validity: A change or delete requires that there be a master record with matching account number, while an update to add a record requires that there *not* be a master record with matching account number. We will show how add-change-delete updates are organized and programmed. We use the BIGWIG file as a fairly simple example; both add-change-delete updates and transaction updates are very common in data processing systems.

Let us next consider the format of records in the update file. First, each record must carry the account number of the master record to be changed or deleted, or the account number to be given to the record added to the file. Second, there must be some indication of whether each update is an add, a change, or a delete. We provide this indication by including a *transaction code*, which typically is the letter A for add updates, the letter C for change updates, or the letter D for delete updates.

For delete updates, only the account number and the transaction code D are required. For add updates, the record must include account number, the transaction code A, and all other fields whose value should be supplied. For an add update to BIGWIG, these fields would include customer name, address, city-state-zip, and credit limit. In order to maintain auditable control and balance the dollar amounts in the BIG-WIG file against the totals of monthly transactions, we would presume that all fields that are updated by transactions fields—balance, charges total, number of charges, credits total, payments total—are to be set to zero as the record is added. The update program should do that as a matter of course, and need not ask for zeros to be supplied in an update record.

Change updates should be permitted to change the same fields that add updates can initiate. They should not be allowed to change the fields that are updated by transactions, for the same reasons that add updates should not set those fields to anything but zero. Program designers may adopt either of two formats in which update records specify which fields are to be updated, and the new values. One format includes all such fields in the update record, with the convention that if a field in the update record is null, the corresponding field in the master record is not to be changed. For example, the format of a change record for BIGWIG could be:

Account number,

Transaction code,

Customer name,

Address,

City, state, zip,

Credit limit.

A particular record might contain

    1361   C   ""   "2730 MAIN ST"   "SPRING, PA   16816"   ""

which would be direction to leave the name and credit limit unchanged,

but to replace address and city, state, zip by the fields given in the update record. One disadvantage of this way of coding updates is that it is
not possible (without some further convention) to replace a field in a
master record *by* a null field.

The second format of change updates allows only one field to be updated by each update record, and requires a *field code* that identifies
which field is to be updated. We could adopt field codes for the BIGWIG
file:

CN   customer name;

CA   customer address;

CC   customer city, state, zip;

CL   credit limit.

The update coded above would have to be done by the *two* update records

```
1361   C   CA   "2730 MAIN STREET"
1361   C   CC   "SPRING, PA  16816"
```

We will adopt this second format for change updates as we develop a
program to update BIGWIG.

The program to do the add-change-delete update follows the same
general pattern as the transaction updates. We again have two files, and
must do everything possible to match account numbers. We will always
keep one record from each file in main storage, and we will use high-
values as an end-of-file indicator. As in the transaction updates, we follow
the pattern of processing whatever record has the lower account number,
if account numbers from the two records currently in main storage are
different; when we find the two account numbers matching, we do an
update and read a new update record.

Some of the processing is different, of course. We will explore differences in the way we read update records, the actions we take when we
find records with matching account numbers, and the actions we take
when the account number in the update record is low.

The format of an update record depends on the transaction code:

1. Acct. no.   A   name   address   city-state-zip   credit limit
2. Acct. no.   C   field code   value
3. Acct. no.   D

In most languages we would execute an instruction to read a record, and
then see what was in the record. In BASIC, our INPUT statements to
read from a file must specify exactly how many fields are to be read.

1. LOOP
    1.1 IF there are more update records to be read
        THEN read acct. no. and transaction code
        ELSE set acct. no. to high-values
    1.2 EXIT WHEN acct. no. = high-values
        or transaction code = "A", "C", or "D"
    1.3 Print an error message for invalid transaction code
2. IF acct. no. $\neq$ high-values
    THEN 2.1 Case 1: Transaction code = "A":
                Read name, address, city-state-zip, credit limit
          Case 2: Transaction code = "C":
                Read field code, value

Figure 9.21 Procedure for reading an A-C-D update record.

Therefore, our program must read account number and transaction code, and then, by testing the transaction code, determine how many more fields to read. Figure 9.21 shows the procedure to be used in reading an update record.

The actions that our program takes when it finds matching records must depend on the transaction code. If the transaction code is A, the update is invalid, and all our program can do is print an error message and go on to the next update. If the transaction code is C, the program should replace the appropriate field in the master record, as determined by the field code, by the value in the update record. There is, of course, the possibility that the field code is invalid, and in that case too, the program must print an error message and go on to the next update. If the transaction code is D, the program should delete the corresponding master record. In what sense can it be deleted? We are not changing the old BIGWIG file, so it cannot be deleted there. We are writing a new file, EARWIG, which will replace the BIGWIG file in further operations, so that if the record is not carried forward to EARWIG, it is effectively deleted from the file. We accomplish this simply by reading a new master record without writing the current one. (Think about it; it is sort of a sneaky idea!) The procedure that represents the actions outlined in this paragraph is shown in Fig. 9.22.

When our program finds the update record to have the low account number, the action again depends on the transaction code. The transaction code should be A; anything else is invalid and should generate an error message. If the code is A, a new master record will be inserted into EARWIG; it will contain account number, name, address, city-state-zip, and credit limit from the update record, and zeros to represent the other fields: balance, number of charges, charges total, credits total, and payments total.

Figures 9.23 and 9.24 show the program itself. The skeleton, in Fig.

1. Case 1: Transaction code = "A":
        Print error message
     Case 2: Transaction code = "C":
        Case 2.1: Field code = "CN":
                Replace name field by value from update record
        Case 2.2: Field code = "CA":
                Replace address field
        Case 2.3: Field code = "CC":
                Replace city-state-zip
        Case 2.4: Field code = "CL":
                Replace credit limit
        Case 2.5: Field code = anything else:
                Print error message
     Case 3: Transaction code = "D":
        Read a master record

Figure 9.22 Procedure for handling matching records in A-C-D update.

```
10    REM    PROGRAM TO UPDATE BIGWIG - ADD, CHANGE, OR DELETE RECORDS
11    REM    FROM UPDATES SPECIFIED IN BIGACD FILE
12    REM    PRODUCING UPDATED FILE EARWIG
14    REM    USING SUBROUTINES:
16    REM       1000 TO READ MASTER RECORD
18    REM       1500 TO READ BIGACD RECORD
20    REM       2000 TO WRITE A MASTER RECORD
22    REM       3000 TO UPDATE OR DELETE A MASTER RECORD
24    REM       4000 TO ADD A NEW MASTER RECORD
30    REM       K1 = RECORD KEY (ACCT NO.) FROM MASTER RECORD
32    REM       K2 = RECORD KEY (ACCT NO.) FROM BIGACD RECORD
34    REM       H9 = HIGH-VALUES, LARGER THAN ANY ACTUAL ACCT NO.
50    REM  G STRUBLE    BIGGLE-WIGGLE CORP    JAN 1980
70        FILES BIGWIG, BIGACD, EARWIG
80        SCRATCH #3
90        QUOTE #3
100       LET H9 = 99999
110       GOSUB 1000
120       GOSUB 1500
190 REM   BEGINNING OF MAIN PROCESSING LOOP
200       IF K1 <> H9 GO TO 220
210       IF K2  = H9 GO TO 9970
220       IF K1 >= K2 GO TO 260
225 REM   CASE 1: MASTER ACCT. NO. < UPDATE ACCT. NO.
230       GOSUB 2000
240       GOSUB 1000
250       GO TO 200
260       IF K1 > K2 GO TO 300
265 REM   CASE 2: ACCOUNT NUMBERS MATCH
270       GOSUB 3000
280       GOSUB 1500
290       GO TO 200
295 REM   CASE 3: UPDATE ACCT. NO. < MASTER ACCT. NO.
300       GOSUB 4000
310       GOSUB 1500
320       GO TO 200
9970      END
```

Figure 9.23 Skeleton program for A-C-D update.

```
965  REM   SUBROUTINE TO READ MASTER RECORD
970  REM      K1  = RECORD KEY (ACCOUNT NUMBER)
972  REM      N1$ = CUSTOMER NAME
974  REM      A1$ = CUSTOMER ADDRESS
976  REM      C1$ = CITY, STATE, ZIP
978  REM      L1$ = CREDIT LIMIT
980  REM      B1  = BALANCE AT BEGINNING OF CURRENT MONTH
982  REM      C1  = NUMBER OF CHARGES IN CURRENT MONTH
984  REM      C3  = TOTAL CHARGES IN CURRENT MONTH
986  REM      C5  = TOTAL CREDITS IN CURRENT MONTH
988  REM      P1  = TOTAL PAYMENTS IN CURRENT MONTH
1000    IF END #1 GO TO 1030
1010    INPUT #1, K1, N1$, A1$, C1$, L1$, B1, C1, C3, C5, P1
1020    GO TO 1040
1030    LET K1=H9
1040    RETURN
1475 REM   SUBROUTINE TO READ TRANSACTION RECORD
1480 REM      K2  = RECORD KEY (ACCOUNT NUMBER)
1482 REM      T2$ = TRANSACTION CODE: "A"=ADD, "C"=CHANGE, "D"=DELETE
1484 REM      N2$ = CUSTOMER NAME,      FROM "A" RECORD
1486 REM      A2$ = ADDRESS,            FROM "A" RECORD
1488 REM      C2$ = CITY, STATE, ZIP,   FROM "A" RECORD
1490 REM      L2$ = CREDIT LIMIT,       FROM "A" RECORD
1492 REM      F2$ = FIELD CODE,         FROM "C" RECORD
1494 REM      V2$ = REPLACEMENT VALUE,  FROM "C" RECORD
1500    IF END #2 GO TO 1530
1510    INPUT #2, K2, T2$
1520    GO TO 1540
1530    LET K2 = H9
1540    IF K2 = H9 GO TO 1600
1550    IF T2$ = "A" GO TO 1600
1560    IF T2$ = "C" GO TO 1600
1570    IF T2$ = "D" GO TO 1600
1580    PRINT "INVALID TRANSACTION CODE "; K2; T2$
1590    GO TO 1500
1600    IF K2 = H9 GO TO 1660
1610    IF T2$ = "A" GO TO 1650
1620    IF T2$ <> "C" GO TO 1660
1630    INPUT #2, F2$, V2$
1640    GO TO 1660
1650    INPUT #2, N2$, A2$, C2$, L2$
1660    RETURN
1995 REM   SUBROUTINE TO WRITE A MASTER RECORD
2000    PRINT #3, K1, N1$, A1$, C1$, L1$, B1, C1, C3, C5, P1
2010    RETURN
2995 REM   SUBROUTINE TO CHANGE OR DELETE MASTER RECORD
3000    IF T2$ = "A" GO TO 3040
3010    IF T2$ = "C" GO TO 3060
3015 REM   T2$="D"; DELETE MASTER RECORD BY NOT WRITING IT; READ NEW ONE
3020    GOSUB 1000
3030    GO TO 3190
3035 REM   T2$ = "A"; ERROR
3040    PRINT "MASTER RECORD ALREADY EXISTS";K2;T2$,N2$,A2$,C2$,L2$
3050    GO TO 3190
3055 REM   T2$ = "C"; REPLACE APPROPRIATE FIELD
3060    IF F2$ = "CN" GO TO 3120
3070    IF F2$ = "CA" GO TO 3140
3080    IF F2$ = "CC" GO TO 3160
3090    IF F2$ = "CL" GO TO 3180
3100    PRINT "INVALID FIELD CODE"; K2; T2$, F2$, V2$
3110    GO TO 3190
3120    LET N1$ = V2$
3130    GO TO 3190
3140    LET A1$ = V2$
3150    GO TO 3190
3160    LET C1$ = V2$
3170    GO TO 3190
3180    LET L1$ = V2$
3190    RETURN
3995 REM   SUBROUTINE TO ADD A NEW MASTER RECORD
4000    IF T2$ = "A" GO TO 4040
4010    PRINT "CHANGE OR DELETE - NO MASTER RECORD"; K2; T2$
4020    GO TO 4050
4040    PRINT #3, K2, N2$, A2$, C2$, L2$, 0, 0, 0, 0, 0
4050    RETURN
```

Figure 9.24 Subroutines to complete A-C-D master update program.

9.23, is very much like the transaction update skeleton shown in Fig.
9.18. The subroutines are shown in Fig. 9.24; subroutines 1000 and 2000,
to read and write master records, are identical to the corresponding subroutines in Fig. 9.20; after all, they are reading and writing the same
files. Subroutines 1500 and 3000 follow the discussion above and the procedures in Figs. 9.21 and 9.22. Subroutine 4000 is different from the
corresponding subroutine in Fig. 9.20, but is fairly simple.

9.8 MERGING AND SORTING

We will explore two more operations on the Biggle-Wiggle Store's files.
First, consider the transactions—charges, credits, and payments—that
are posted daily to the BIGWIG file. At the end of the month, when we
print customer billing statements, Biggle-Wiggle may want to list each
transaction on the customer's billing statement. Some companies include
this detail and some do not. If Biggle-Wiggle wants to provide those
data, how can it be done? Transactions for the month are in about 22
files, one for each working day in the month. For a program to manage
access to 22 files is difficult; it is even likely that at least one of the files
has been lost or at least misnamed. To make the entire task more man-
ageable, we will build a transactions month-to-date file, which will contain all transactions during the month, up to and including today's transactions. If we can generate and maintain that file during the month, the
contents at the end of the month will be all the transactions for the
month, and if the file is well organized, the task of the program that
prints monthly billing statements will be simplified enormously.

How should the transactions month-to-date file be organized? From
the fact that we want to print the transactions for each account together,
and on the statement with data from BIGWIG, which is in sequence by
account number, we can easily conclude that the transactions must also
be in sequence by account number. All transactions for each account
should be grouped together, regardless of the transaction date. However,
since the statement will list the transactions in the order in which they
appear in the transaction month-to-date file, the statement will appear
more orderly if the transactions for each account are in sequence by date.
There is a date in each transaction record, and we will soon learn how
we might sort records by a key such as date; for the present, we can
approximate that date sequence by arranging the transactions according
to the date on which they were posted to BIGWIG.

Our strategy in building the transaction month-to-date file is what
we call *merging*. Yesterday's month-to-date file is merged with today's
transactions to produce a new month-to-date file. The attempt to group

today's transactions for each account with the others this month from the same account requires the matching of account numbers, very much as we did in both update programs. The desire to arrange transactions for each account by date of posting requires that records from the old month-to-date file be written into the new file before today's transactions are written. In the framework of our update programs then, we will take the following actions:

Case 1: Account number in the month-to-date file is low: Write the month-to-date record into the new file, and read another month-to-date record.

Case 2: Account numbers in the two files match: Write the month-to-date record, and read another month-to-date record.

Case 3: Account number in today's transaction file is low: Write today's transaction into the new file, and read another today's transaction.

Since the actions of Cases 1 and 2 are identical, we can combine them. Furthermore, since the actions to be taken are such simple ones, we can keep the use of subroutines to those that read records. Figure 9.25 shows a complete program that merges the files. The program looks very similar to those that perform updates to BIGWIG, and it should, since it uses the same ideas and central strategy.

The technique of synchronizing progress through two files, exhibited in both update programs and in the merging program, is a very common and useful technique; we call it a *merge* process even when the effect is updating, and not strictly a merging of records.

We have assumed that the transactions in the file TRANS were in sequence by account number. We showed that this was a necessary assumption, and with that assumption we were able to preserve the sequence of the BIGWIG file and the WIGMTD file. We had to make the same assumption about the update records in BIGACD. How do the records get into the proper sequence? One possible way, of course, is for clerks to sort the transactions or the updates manually before entering them into the computer. This is not wise for the following reasons:

1. Clerks will make errors, and records will be out of sequence. Our programs will have to check for sequence, and it will be awkward to fix the error when records are found to be out of sequence.

2. Computers exist to help people do clerical work better. Sorting records is the kind of task that ought to be done by computer: It is repetitious, and needs no human judgment.

```
10    REM    PROGRAM TO BUILD MONTH-TO-DATE TRANSACTION FILE WIGMTD
11    REM    FROM YESTERDAY'S MONTH-TO-DATE FILE BIGMTD
12    REM    AND TODAY'S TRANSACTION FILE TRANS
14    REM    USING SUBROUTINES:
16    REM       1000 TO READ MASTER RECORD
18    REM       1500 TO READ TRANSACTION RECORD
30    REM       K1 = RECORD KEY (ACCT. NO.) FROM BIGMTD
32    REM       K2 = RECORD KEY (ACCT. NO.) FROM TRANS
34    REM       H9 = HIGH-VALUES, LARGER THAN ANY ACTUAL ACCT NO.
50    REM    G STRUBLE     BIGGLE-WIGGLE CORP     JAN 1980
70       FILES BIGMTD, TRANS, WIGMTD
80       SCRATCH #3
90       QUOTE #3
100      LET H9 = 99999
110      GOSUB 1000
120      GOSUB 1500
190   REM   BEGINNING OF MAIN PROCESSING LOOP
200      IF K1 <> H9 GO TO 220
210      IF K2  = H9 GO TO 9970
220      IF K1  > K2 GO TO 270
225   REM   MTD ACCT. NO. <= TODAY'S ACCT. NO.
230      PRINT #3, K1, D1$, D3$, T1$, A1
240      GOSUB 1000
250      GO TO 200
265   REM   TODAY'S ACCT. NO. IS ,LOW
270      PRINT #3, K2, D2$, D4$, T2$, A2
280      GOSUB 1500
290      GO TO 200
975   REM   SUBROUTINE TO READ A MONTH-TO-DATE TRANSACTION RECORD
980   REM       K1  = RECORD KEY (ACCOUNT NUMBER)
982   REM       D1$ = DATE OF TRANSACTION
984   REM       D3$ = DOCUMENT NUMBER
986   REM       T1$ = TRANSACTION CODE: "CH" = CHARGE,
987   REM             "CR" = CREDIT, "P" = PAYMENT
990   REM       A1  = TRANSACTION AMOUNT
1000     IF END #1 GO TO 1030
1010     INPUT #1, K1, D1$, D3$, T1$, A1
1020     GO TO 1040
1030     LET K1=H9
1040     RETURN
1475  REM   SUBROUTINE TO READ TODAY'S TRANSACTION RECORD
1480  REM       K2  = RECORD KEY (ACCOUNT NUMBER)
1482  REM       D2$ = DATE OF TRANSACTION
1484  REM       D4$ = DOCUMENT NUMBER
1486  REM       T2$ = TRANSACTION CODE: "CH" = CHARGE,
1487  REM             "CR" = CREDIT, "P" = PAYMENT
1490  REM       A2  = TRANSACTION AMOUNT
1500     IF END #2 GO TO 1530
1510     INPUT #2, K2, D2$, D4$, T2$, A2
1520     GO TO 1540
1530     LET K2=H9
1540     RETURN
9970  END
```

Figure 9.25 Program for building month-to-date file.

In fact, virtually every computer comes with a sort program supplied by the vendor; the user describes the file and the keys on which the file is to be sorted, and the system does the rest.

There are several techniques used in sorting by computer. If the entire file can be read and kept in main storage, we can use one of a class of *internal sorting techniques.* If not, it may still be possible to use an internal sorting method with records in direct access storage. We will describe (but not program) one of a class of *serial* sorting techniques, which process records serially or sequentially. This particular technique is called *sorting by merging,* using the merging strategy we have just developed.

We may speak of a *group* of records, meaning a sequence of records whose keys are in ascending order. The entire purpose of the sort is to merge the whole file into one group, and we do that, in stages. Our procedure will use four files, and as often as necessary merge two groups into one. The first stage of the procedure is to divide the original file into two files, with an equal number of groups in each file. Figure 9.26 illustrates the process; for simplicity, we assume that the sort keys are two-digit numbers. In the next stage we merge each pair of groups, one from each file, into a larger group. The groups thus formed are written alternately into files 3 and 4. What have we accomplished? We have only half as many groups as we started with, and because the groups are distributed between two files, they are ready for another merge. We can reverse the roles of the file pairs 1,2 and 3,4, and merge groups from files 3 and 4, writing the merged groups alternately between files 1 and 2. We can continue the process of merging and reversing roles of the pairs of files until all records are merged into one group, which completes the sort. If a file of, say, 16,000 records is in essentially random sequence, there will be about 8000 groups. The first merge phase will reduce the number of groups to 4000, the second to 2000, etc. Thirteen merges will sort the

Original file: 01,27,82,34,19,12,74,13, 69,53,58,84,95,11,87,92

    split into

File 1: 01,27,82,19,13,69,11,87,92

File 2: 34,12,74,53,58,84,95

    merge into

File 3: 01,27,34,82,13,53,58,69,84,95

File 4: 12,19,74,11,87,92

    merge into

File 1: 01,12,19,27,34,74,82

File 2: 11,13,53,58,69,84,87,92,95

    merge into

File 3: 01,11,12,13,19,27,34,53,58,69,74,82,84,87,92,95

File 4: - - - -

Figure 9.26 Sort by merge.

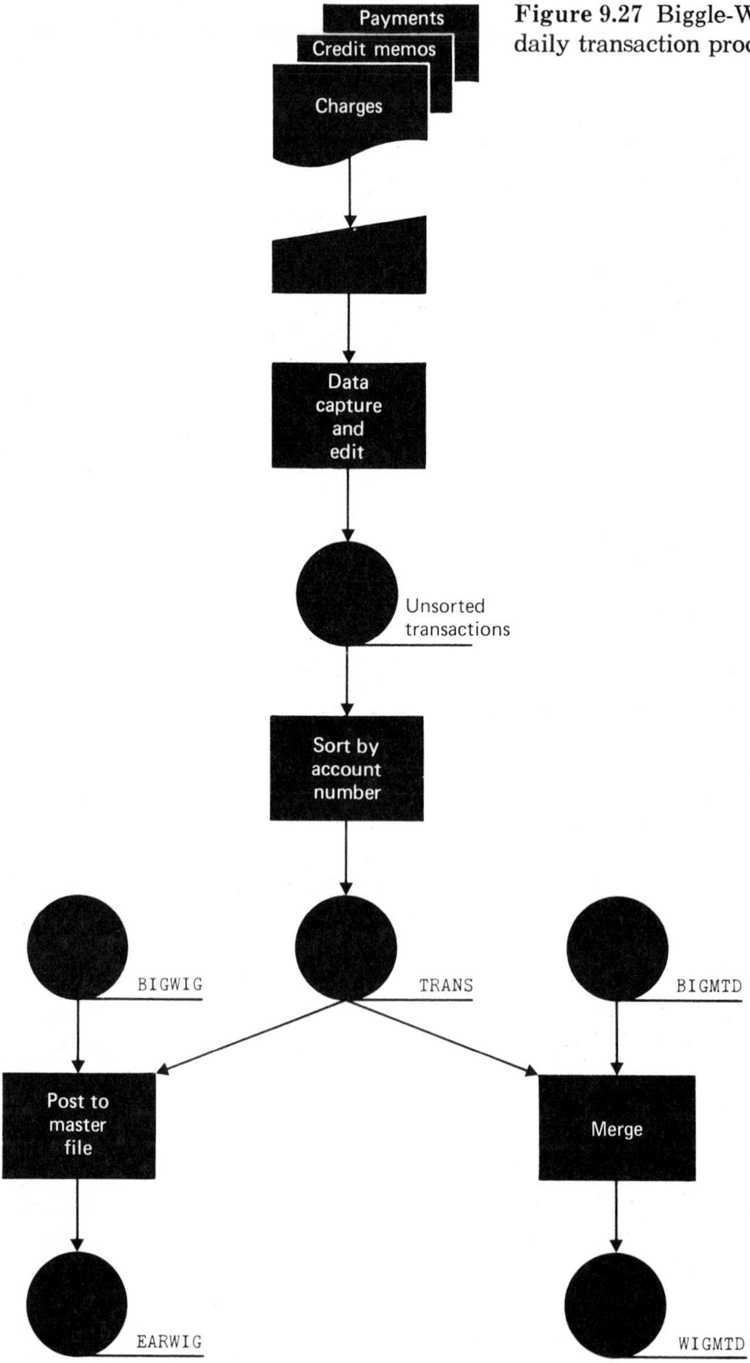

Figure 9.27 Biggle-Wiggle daily transaction processing.

entire file; starting with twice as many records requires only one more merge phase.

Keeping track of the end of a group, alternating the writing of groups between two files, and reversing the roles of the pairs of files make the programming of a sort by merge more complex than is worth pursuing here. The student who wants a challenge may try.

We close this section by reviewing the processing steps for the Biggle-Wiggle Store. Figure 9.27 shows a systems flowchart for the daily transaction processing. First the transactions are entered through a data capture and edit program similar to the program in Fig. 9.2. Second, the transactions are sorted into sequence by account number, using a sort by merge program. Then the transactions are posted to the master file and also merged into a month-to-date transaction file. Files are then copied and backed up; old versions of BIGWIG, BIGMTD, and today's TRANS are kept for backup, preferably away from the computer site. EARWIG is copied to BIGWIG and WIGMTD to BIGMTD, ready for further processing. A similar flowchart would be followed for add-change-delete updating of BIGWIG; that process does not include a merge program, however. The add-change-delete update is perhaps not performed every day, but when it is performed, it should precide the daily transaction processing.

9.9 MAIN IDEAS

a. To write a file in BASIC, the statement

> *line no.*   SCRATCH *#k*

prepares the file for writing: It deletes any previous contents of the file, and establishes the file in the user's directory if it did not exist previously. The statement

> *line no.*   QUOTE *#k*

sets a switch so that strings that contain commas or spaces are enclosed in quotation marks as they are written to a file. The statement

> *line no.*   PRINT *#k, list*

writes a record into the file. The record is determined by *list*, which has the same format as PRINT statements to the terminal.

b. Data enter a data processing system through a *data capture and edit* program, which checks each field for validity, as much as possible, and permits correction of invalid data.

c.   When we add to or update a file, we create a new file containing the updated data. The old file, and often one previous file, are kept for backup. As each new file is created, it becomes a "son" and an old file is deleted, keeping a "grandfather-father-son" relationship.

d.   A BASIC subroutine is a section of program that is called by a GOSUB statement and returns via a RETURN statement to the statement following the GOSUB. A subroutine may perform a task that is required by—and therefore called from—two or more points in the program, thus requiring the programming of the task only once. A subroutine may also be used to implement stepwise refinement of a procedure, thus making the general structure of the program clearer.

e.   Many processes require the use of two sequential input files, with matching of keys of records where possible. This requires that both files be in sequence on the same key. The *zipper* or *merging strategy* used always processes the current record whose key is low, if they do not match.

f.   Processes using a merging strategy include updating a master file from transactions, add-change-delete updates, and merging the records from two files.

g.   In a master file, each field may be updated by adding or subtracting a quantity from a transaction, or by replacement from an add-change-delete update, but not both.

h.   Records must sometimes be sorted into sequence on some key. A common file sorting technique uses successive merges to increase the lengths of groups of records in sequence.

9.10 QUESTIONS FOR IMAGINATION AND REVIEW

1. What would be the result if, in Fig. 9.4, the SCRATCH statement were renumbered 115? 140?

2. The transcript of program execution in Fig. 9.5 shows recovery from the mistake of neglecting to enter an account number. What happens if the clerk neglects to enter a customer name and goes on to enter the next account number? Modify the procedure in Fig. 9.3 to ask the clerk's OK just before each record (that is entered by the clerk) is written in the new file. If the response is *not* OK, the procedure should permit reentry of the record. This is a safeguard often built into production programs. Rewrite the program to incorporate your modification to the procedure.

3. Write a procedure and then a program for data capture and edit for a college's time schedule of courses. Figure out what fields would be necessary information if the resulting file were to be used for:

    a) Printing the time schedule of courses, and

    b) Reference for course data in printing transcripts or grade rosters.

You may simplify in order to keep your program from getting too repetitive.

4. The Biggle-Wiggle Store has an opportunity to rent the mailing list of its charge account customers to another company. Write a procedure and then a program that will create from BIGWIG a new file containing only the name, address, and city, state, zip for each customer.

5. The Biggle-Wiggle Store wants to do a special analysis on its most active customers. For this purpose, we classify a customer as active if there were any charges made to the account within the current month. Write a procedure and then a program that will create a new file containing only the records of BIGWIG that represent active customers.

6. Outline, and program as much as you wish, the program that prints the monthly customer statements for the Biggle-Wiggle Store. Can you include a listing of the transactions in the WIGMTD file? Show the layout of the statement that your program will produce.

7. It is possible to combine the two monthly Biggle-Wiggle programs; monthly statements and the NEWWIG file can be produced by the same program. For what reasons would you consider that to be desirable? For what reasons would it be undesirable?

8. The Biggle-Wiggle Store probably levies a service charge on accounts that do not pay their entire bill during the month. Speculate on how that charge might be computed; then, if you can, check on how actual companies compute a service charge. Build your computation of service charge into the computations of the new account balance in the program of Fig. 9.11. This same service charge computation must be included in the program that prints the monthly statements. Does this change your judgment on whether the two programs should be combined?

9. Write a data capture and edit program that will accept and file payroll data: social security number, number of regular hours worked, number of overtime hours worked. Because the sections that accept and validate regular hours and overtime hours are similar, try to incorporate them into a general subroutine that accepts numeric data. You may wish to supply a variable P$, which could be set *outside* the subroutine to "REGULAR HOURS" or "OVERTIME HOURS" and used *inside* the subroutine as part of a message to prompt the user. We would call such a variable a *parameter* of the subroutine. In other computer languages, there are explicit provisions for passing parameters to and from subroutines.

10. Trace the following program and determine what is printed by its execution.

```
100   LET K = 5
110   GOSUB 400
120   PRINT K,W
130   LET K = -4
140   GOSUB 400
150   PRINT K,W
160   GO TO 970
400   IF K < 0 GO TO 450
410   LET W = 2 * K
420   GO TO 460
450   LET W = 1 - K/2
460   RETURN
970   END
```

11. Take one of the more complex programs that you have written, and reorganize it to use subroutines for some processing detail so that the main structure or flow of control of the program is clarified.

12. Construct for yourself a few records in a BIGWIG file, and a few transactions in a file TRANS that could apply to the records in your BIGWIG file. Then trace execution of the program shown in Figs. 9.18 and 9.20 to see how the program actually applies transactions and creates a new file.

13. A payroll system includes a payroll master file, and often a file containing pay data for the current pay period. Adapt the skeleton program in Fig. 9.18, and write subroutines similar to those in Fig. 9.20, to form a program that will update a payroll master file by adding the wages for the current pay period to the year-to-date wages for each employee.

14. The add-change-delete update program determines its actions at any moment by the comparison of account numbers and by the transaction code. The program in Figs. 9.23 and 9.24 compares account numbers first and examines the transaction code second. Rewrite the program to examine the transaction code first and compare account numbers second. Which version of the program do you think is preferable? Why?

15. Sometimes we discover that an error has been made in a transaction and, therefore, the current balance due and totals of charges, credits, or payments is incorrect. Why do we not permit such errors to be corrected by add-change-delete updates that replace incorrect amounts by the correct ones?

16. It is important that all data entered into a computer be as accurate as possible. We do all that we can to prevent incorrect input, but not all errors can be prevented. The fields that are updated by add-change-delete updates generally cannot be checked very thoroughly by the usual methods: ensuring that a number is within a specified range, or requiring that a batch of transactions add up to some total. Therefore, the usual way to monitor add-change-delete updates for accuracy is to print a *change report* showing the result of all updates: records added, records deleted, records changed (at least the new contents, and some programs print the previous contents, too). Modify the add-change-delete program in Figs. 9.23 and 9.24 to print such a report as well as updating the file BIGWIG.

17. If updates for an add-change-delete program are accumulated for a few days, and then sorted and applied all at once, it is possible that we will find an update to change a record that is just being added in the same run. The program in Figs. 9.23 and 9.24 will not perform such changes. Why not? How would you modify the program to permit a change to a record just being added?

18. When an add-change-delete program encounters an invalid transaction, it displays an error message and goes on to the next transaction. In BASIC, there may be problems when the update record is of incorrect form. What happens if the program in Figs. 9.23 and 9.24 encounters, say, a record whose transaction code is C but which contains six fields (as a valid *add* update does) or only two fields (as a valid *delete* transaction does)? What adjustments would you make to the program to handle this sort of problem better?

19. Part of the answer to Question 18 is that the data capture and edit program that accepts add-change-delete updates should refuse to create records that have invalid transaction codes or incorrect length. Write such a program.

20. What change must be made in the merge program in Fig. 9.25 if the records in each file (and the resulting file) are in *descending*, rather than ascending, sequence by account number?

21. What should the Biggle-Wiggle Store do at the beginning of each month to preserve the file of all transactions for the previous month and to initialize the BIGMTD file for the new month? What would any of the programs (Figs. 9.18 and 9.20, 9.23 and 9.24 or 9.25) do if fed a file with no records in it?

22. In Question 19 you were asked to write a data capture and edit program for add-change-delete updates. Combine this program with the update program in Figs. 9.23 and 9.24 so that updates are applied immediately upon entry. The data-capture-and-edit portion can essentially replace subroutine 1500, and the file BIGACD becomes unnecessary. One additional feature must be built into the program: We had assumed that BIGACD was sorted into ascending account number sequence. Your program will now have to *verify* that updates are *entered* in ascending account number sequence.

CHAPTER 10
ARRAYS

One more feature is necessary for our programs to realize the full power of the computer. Each loop we have constructed has used the same few variables each time, and the variables have been input from the terminal or a file or updated through an arithmetic process. But each set of data was used and replaced by new values for the next pass through the loop; once used and replaced, the data were no longer available. A computer's main storage is not made up of simple unrelated variables; there are locations, each holding a byte or a word, with consecutive addresses, and we should be able to set aside a block of main storage locations that will hold a set of similar data, all accessible to the program. After all, addresses are numbers and instructions are coded as numbers, so it ought to be possible to do computations that result in an address of a particular location within a block of main storage, and to use that address in further instructions. This is, in fact, feasible in machine language, and as we shall see, it is a powerful capability. That capability is provided within BASIC in what are called *arrays;* in this chapter we will discuss methods of setting up and using arrays.

10.1 ONE-DIMENSIONAL ARRAYS

An *array* is a list or block of numbers or strings that are accessed by the same variable name. An array can therefore hold several items (numbers or strings) that a program can treat in the same way, repeatedly or in any desired sequence. All the items are available without pushing each other out of the same single main storage location.

We can regard each item in an array as stored in a *cell*. Each cell thus represents a main storage location that holds a number or a string. In most versions of BASIC, each array name consists of:

1. A single letter, in which case it is a numeric array and all cells in the array contain numbers, or

2. A single letter followed by the dollar sign ($), in which case it is a character string array and all cells in the array contain strings.

Thus, A, T, and W may be names of numeric arrays and A$, C$, and P$ may be names of string arrays. There are no conflicts between simple variables A and A$ and the arrays A and A$; they may be used in the same program, and are assigned completely separate main storage locations. However, as a matter of avoiding confusion and possible errors, I recommend *against* having simple variables with the same names as arrays in the same program.

Since all cells in any array have the same array name, the language must provide a means of accessing each cell and distinguishing among the cells. The means provided is a *subscript* or *index* (in BASIC, subscript and index are synonymous; in some other languages, like COBOL, they are not), which is enclosed in parentheses after the array name. Figure 10.1 shows a diagram of an array that has a maximum subscript of 7. The

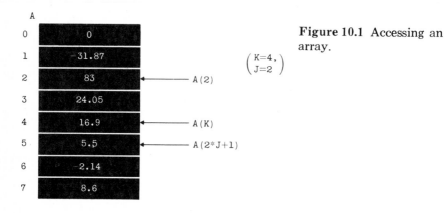

Figure 10.1 Accessing an array.

first cell in the array is accessed with subscript 0; we often ignore this cell if the logic of the use of the array is most naturally expressed with a minimum subscript of 1. Figure 10.1 also shows that the cell with subscript 2 is called A(2) in a BASIC program. If K = 4, A(K) will access the cell with subscript 4, and if J = 2, A(2*J+1) will access the cell with subscript 5. The subscript may be represented in a program by any arithmetic expression. Even a fractional value is permitted; the value is rounded *down*, so A(2.9) is really A(2). Negative subscripts are not permitted, nor are subscripts above the range for which cells actually exist; for example, A(−1) and A(8) are invalid in accessing the array in Fig. 10.1, and if a program attempts to use A(−1) or A(8), the computer will stop the program with an error message.

To distinguish arrays from the variables we have been using, we will call those without subscripts *simple variables*. A cell of an array may be used anywhere in a program that a simple variable can—in LET, IF, INPUT, PRINT statements—for example:

```
80    LET A(3) = 0
90    LET T = T + A(K)
160   LET B(J) = A(J) − A(J − 1)
170   INPUT A(K)
180   INPUT #1,A(1),A(2),A(3)
220   PRINT K; TAB(6); A(K)
230   PRINT #2,A(K),B(K)
320   IF A(K) > A(K − 1) GO TO 370
```

If a program is to use an array, we should declare our intention at the beginning of the program, so that:

1. When the translator finds a subscripted variable used in the program, it can translate the subscripted variable correctly;

2. The translator can set up the block of space needed for the array.

The declaration is a DIM statement (DIM stands for *dimension*). Each array name is followed by the maximum subscript desired, in parentheses; several arrays may be declared in one DIM statement. For example,

```
60   DIM A(15),V$(75)
```

will reserve space for an array named A; its 16 cells are accessed by subscripts 0 to 15. The same DIM statement also reserves space for a string array V$, whose 76 cells will hold strings with subscripts 0 to 75. The

DIM statements should appear early in the program, certainly before any mention of the arrays in executable statements. I prefer to place DIM statements just before FILES statements, though just after FILES statements would do just as well.

In fact, most BASIC systems permit use of an array without a DIM statement; if a variable is used with a subscript, the translator sets aside space for an array with maximum subscript 10. I encourage you not to rely on this feature, which is *not* included in other computer languages.

Let us consider an example. A file SLSMO contains a record for each salesperson:

Salesperson number,

Salesperson name,

Sales total for the previous month.

We know the company has fewer than 200 salespersons. The sales manager wants a list of all salespersons whose sales for that month are at least twice the average sales of all salespersons. What strategy can a computer program use in generating this list? It will have to be in two parts:

1. Find the average sales per salesperson.

2. List the salespersons whose sales are at least twice this average.

To find the average, the program must read all the records in the file, accumulate the total sales, and divide by the number of salespersons. Then in the second step each salesperson's data must be examined *again*. There are two ways to do that:

1. Reread the entire file.

2. During the first step, store all the data in a set of arrays, and use the data in the arrays during the second step.

In nearly all data processing programs, input and output are the chief bottlenecks; a program that must read its data from a file twice will take nearly twice as long to run and cost nearly twice as much. Therefore, it is more effective to use arrays for this program than to read the file a second time.

Figure 10.2 shows a quite detailed procedure for carrying out the task. One part of the procedure that is not obvious is Step 1.4, which

---

1. Read data into arrays and find average sales
   1.1 Set total sales T = 0
   1.2 Set K = 1
   1.3 WHILE there are records left
      1.3.1 Read a record into K'th cells of arrays
      1.3.2 Add sales to total
      1.3.3 Increase K by 1
   1.4 Find no. of salespersons M = K − 1
   1.5 Compute and print average A = T/M
2. List salespersons whose sales are at least twice average
   2.1 Set K = 1
   2.2 WHILE K ≤ M
      2.2.1 IF Sales for K'th salesperson ≥ 2 × average
            THEN print salesperson's number, name, sales

Figure 10.2 Procedure for listing best salespersons.

finds the number of salespersons as K − 1. Why not K itself? Let us concentrate on K as a counter; it is set to 1, and incremented inside the WHILE loop. Always, when the test for continuation of the loop is made, K indicates which record will be read next: When K = 1, we are about to read the first record; when K = 2, we are about to read the second record, and so on. Suppose when the test finds there are no more records, the value of K is 158. That means we were about to read the 158th record, and therefore we *have read* 157 records. Step 1.4 will correctly set M to 157. This is an example of the care we must take in constructing procedures or programs; it would be easy to ignore the analysis of the relationship between K and the number of records, so be careful and precise in thinking out a procedure.

There are two loops in the procedure; both loops examine the same data. Exit from the first loop is controlled by the IF END #1 test. In the second loop we use a comparison between K and M as the exit criterion. What is different? Why not test for end of file in the second loop, too? In fact, at any time after statement 170, an IF END #1 test would show that we were at the end of the file. We are using arrays precisely because we do not want to touch the file again. The data for the program to use in Step 2 are in the arrays, not the file, so a test based on the status of the file would be inappropriate and ineffective.

Figure 10.3 shows the program that follows the procedure in Fig. 10.2. The variable K is used not only as a counter but as a subscript into the three arrays. Note that the use of K in the second loop is independent of the value of K left from the first loop; if all references to K in statements 200 to 250 were replaced by J or, in fact, any variable except A or M, the results would be identical.

```
10   REM   PRINT NUMBERS AND NAMES OF SALESPERSONS
12   REM   WHOSE SALES ARE AT LEAST TWICE THE AVERAGE
20   REM   G STRUBLE    FEB 1980
30   REM      ARRAY N:  SALESPERSON NUMBERS
32   REM      ARRAY N$: SALESPERSON NAMES
34   REM      ARRAY S:  SALES FOR THE MONTH
36   REM      T = TOTAL SALES
38   REM      K = COUNTER AND SUBSCRIPT OF SALESPERSONS
40   REM      M = NUMBER OF SALESPERSONS
42   REM      A = AVERAGE SALES PER SALESPERSON
60       DIM N(200), N$(200), S(200)
70       FILES SLSMO
98   REM   1. READ DATA INTO ARRAYS, FIND AVERAGE SALES
100      LET T = 0
110      LET K = 1
120      IF END #1 GO TO 170
130      INPUT #1, N(K), N$(K), S(K)
140      LET T = T + S(K)
150      LET K = K + 1
160      GO TO 120
170      LET M = K - 1
180      LET A = T / M
190      PRINT "AVERAGE SALES = $"; A
198  REM   2. LIST SALESPERSONS WHOSE SALES ARE AT LEAST TWICE AVERAGE
200      LET K = 1
210      IF K > M GO TO 970
220      IF S(K) < 2 * A GO TO 240
230      PRINT N(K); TAB(10); N$(K); TAB(35); S(K)
240      LET K = K + 1
250      GO TO 210
970  END
```

Figure 10.3 Program for listing best salespersons.

The second step of the procedure is a good example of a counting loop that is simplified by the use of FOR and NEXT in BASIC. Statements 200 to 250 could be replaced by

```
200   FOR K = 1 TO M
220   IF S(K) < 2*A GO TO 240
230   PRINT N(K); TAB(10); N$(K); TAB(35); S(K)
240   NEXT K
```

Suppose we were not asked to print each salesperson's number, but only his or her name. In that case our program does not need an array holding all salesperson numbers, and we would rewrite the program to do without this array. The statements changed would be

```
60    DIM N$(200), S(200)
```

(delete line 62)

```
130   INPUT #1,N,N$(K),S(K)
230   PRINT TAB(10);N$(K);TAB(35);S(K)
```

When a change like this can be made, it should be; a needless use of arrays wastes space and some time spent in computing the address of a desired cell in an array.

We have seen one use of arrays: holding data to avoid the necessity of rereading them from a file. When very large files are involved, main storage is not large enough to hold the file contents in arrays, so we look for other techniques, such as the merge logic discussed in Chapter 9. Another use of arrays is to hold tables needed by a program. For example, suppose a file ASSESS contains a record for each property in a county:

Tax-lot-number (a string),

Owner name,

Owner address,

Tax district number (a string),

Assessment.

An actual file would contain much more data in each record, but this is sufficient to illustrate the use of a table. Each district has adopted a tax rate, and all properties in each district are assessed at that rate (an oversimplification), and it is time to print the tax bill for each property. Suppose there are approximately 100 tax districts in the county. The program must follow this strategy:

WHILE there are records

    Read a record

    Find the rate to be applied

    Tax = rate × assessment

    Print the data and the tax

The program could use a CASE structure for finding the rate:

CASE 1: District = "4J":

    Set rate = .02374

CASE 2: District = "6SW":

    Set rate = .01756

CASE 3: District = "7P":

    Set rate = .02280

    etc.

For 100 districts or so, this is very tedious, and it could be difficult ensuring there were no errors in the necessary 300 statements or so that implement the CASE structure. If we can keep a table in main storage, with district numbers in one array and the corresponding tax rates in another, our program can use the logic of a search for equality to find the district number and corresponding tax rate for each property. The program will be much shorter, though a little more complex. The arrays could be named D$ and R, and, using the same districts and rates as above, would have the following contents:

```
D$(1) = "4J"     R(1) = .02374
D$(2) = "6SW"    R(2) = .01756
D$(3) = "7P"     R(3) = .02280
etc.
```

Figure 10.4 shows a procedure for printing the tax bills. The procedure is in two parts: The first loads the table, and the second handles the assessment records, using the table. Let us consider the first step in the program first. The best way to maintain the data that belong in the table is to keep them in a file. The tax bill program can read the data from the file and other programs can also use the file and update it. An alternative would be to keep the table in DATA statements in the tax bill program. This is a reasonable use of DATA statements (see Section 6.5), and would make it easy to update the table using the BASIC editor, but the table would not be accessible to any other program. And to maintain a copy in DATA statements in *each* program that needs the table invites disaster, for it would be very difficult to ensure that an update to the table is applied correctly to all copies.

The procedure for loading the table is very similar to the first step of the previous program, and so is the corresponding portion of the program

---

1. Load the table from file RATES
   1.1 Set K = 1
   1.2 WHILE there are records in RATES
      1.2.1 Read district number and tax rate into arrays
      1.2.2 Add 1 to K
   1.3 Set M = K − 1 = no. of entries in table
2. Read records, compute and print tax bill
   2.1 WHILE there are records in ASSESS
      2.1.1 Read a record
      2.1.2 Search table for district no.
      2.1.3 IF district found,
            THEN compute tax = corresponding rate × assessment
                print tax bill
            ELSE print error message

Figure 10.4 Procedure for printing tax bills.

in Fig. 10.5. The variable K is used both as counter and as subscript, and the WHILE structure forms the loop that reads the records as consecutive entries in the table. In view of the discussion of data laundering in Chapter 8, there should be a test in both of these programs to make sure that we have room for all the records in the arrays. Actually, in BASIC the computer will stop the program with an error message if we attempt to read a record into the arrays beyond the maximum declared subscript.

The second step of the tax bill procedure in Fig. 10.4 is fairly simple and obvious. It makes allowance for the possibility that any particular tax district number will not be found in the file. This step of the procedure appears simple because the logic of searching the table is submerged in Step 2.1.3. This helps show the overall logic of the program and postpones the detail. When the procedure is implemented in the program in Fig. 10.5, we implement the procedure as shown, and submerge the de-

```
10    REM   PROGRAM TO COMPUTE PROPERTY TAXES AND PRINT THE TAX BILLS
20    REM   NORGE GUDDLE   FEB 1980
30    REM      ARRAY D$: DISTRICT NUMBERS IN TABLE
32    REM      ARRAY R:  RATES IN TABLE
34    REM      K  = SUBSCRIPT IN TABLE
36    REM      M  = NUMBER OF DISTRICTS IN TABLE
38    REM      L$ = TAX LOT NUMBER,           IN ASSESSMENT RECORD
40    REM      N$ = OWNER NAME,               IN ASSESSMENT RECORD
42    REM      A$ = OWNER ADDRESS,            IN ASSESSMENT RECORD
44    REM      T$ = TAX DISTRICT OF PROPERTY, IN ASSESSMENT RECORD
46    REM      A  = ASSESSMENT AMOUNT,        IN ASSESSMENT RECORD
48    REM      T  = TAX COMPUTED
60       DIM D$(150), R(150)
70       FILES RATES, ASSESS
98    REM   1. LOAD THE TABLE FROM THE FILE RATES
100LET K = 1
110      IF END #1 GO TO 150
120      INPUT #1, D$(K), R(K)
130      LET K = K + 1
140      GO TO 110
150      LET M = K - 1
198 REM   2. READ ASSESSMENT RECORDS, COMPUTE AND PRINT TAX BILL
200      IF END #2 GO TO 970
210      INPUT #2, L$, N$, A$, T$, A
220      GOSUB 400
222 REM   SUBROUTINE 400 SEARCHES TABLE FOR TAX DISTRICT T$
223 REM   IF SUCCESSFUL, K = SUBSCRIPT.  IF NOT, K = 0.
230      IF K = 0 GO TO 290
240      LET T = A * R(K)
250      PRINT
260      PRINT N$; TAB(40); L$; TAB(60); T$
270      PRINT A$; TAB(40); A; TAB(50); R(K); TAB(60); T
280      GO TO 320
290      PRINT
300      PRINT N$; TAB(40); L$; TAB(60); T$
310      PRINT A$; TAB(40); A; TAB(60); "DISTRICT NOT ON FILE"
320      GO TO 200
970   END
```

Figure 10.5 Tax bill program.

tails of the search in a subroutine. We have to set out some specifications for the subroutine, and it is wise to show them in REM statements as we have in statements 222 and 223. The data printed onto what is presumably a tax bill form are printed on three lines (one blank), which is less than adequate design. In Chapter 13 we will discuss the layout of printed reports and methods in BASIC of formatting reports more nicely than we now can.

Figure 10.6 shows the procedure for carrying out the search of the table and the subroutine that follows the procedure. The logic of the procedure is adapted from Fig. 7.10. The variable K is used as an indicator: If the search is successful, K is set to the subscript of the table entry where the match is found, but to zero if not successful. This enables the main program to get and use (in statements 240 and 270) the tax rate that corresponds to the district found in the table. The variable J is used as the subscript in the search loop itself.

I encourage you to draw some boxes representing the two arrays, lay out on paper some sample contents of the two files RATES and ASSESS, and follow the program's execution, step by step; the program includes enough features, including a loop within a loop, that I believe some program tracing is necessary before most of you understand fully the function of each procedure substep and statement.

What can we say about when to use an array? The first advice is not to use one unless it is necessary or really promotes the efficiency of the

---

```
2.1.3 Search table for district number
    2.1.3.1 Set indicator K to zero
    2.1.3.2 Set subscript J = 1
    2.1.3.3 WHILE J ≤ M and K = 0
        2.1.3.3.1 IF D$(J) = T$
                THEN Set K = J
        2.1.3.3.2 Increase J by 1
```

(a)

```
397 REM   SUBROUTINE TO SEARCH TABLE FOR TAX DISTRICT T$
398 REM   IF T$ = D$(K), K IS RETURNED
399 REM   IF NO D$ MATCHES T$, K IS SET TO ZERO
400     LET K = 0
410     LET J = 1
420     IF J > M GO TO 490
430     IF K <> 0 GO TO 490
440     IF D$(J) <> T$ GO TO 460
450     LET K = J
460     LET J = J + 1
470     GO TO 420
490   RETURN
```

(b)

Figure 10.6 (a) Procedure to search a table. (b) Program to search a table.

program. In our first example, use of the arrays N, N$, and S enabled us to avoid reading a file a second time. In the tax bill program, the alternatives to using arrays for the table were either a very long CASE structure or rereading a portion (on the average, half) of the table file for *every* record read from ASSESS. A third alternative would be to sort the ASSESS file into ascending order by tax district number, do the same with the RATES file, and apply the merge logic. Sorting the files would take quite a bit of time, and this strategy would print the tax bills in sequence by tax district, which is probably not what the tax collector wants.

We will see some other uses for arrays in the following section, as we discuss some common operations that are performed on arrays. Then in Section 10.3 we will discuss one method of performing a sort on items in arrays—one of the class of so-called internal sorting methods. As you become more familiar with the concept of arrays and more skillful in applying the concept, you will find still other effective ways to use arrays in your programs.

10.2 COMMON ARRAY OPERATIONS

In Section 10.1 we discussed two examples of the use of arrays in complete programs, as well as introducing the concept and the representation in the BASIC language. In this section we show several common tasks that are performed on arrays as a part of a variety of procedures.

First, we may want to initialize all values in an array to zero. This was not necessary in the programs in Figs. 10.3 and 10.5, but would be necessary if we were to use an array as a set of totals. If an array T has a maximum subscript of 150, the following procedure sets all cells to zero:

1. Set subscript J to zero
2. WHILE J $\leq$ 150,
   > 2.1 Set T(J) to zero
   > 2.2 Increase J by 1

This can be implemented by the BASIC statements

```
100   LET J = 0
110   IF J > 150 GO TO 150
120   LET T(J) = 0
130   LET J = J + 1
140   GO TO 110
150   next step
```

or more simply by the FOR-NEXT loop

```
100   FOR J = 0 TO 150
120   LET T(J) = 0
130   NEXT J
150   next step
```

By now the program looks simpler than the procedure, and we would like to simplify the procedures along the lines of the FOR-NEXT loop. So I suggest an equivalent representation

1. FOR J from 0 to 150

    1.1 Set $T(J)$ to zero

Please compare this with the first procedure version, which is supposed to mean the same thing; we don't want to make our lives complicated, but neither do we want to suggest procedure language elements that are not understood!

As a second example, suppose we have two arrays, A and B, and 12 numbers in each (subscripts 1 to 12). We want to construct an array C, in which each cell will contain the sum of the corresponding cells of A and B:

$$C(1) = A(1) + B(1)$$
$$C(2) = A(2) + B(2)$$
$$\cdot$$
$$\cdot$$
$$\cdot$$
$$C(12) = A(12) + B(12)$$

A procedure for computing the numbers in array C could be

1. FOR J from 1 to 12

    1.1 Compute $C(J)$ as $A(J) + B(J)$

and the program is hardly more complex:

```
200   FOR J = 1 TO 12
210   LET C(J) = A(J) + B(J)
220   NEXT J
```

Any desired arithmetic operation can, of course, be substituted for the addition operation. One of the important points is that a single variable can be used as subscript for several arrays, as both example programs in Section 10.1 also showed. Conversely, several variables may be used as subscripts for one array. There is no mystical association between a variable used as a subscript and an array; the *value* of a subscript is the important thing, and any variables or expressions that will generate the pattern of values that access the desired cells in an array or set of arrays will be correct.

A third common operation is to print the contents of an array or a set of arrays. Suppose the array D$ contains the tax district numbers and R contains corresponding tax rates. We may want the schedule of districts and rates printed, and identified with the place of each in the array. For example, if

```
D$(1) = "4J",   R(1) = .02374
D$(2) = "6SW",  R(2) = .01756
D$(3) = "7P",   R(3) = .02280
```

we would like a schedule printed as

```
1   4J      .02374
2   6SW     .01756
3   7P      .02280
```

A procedure to print a schedule in this form is simply

   1. FOR J from 1 to M

      1.1 Print J, district no. (J), rate (J)

and the portion of program is

```
400   FOR J = 1 TO M
410   PRINT J; TAB(10); D$(J); TAB(20); R(J)
420   NEXT J
```

The variable J can be printed; its use as a subscript does not deprive us of the right to use it in any other way we wish.

We may also use expressions as subscripts to access different cells of the same array. Suppose an array E contains values of an economic indicator for the 13 months from January 1979, through January 1980. We may want the twelve two-month moving averages:

Average of January and February 1979,

Average of February and March 1979,

etc.

We might print these averages directly, but if we wanted them for later use we could put them in an array V:

   1. FOR J from 1 to 12

       1.1 Compute $V(J)$ as the average of $E(J)$ and $E(J+1)$

or, in BASIC:

```
500   FOR J = 1 TO 12
510   LET V(J) = (E(J)+E(J+1))/2
520   NEXT J
```

A similar strategy could be used to compute, for example, the changes from each month to the next. Note that all 13 values of the array E are used, even though J goes only from 1 to 12. What would you expect to happen if the FOR statement in line 500 varied J from 1 to 13?

We saw in the tax bill program in Section 10.2 how an array can be used as a table, and the subroutine of Fig. 10.6 showed how we look up items in such a table. This process can be somewhat time-consuming, since if there are 100 items in a table, we would expect, on the average, to examine 50 of them before finding a match. There is a more complex procedure known as *binary search* that can be used if the table is arranged in ascending order by its argument—say, tax district number. The binary search first compares the search key (T$ in the tax bill program) with the tax district number in the middle of the table. This comparison determines which *half* of the table the desired item must be in (if we weren't lucky enough to have found that it *was* the middle one itself). The next comparison is with the item in the middle of the appropriate half. The process continues, each comparison halving the segment of the table that may contain the desired item. At most seven comparisons will find a match (or conclude there is none) in a 100-item table. The programming of a binary search is significantly more complex than the sequential search used in Fig. 10.6, but the binary search should be used for large tables that will be consulted many times. You may attempt to write a program for a binary search as a challenge, but we will not do the programming here.

Sometimes we can do better yet, and more simply. Suppose the table RATES were available when the records were generated and written into the file ASSESS. Through a table lookup similar to the one in Fig. 10.6, we could derive and store in ASSESS the number 1 rather than 4J for any property in district 4J, the number 3 rather than 7P for any property in district 7P, etc. If these numbers, which we might call district indexes, are included in ASSESS rather than the more cumbersome strings, the district indexes can be used as subscripts directly into the table to find

Chapter 10. ARRAYS

"What?" exclaimed Roger, as Karen rolled over on the bed and rested her warm
body against his. "I know you can search a file, and sequentially search a table in
an array, but how can you retrieve data from a table without a search?"
Karen pursed her lips. "We can use a district index directly as a subscript..."

the tax rate and, if wanted on the tax bill, the strings 4J, and so forth,
as well. Figure 10.7 shows the revised second half of the program. The
variable I, the district index, is read in statement 210 and used *directly
as a subscript* in statement 240 to get the appropriate tax rate. The tax
index is also used in statement 260 to print the tax district number, as
before. Note that statements 220 and 230 ensure that I can be used as a

```
44   REM     I  =  TAX DISTRICT INDEX,         IN ASSESSMENT RECORD
198  REM   2.  READ ASSESSMENT RECORDS, COMPUTE AND PRINT TAX BILL
200      IF END #2 GO TO 970
210      INPUT #2, L$, N$, A$, I, A
220      IF I < 1 GO TO 290
230      IF I > M GO TO 290
240      LET T = A * R(I)
250      PRINT
260      PRINT N$; TAB(40); L$; TAB(60); D$(I)
270      PRINT A$; TAB(40); A; TAB(50); R(I); TAB(60); T
280      GO TO 320
290      PRINT
300      PRINT N$; TAB(40); L$; TAB(60); "DISTRICT INDEX"; I
310      PRINT A$; TAB(40); A; TAB(60); "OUTSIDE TABLE RANGE"
320      GO TO 200
970  END
```

Figure 10.7 Revised second step of tax bill program.

subscript; if it is not in the range 1 to M, we print the error message. This is absolutely necessary: Using an index value outside the range will either blow up the program, produce weird results, or worse.

We can use arrays to generate totals that will then be printed or written to a file. Let us take as an example the construction of the file SLSMO, which we used in Section 10.1. The company's sales records for the month may be accumulated in a file SLSDET whose records contain

Date,

Account number of customer,

Salesperson number,

Amount of sale.

There is also a file SLSPR, which has the same format as SLSMO but with data for the month before. Ignoring the problem of salesperson turn-over, we can use the file SLSPR to load salesperson numbers and names into arrays. Then in a third array S we will accumulate, sale by sale, all the sales for each salesperson for the month, by reading each SLSDET record and adding its sale amount to the appropriate cell of the array S.

Let us be more specific about the data structure we propose to use and the interpretation we place on each array and cell within an array.

$N(1)$ = Salesperson number of the first salesperson

$N\$(1)$ = Name

$S(1)$ = Sales by the first salesperson. At any time during the read-ing of SLSDET, $S(1)$ will contain the total of sales by the first salesperson *in records read up to that time*.

The strategy is just like that of other programs that accumulate totals, except that in this program we must decide into which of several totals to add the current amount. How do we do that? The table lookup pro-cedure in Fig. 10.6 enables our program to determine the total associated with the salesperson in the current record.

A procedure following the strategy we have outlined is shown in Fig. 10.8. The procedure need not be very detailed, because most of the pro-gram is borrowed from other programs we have developed. The program is shown in Fig. 10.9. The first step, statements 110–170, is adapted from the first step in Fig. 10.3. The totalling of sales records is omitted, and in fact the sales figure read from each record is thrown away into a vari-able S9 rather than being loaded into an array. The second step, initial-izing the totals in the array S to zeros, is completely straightforward. In fact, the first two steps could be combined; if statement 210 were re-

---

1. Load salesperson names and numbers into table from SLSPR
2. Set all totals to zero
3. WHILE there are records in SLSDET
   3.1 Read a record
   3.2 Find subscript K in table corresponding to salesperson
   3.3 Add sales to total (K)
4. Write contents of table into the file SLSMO

Figure 10.8 Procedure for generating totals by salesperson.

numbered 140, each total would be initialized in the same pass through the loop that reads the corresponding salesperson number and name, and the entire step, statements 200–220, could be deleted.

The third step of the program is the one for which we constructed this example. The important fields in each SLSDET record are N1, the salesperson number, and S1, the sales amount. Again we use a subroutine to look up the salesperson number in the table; the subroutine is almost identical to that in Fig. 10.6. If some particular record reports a sale of $1450 by salesperson 539, the subroutine may find that $N(53)$ contains the salesperson number 539. If so, the subroutine sets K to 53 and returns. Statement 340 then adds the sale amount of $1450 to $S(53)$, which holds the total sales for salesperson 539. Statements 360 and 370 report an error message if the salesperson number cannot be found in the table.

The fourth step of the program is again quite a simple one. The sales totals for the month, as accumulated in Step 3, are written with the corresponding salesperson numbers and names to the new file.

The ideas and techniques can be combined and extended in different ways. The idea of using data directly as a subscript can be applied to problems of accumulating totals, and can also be extended to situations in which arithmetic manipulation on data yields subscripts. For example, suppose a file CENS contains some census data, with a record for each person:

Identifying number,

Age,

Six other fields.

We want an age profile, in five-year groups:

The number of people ages 0–4,

The number of people ages 5–9,

The number of people ages 10–14,

etc.

```
10   REM   GENERATE THE FILE SLSMO OF SALES PER SALESPERSON FOR THE MONTH
12   REM   SALESPERSON NUMBERS AND NAMES ARE TAKEN FROM THE FILE SLSPR
14   REM   SALES ARE ACCUMULATED FROM THE FILE SLSDET
20   REM   NORGE GUDDLE    FEB 1980
30   REM     ARRAY N:   SALESPERSON NUMBERS
32   REM     ARRAY N$:  SALESPERSON NAMES
34   REM     ARRAY S:   ACCUMULATED SALES FOR SALESPERSON IN MONTH
36   REM     S9 = SALES FOR PREVIOUS MONTH, IN SLSPR RECORD
38   REM     D$ = DATE OF SALE,           IN SLSDET RECORD
40   REM     C$ = CUSTOMER ACCOUNT NO.,   IN SLSDET RECORD
42   REM     N1 = SALESPERSON NUMBER,     IN SLSDET RECORD
44   REM     S1 = SALE AMOUNT,            IN SLSDET RECORD
46   REM     K  = SUBSCRIPT TO ACCESS TABLE ENTRIES
48   REM     M  = NUMBER OF SALESPERSONS IN TABLE OR IN SLSPR FILE
50   REM     J  = TABLE SUBSCRIPT USED IN SEARCH SUBROUTINE 400
60      DIM N(150), N$(150), S(150)
70      FILES SLSPR, SLSDET, SLSMO
80      SCRATCH #3
90      QUOTE #3
98   REM   1. LOAD SALESPERSON NUMBERS AND NAMES INTO TABLE FROM SLSPR
110     LET K = 1
120     IF END #1 GO TO 170
130     INPUT #1, N(K), N$(K), S9
150     LET K = K + 1
160     GO TO 120
170     LET M = K - 1
198  REM   2. SET SALES TOTALS FOR EACH SALESPERSON TO ZERO
200     FOR K = 1 TO M
210     LET S(K) = 0
220     NEXT K
298  REM   3. ACCUMULATE SALES TOTALS FROM SALES IN SLSDET
300     IF END #2 GO TO 400
310     INPUT #2, D$, C$, N1, S1
320     GOSUB 500
322  REM   SUBROUTINE 500 SEARCHES TABLE FOR SALESPERSON NUMBER N1
323  REM   IF SUCCESSFUL, K = SUBSCRIPT.   IF NOT, K = 0.
330     IF K = 0 GO TO 360
340     LET S(K) = S(K) + S1
350     GO TO 380
360     PRINT "SALESPERSON NO."; N1; "NOT IN TABLE."
370     PRINT TAB(5); D$; TAB(15); C$; TAB(25); S1
380     GO TO 300
398  REM   4. WRITE CONTENTS OF THE TABLE TO SLSMO
400     FOR K = 1 TO M
410     PRINT #3, N(K), N$(K), S(K)
420     NEXT K
430     GO TO 970
498  REM   SUBROUTINE TO SEARCH THE TABLE
500     LET K = 0
510     LET J = 1
520     IF J > M GO TO 590
530     IF K <> 0 GO TO 590
540     IF N(J) <> N1 GO TO 560
550     LET K = J
560     LET J = J + 1
570     GO TO 520
590  RETURN
970  END
```

Figure 10.9 Program for generating totals by salesperson.

The records are not in any particular order by age. Our strategy will be to use a cell in an array C as a counter for each age group. We may allocate 21 cells, and let the 21st cell count all those whose ages are 100 or over.

Figures 10.10 and 10.11 show the procedure and program that generate the age distribution report. The subscript of the cell in which each person should be counted is derived from the age itself; for example, if a person is age 21, the subscript generated is

$$21/5 + 1 = 4.2 + 1 = 5.2.$$

When 5.2 is used as a subscript, 1 will be added to the cell $C(5)$. We pre-

---

1. Initialize the array C to zeros
2. WHILE there are records
   2.1 Read a record
   2.2 IF age $\geq$ 100
       THEN set $J = 21$
       ELSE compute $J = $ age/5 $+ 1$
   2.3 IF $J \geq 1$
       THEN add 1 to $C(J)$
3. Print the counts

Figure 10.10 Procedure for deriving age distribution.

```
10   REM   PRINT AGE DISTRIBUTION IN FIVE-YEAR GROUPS
20   REM   NORGE GUDDLE    FEB 1980
30   REM      ARRAY C: COUNTS OF POPULATION IN EACH 5-YEAR AGE GROUP
32   REM      J  = SUBSCRIPT USED TO ACCESS ARRAY C
34   REM      A  = AGE OF PERSON IN CENS RECORD
36   REM      I1$, I2$, I3$, I4$, I5$, I6$, I7$ = IRRELEVANT ITEMS IN CENS
60      DIM C(21)
70      FILES CENS
98   REM   1. INITIALIZE ARRAY C TO ZEROES
100     FOR J = 1 TO 21
110     LET C(J) = 0
120     NEXT J
198  REM   2. COUNT PEOPLE IN THE 21 GROUPS
200     IF END #1 GO TO 300
210     INPUT #1, I1$, A, I2$, I3$, I4$, I5$, I6$, I7$
220     IF A >= 100 GO TO 250
230     LET J = A/5 + 1
240     GO TO 260
250     LET J = 21
260     IF J < 1 GO TO 280
270     LET C(J) = C(J) + 1
280     GO TO 200
298  REM   3. PRINT THE COUNTS ACCUMULATED IN THE TABLE
300     FOR J = 1 TO 20
310     PRINT 5*J-5; "TO"; 5*J-1; TAB(15); C(J)
320     NEXT J
330     PRINT "OVER 100"; TAB(15); C(21)
970  END
```

Figure 10.11 Program for deriving age distribution.

sume that if a negative age is found, we can ignore it; however, we must protect our program against such things, as the test in statement 260 does. Step 3 of the program shows essentially the reverse of the subscript derivation process; we compute and print the age range corresponding to each count, deriving the range from J.

We show one last use of arrays in this section. Functions such as economic activity, product demand, and so forth, are often approximated by polynomials in a variable x. We call the highest power of x the *degree* of the polynomial. If the degree is n, the polynomial can be represented as

$$p(x) = a_0 x^n + a_1 x^{n-1} + a_2 x^{n-2} + \cdots + a_{n-1} x + a_n,$$

where the coefficients $a_0, \ldots, a_n$ are constants (perhaps derived from a least-squares curve-fitting program). We may wish to compute the value of the polynomial for a given value of x. The values of the coefficients may be stored in an array A (you must have seen this coming), and here it is most convenient to use the cell with subscript zero. The most efficient general scheme for evaluation of a polynomial is variously called *nesting*, or *synthetic division*, or *Horner's method:*

1. Set $V = a_0$
2. FOR j from 1 to n
   Compute $V = Vx + a_j$

This scheme can be programmed very simply:

```
400   LET V = A(0)
410   FOR J = 1 TO N
420   LET V = V * X + A(J)
430   NEXT J
```

The final value of V is the value of the polynomial at X. This scheme is not only simple, but uses only n multiplications, whereas other schemes would require $2n$ or $n(n+1)/2$ multiplications. Convince yourself that the procedure does properly compute the value of the polynomial; you can do it by expanding algebraically just what each of the successive values of V will be.

10.3 SORTING

In Chapter 9 we outlined the strategy for sorting a file by merging, and mentioned that there are internal sorting techniques for sorting data within main storage. In this section we present one of those techniques, partly because sorting is a fairly common operation and partly because it is a good example of the use of arrays and of nested FOR-NEXT loops.

There are several internal sorting methods, and variations of most. We will present what is called an *exchange* method. The set of data to be sorted is loaded into a set of arrays, as we have done in several other examples in the last two sections. The field that we wish to sort into sequence (we will presume *ascending* sequence) will be called the *sort key*. The general idea of the exchange strategy is to pass through the arrays, comparing each sort key with its neighbor. If the pair are not in the desired sequence, we exchange the two (and the rest of the data that belong with each sort key) so the pair will be in the proper sequence. Then we compare the higher sort key of that pair with the next sort key and repeat the process. The result in one pass through the arrays is that the largest sort key will sink to the bottom of the array.

Figure 10.12 shows a small example, with names and corresponding telephone extensions to be sorted into alphabetical order. In the first pass through the array, the first comparison is between JONES and SMITH, which need not be exchanged. SMITH is then compared to OLSEN, and the two are interchanged. Then the third and fourth cells are compared and SMITH is exchanged with KIMURA. One last exchange puts

JONES	1249
SMITH	1637
OLSEN	2619
KIMURA	2065
AMATO	1891

(a)

JONES	1249
OLSEN	2619
KIMURA	2065
AMATO	1891
SMITH	1637

(b)

JONES	1249
KIMURA	2065
AMATO	1891
OLSEN	2619
SMITH	1637

(c)

AMATO	1891
JONES	1249
KIMURA	2065
OLSEN	2619
SMITH	1637

(d)

Figure 10.12 Example of an exchange sort: (a) arrays as first loaded; (b) after first pass; (c) after second pass; (d) after fourth pass.

SMITH, the highest name, into the bottom cell, as shown in Fig. 10.12(b). The process now starts over, with comparison between JONES and OLSEN, then between OLSEN and KIMURA. OLSEN sinks through the array until it lodges in the second-to-last position, as shown in Fig. 10.12(c). There is no need to compare OLSEN with SMITH in the second pass, since SMITH was already known to belong last. The third pass needs only two comparisons, and the fourth pass only one comparison. Four passes are needed, since AMATO must work its way to the top and can rise only one cell each pass.

We may take as an example that relates to previous examples the file SLSMO, and suppose we want the file printed in alphabetical order by salesperson name. The procedure we have described informally is shown in Fig. 10.13. Step 2.1 sets up the repetition of passes through the arrays, and J represents the last cell to be examined in each pass. The first pass must consider all cells, and each successive pass may ignore one more at the bottom of the array, until the last pass need only compare the first and second cells. The second FOR, in Step 2.1.1, implements a pass through the arrays. The variable K represents the *first* subscript of each pair to be compared, so K must begin at 1 and go to $J - 1$; since the comparison involves Kth and $(K + 1)$th entries, the Jth entry will be the $(K + 1)$th cell in the last comparison of each pass. Figure 10.14 shows the pattern of comparisons and potential exchanges carried out in each pass.

---

1. Load arrays from the file SLSMO
2. Sort into ascending order by salesperson name
   2.1 FOR J from M down to 2
      2.1.1 FOR K from 1 to $J - 1$
         2.1.1.1 IF name (K) $>$ name $(K + 1)$
                 THEN exchange K'th and $K + 1$'th entries
3. Print the sorted data

Figure 10.13 Procedure for an exchange sort.

Pass 1: $J = M$	Pass 2: $J = M - 1$ ...	Pass $M - 2$: $J = 3$	Pass $M - 1$: $J = 2$
Compare 1,2	Compare 1,2	Compare 1,2	Compare 1,2
Compare 2,3	Compare 2,3	Compare 2,3	
Compare 3,4	...		
...	Compare $M - 2$, $M - 1$		
Compare $M - 1$, M			

Figure 10.14 Comparisons made in each pass of exchange sort.

Figure 10.15 shows a program that follows the exchange sort procedure of Fig. 10.13. The first step, which loads the arrays, should look very familiar by now. The difficult part of Step 2 is control of the looping, making sure the program follows the proper number of passes through the arrays and does the proper comparisons in each pass. But that was figured out in the procedure, and is implemented by a nested pair of FOR-NEXT loops. Note that each interchange requires *three* statements; one of the numbers or strings must be moved to a temporary location so it will not be lost when the other is moved to its place.

This is the first time we have seen nested FOR-NEXT loops. One rule is that the second FOR in such a sequence must be terminated *before* the first one, so one FOR-NEXT is entirely *inside* the other. I encourage you to transcribe these FOR-NEXT pairs into the equivalent

```
10    REM    SORT AND PRINT THE FILE SLSMO IN ALPHABETIC ORDER
20    REM    NORGE GUDDLE     FEB 1980
30    REM         ARRAY N:  SALESPERSON NUMBERS
32    REM         ARRAY N$: SALESPERSON NAMES
34    REM         ARRAY S:  SALES FOR EACH SALESPERSON
36    REM         J = SUBSCRIPT USED FOR MAJOR CONTROL IN ARRAYS
38    REM         K = SUBSCRIPT USED IN INNER LOOP
40    REM         M = NUMBER OF ENTRIES IN THE TABLE
42    REM         T, T$ = TEMPORARY LOCATIONS USED IN EXCHANGE OF ITEMS
60        DIM N(200), N$(200), S(200)
70        FILES SLSMO
98    REM    1. LOAD ARRAYS FROM THE FILE SLSMO
100       LET J = 1
110       IF END #1 GO TO 170
120       INPUT #1, N(J), N$(J), S(J)
130       LET J = J + 1
140       GO TO 110
170       LET M = J - 1
198   REM    2. SORT INTO ASCENDING SEQUENCE BY NAME N$
200       FOR J = M TO 2 STEP -1
210       FOR K = 1 TO J - 1
220       IF N$(K) <= N$(K+1) GO TO 260
228   REM    EXCHANGE TWO ENTRIES
230       LET T = N(K)
232       LET N(K) = N(K+1)
234       LET N(K+1) = T
240       LET T$ = N$(K)
242       LET N$(K) = N$(K+1)
244       LET N$(K+1) = T$
250       LET T = S(K)
252       LET S(K) = S(K+1)
254       LET S(K+1) = T
258   REM    FINISH LOOP CONTROL
260       NEXT K
270       NEXT J
298   REM    3. PRINT THE SORTED DATA
300       FOR J = 1 TO M
310       PRINT N$(J); TAB(28); N(J); TAB(38); S(J)
320       NEXT J
970   END
```

Figure 10.15 Program for an exchange sort.

BASIC using LET, IF, and GO TO statements, and, with a small example (as in Fig. 10.12 perhaps), trace the execution of the second step of the procedure.

10.4 TWO-DIMENSIONAL ARRAYS

An array need not be only a list, with one subscript. A *numeric* array (not a string array in most systems) may be a two-dimensional table, accessed by two subscripts. We may think of the first subscript as a *row index*, determining the row of the cell being accessed. The second subscript is a *column index*, and determines the column within the array. Figure 10.16 shows such an array. The BASIC translator allocates space for a row and a column with subscript zero whether we want them or not. The array must be declared in a DIM statement, which is different from the declaration of a one-dimensional array only in the specification of the maximum subscript for the second dimension. Thus, the array shown in Fig. 10.16 is set up by

```
60   DIM A(5,3)
```

Declarations of one- and two-dimensional arrays can be intermixed in any fashion in one or more DIM statements.

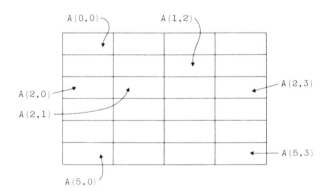

Figure 10.16 The array dimensioned $A(5,3)$.

The use of two-dimensional arrays is also very similar to the use of one-dimensional arrays. Our programs may include statements like

```
160   LET A(J,K) = S(J)
170   LET T = T + A(2,J - 1)
180   IF A(J,J) = 0 GO TO 230
```

```
410   INPUT A(K + 1,2)
420   INPUT #1,A(J,1),A(J,2),A(J,3)
530   PRINT A(K,J)
```

One thing to avoid is having a one-dimensional array *and* a two-dimensional array of the same name. Some systems would have the two share the same space, which ought to scare you, and the likelihood of programming error is increased beyond reasonable bound.

Let us illustrate the use of a two-dimensional array with an example. Suppose the Biggle-Wiggle Company has several (but no more than 20) production plants, and production for each plant for each month of last year is in a file named PRODTN. There is a record for each plant, which contains:

Plant name,

Production in each of the twelve months (Jan. through Dec.)

We want to do some analysis of the production, so our program will read the production statistics into a two-dimensional array P. Let us decide that the first subscript (row index) of P will indicate the plant number, and the second subscript (column index) will indicate the month. A portion of the procedure and program that load the data from the file into the arrays is shown in Fig. 10.17. The procedure is very familiar; what is new is the portion of program in statements 210–240, which read a single record into the Jth row of P. In practically any other language than BASIC we read a record with one input statement, but in BASIC

---

1. Set J = 1
2. WHILE there are records in PRODTN
   2.1 Read a record into N$(J), J'th row of P
   2.2 Increase J by 1
3. Set M = number of plants = J − 1

                         (a)

```
60      DIM P(20,12), N$(20)
70      FILES PRODTN
100     LET J = 1
200     IF END #1 GO TO 300
210     INPUT #1, N$(J)
220     FOR K = 1 TO 12
230     INPUT #1, P(J,K)
240     NEXT K
250     LET J = J + 1
260     GO TO 200
300     LET M = J - 1
```

                         (b)

Figure 10.17 Loading a two-dimensional array: (a) procedure; (b) program segment.

the loop to read the twelve monthly production figures is easier to write than a single (equivalent) statement

```
220   INPUT #1, N$(J), P(J,1), P(J,2), P(J,3),
         P(J,4), P(J,5), P(J,6), P(J,7), P(J,8), P(J,9),
         P(J,10), P(J,11), P(J,12)
```

Let us also note that if we know that there are *exactly* 20 records in the file, we can replace statements 100, 200, 250, 260, and 300 by

```
200   FOR J = 1 TO 20
250   NEXT J
300   LET M = 20
```

What was the production of the sixth plant in March? It is available to the program as P(6,3). What was the production for the sixth plant for the entire year? That can be accumulated as the result T of a simple segment

```
400   LET T = 0
410   FOR L = 1 TO 12
420   LET T = T + P(6,L)
430   NEXT L
```

Similarly, the production for all plants for March can be accumulated as the value of T1 by the segment

```
500   LET T1 = 0
510   FOR L = 1 TO M
520   LET T1 = T1 + P(L,3)
530   NEXT L
```

We can develop an elementary inquiry program that allows corporate managers to find the total production for any month or for any plant. We will ask the user to input from the terminal:

P for total for a plant,

M for total for a month,

S to stop the program.

If the user types P or M, the program must also ask for plant or month number. The procedure is shown in Fig. 10.18, and puts together several ideas that we have seen before. It is a simplified example of the kind of programs and systems that are provided for decision support in business.

---

1. Load arrays from file PRODTN
2. LOOP
   2.1 LOOP
      2.1.1 Obtain choice from terminal
      2.1.2 EXIT WHEN choice = P, M or S
      2.1.3 Display error message
   2.2 EXIT WHEN choice = S
   2.3 LOOP
      2.3.1 Obtain number Q
      2.3.2 EXIT WHEN $1 \leq Q \leq 12$ *and* choice = M
          or $1 \leq Q \leq M$ *and* choice = P
      2.3.3 Display error message
   2.4 IF choice = M
      THEN 2.4.1 Compute total production for month Q
            2.4.2 Print total
      ELSE 2.4.3 Compute total production for plant Q
           2.4.4 Print total

Figure 10.18 Procedure for production inquiry program.

The program that follows the procedure is shown in Fig. 10.19 (and Fig. 10.17). The only difficult pieces of this program are:

1. The validation of the plant or month number, which is a combination of conditions, and

2. Keeping the use of subscripts straight.

It could be less confusing not to use L in both segments 700s and 800s; the use of the variable M and the value "M" of C\$ could be confusing. Perhaps you would like to modify the program to straighten out these problems.

In what situations should we use a two-dimensional array? The first answer is that we use a two-dimensional array only when necessary. For example, consider the problem of generating the file PRODTN in the first place. The data may be in detail form in a large file that contains a record for production of each product each day in a plant. If the records are not in any useful order, the best way to generate the file is to set up an array (the array P, really) in which we will accumulate the production figures in each month for each plant. As we read each detail record, we must determine the month K of that production and the plant J that produced it. Then the production D read from the record can be added to the appropriate total:

440   LET P(J,K) = P(J,K) + D

When all detail records are processed (and we get from somewhere the plant *names*), we can write the data into the file in essentially the same way we read them in Fig. 10.17.

```
10    REM    INQUIRY PROGRAM FOR MONTH OR PLANT PRODUCTION TOTALS
20    REM    G STRUBLE    FEB 1980
30    REM       ARRAY P: PRODUCTION BY PLANT BY MONTH
31    REM                FIRST SUBSCRIPT = PLANT NO., SECOND = MONTH
34    REM       ARRAY N$: PLANT NAMES
36    REM       M  = NUMBER OF PLANTS IN TABLE
38    REM       C$ = USER'S REQUEST INDICATOR: "M" FOR TOTAL FOR A MONTH,
39    REM            "P" FOR TOTAL FOR A PLANT, "S" TO STOP
42    REM       Q  = USER'S CHOICE OF MONTH OR PLANT
44    REM       T  = TOTAL COMPUTED FOR A PLANT
45    REM       T1 = TOTAL COMPUTED FOR A MONTH
46    REM       L  = SUBSCRIPT SWEEPING THROUGH MONTHS OR PLANTS
50    REM ** DIM AND FILES DECLARATIONS AND STEP 1 ARE IN FIG. 10.17 **
398   REM   ACCEPT AND FULFILL INQUIRIES
400       PRINT "TYPE M FOR TOTAL FOR A MONTH"
405       PRINT "     P FOR TOTAL FOR A PLANT"
410       PRINT "     S TO STOP THE PROGRAM"
420       INPUT C$
430       IF C$ = "M" GO TO 500
440       IF C$ = "P" GO TO 500
450       IF C$ = "S" GO TO 500
460       PRINT "TYPE ONLY M, P, OR S"
470       GO TO 400
500       IF C$ = "S" GO TO 970
600       PRINT "TYPE NUMBER OF PLANT OR MONTH DESIRED"
610       INPUT Q
618   REM   VALIDATE THE NUMBER Q
620       IF Q < 1 GO TO 670
630       IF C$ = "M" GO TO 660
640       IF Q > M GO TO 670
650       GO TO 700
660       IF Q <= 12 GO TO 700
670       PRINT "MONTH MUST BE 1 - 12, PLANT MUST BE 1 -"; M
680       GO TO 600
700       IF C$ = "M" GO TO 800
708   REM   FORM TOTAL OF PRODUCTION FOR PLANT Q
710       LET T = 0
720       FOR L = 1 TO 12
730       LET T = T + P(Q, L)
740       NEXT L
750       PRINT "TOTAL PRODUCTION FOR PLANT"; Q; N$(Q); " WAS"; T
760       GO TO 870
798   REM   FORM TOTAL OF PRODUCTION FOR MONTH Q
800       LET T1 = 0
810       FOR L = 1 TO M
820       LET T1 = T1 + P(L, Q)
830       NEXT L
840       PRINT "TOTAL PRODUCTION FOR MONTH"; Q; "WAS"; T1
870       PRINT
880       GO TO 400
970   END
```

Figure 10.19 Program for production inquiries.

The key in deciding whether a two-dimensional array is needed is to think about what the subscripts would be. If there are two *different* variables that should both index a cell in an array, we should think about using a two-dimensional array. However, we should think carefully whether we need to keep in main storage all the values in the cells identified by both indexes. For example, if the detail file used in generating the PRODTN file were arranged in sequence by plant number, we need keep only a one-dimensional array of production for each month for the *plant from which we are now reading records*. When we have read all records for that plant we could write the corresponding PRODTN record to the file, then clear the array to be ready for the next plant. The strategy of that kind of program will be developed in Chapter 13. As another example, if we wanted to summarize Biggle-Wiggle's production by month, print the twelve totals, and stop, only one one-dimensional array would be needed. Similarly, if we wanted to summarize the production by plant, print the plant totals, and stop, only a one-dimensional array is needed.

Many statistical analysis procedures, especially those relating some variables to others, require two-dimensional arrays. Most BASIC systems have a set of matrix operations that assist in such procedures and other scientific and mathematical computations. The matrix operations are beyond the scope of this text.

10.5 MAIN IDEAS

a. An array is a block of main storage with one name that is accessed in a BASIC program by that array name and one or two subscripts. A numeric array may be one- or two-dimensional; a string array may be only one-dimensional. The DIM statement tells the translator to allocate space for the array and to expect array use.

b. Cells in arrays may be used in all ways that simple variables are. We set up and use arrays when that can avoid rereading a file or when we need to keep several items in main storage at once, to be treated similarly. Some examples of use are tables for the program to look up data in, and banks of accumulators in which to generate several totals simultaneously.

c. Some common operations on arrays are to:
1. Initialize contents of an array to zero.
2. Add together all, or some, numbers in an array.
3. Retrieve data from a table by a search procedure.
4. Load data from a file into an array or set of arrays.
5. Accumulate totals in cells of an array.
6. Print the contents of an array.
7. Sort the contents of a set of arrays.
8. Use in polynomial evaluation.

d. In some operations we use a WHILE or FOR structure to treat each of a sequence of cells in an array in turn. In other instances, a piece of data itself can be used either directly as a subscript or in some arithmetic formula resulting in a subscript.

e. FOR-NEXT loops are very convenient for dealing with arrays. They can be nested one inside another, as in the exchange sort procedure.

10.6 QUESTIONS FOR IMAGINATION AND REVIEW

1. Our old friend Norge Guddle wants his program to compute B as the product of A and the expression $4*J - 6$. If he writes the statement as

```
260   LET B = A(4*J − 6)
```

what do you expect will be the result?

2. What would you expect to happen during execution of the program in Fig. 10.3 if the file SLSMO contains 236 records? No records? If the program's behavior would not be acceptable, modify the program to improve it.

3. Modify the program in Fig. 10.3 so that, in addition to printing the list of best salespersons, the program writes a file containing name and sales of all salespersons whose sales are *less than half* of the average sales per salesperson.

4. Write a program segment that will store in the array D the differences between successive values of E:

$$D(1) = E(2) - E(1)$$
$$D(2) = E(3) - E(2)$$
$$\vdots$$
$$D(12) = E(13) - E(12)$$

5. Write a program segment that will reverse the sequence of the contents of the cells of an array W; the contents we are concerned about are cells with subscripts 1 to G. That is, $W(1)$ and $W(G)$ are interchanged, $W(2)$ and $W(G - 1)$ are interchanged, etc. What trouble is caused by the fact that G might be even or odd?

6. Write a program segment that will move the contents of an array W (subscripts 1 to G) down one cell each, that is, to cells with subscripts 0 to G − 1.

7. Write a program segment that will print the contents of an array Q$ (subscripts 1 to M) in reverse order, that is Q$(M), Q$(M − 1),..., Q(1).

8. Modify the program in Fig. 10.5 to accumulate the total tax on all properties within each tax district, and print those totals after all the tax bills are printed.

9. Design and write a program that will create the file RATES of tax rates used in the program in Fig. 10.5, but capturing the data from a terminal. Design and write another program that will allow the assessor to type in a new rate for each district when prompted by the district number from the current file, and then create a new file containing the new rates. Note that neither of these programs requires the use of an array.

10. There are various programs in this chapter where:

   a) A GO TO statement leads to another GO TO,

   b) An IF statement leads to a GO TO,

   c) An IF statement leads to another IF that tests the same condition.

Any of these is unappealing, though done to keep the integrity of each procedure step as the procedure is transcribed into BASIC. Eliminate these inefficiencies.

11. Shorten the subroutine in Fig. 10.6(b) by rewriting it using a FOR-NEXT loop.

12. The program and procedure in Figs. 10.10 and 10.11 are an instance where using the array cell with subscript 0 can simplify the procedure and programming somewhat. We would use cells 0–20 rather than 1–21. Make the change.

13. In the program in Fig. 10.15 we might prefer not to use a FOR that counts down. We could achieve the same results by replacing statements 200 and 270 by

```
200   FOR L = 1 TO M − 1
205   LET J = M + 1 − L
270   NEXT L
```

Would we also achieve the same results by replacing statements 200 and 210 by

```
200   FOR J = 1 TO M - 1
210   FOR K = 1 TO M - J
```

14. Make the appropriate changes to the procedure and program in Figs. 10.13 and 10.15 to sort the items into *descending* sequence.

15. The *median* of a set of data is defined as the number *m* such that half of the numbers in the set are greater than *m* and half are lower than *m*. If there are an even number of items in the set, the convention is usually that the median is the average of the largest number in the smaller half and the smallest in the larger half. For example, the median of

   20   40   80   82   84   86

would be 81. To find the median of a set of numbers we must sort them and then take the middle one, or the average of the two in the middle. Actually, it is not necessary to sort all the items, only just over half of them.

Write a procedure and program, adapting the exchange sort method, that will take from a file a set of exam scores and names and print the average (mean) score and the median score.

16. Often a single sort key is not sufficient. We may have a file of employees and want them sorted and listed by birthdate, with the oldest first. Suppose year, month (a number from 1–12), and date are three separate fields in each record. The criterion for which of two records should be listed first is:

Case 1: If years are different, the record with the earlier year should be listed first.

Case 2: If years are the same but months are different, the record with the earlier month should be listed first.

Case 3: If years and months are the same but days are different, the record with the earlier day should be listed first.

Case 4: Otherwise, they are tied, and either may be listed first.

To sort records according to this criterion, the strategy of an exchange sort (or a sort by merge, if we were using that) is not changed in the slightest. Only the test to determine whether to exchange items is affected. Modify the procedure in Fig. 10.13 and the program in Fig. 10.15 to sort and list an employee file by birthdate.

17. In each of the following, the variable K takes on values 1 to M inside a loop and J takes on values 0 to M − 1. What is the difference in effect between the two?

```
200   FOR K = 1 TO M        200   FOR K = 1 TO M
210   LET J = K - 1         210   FOR J = 0 TO M - 1
  .                           .
  .                           .
  .                           .
290   NEXT K                290   NEXT J
                            295   NEXT K
```

18. How many times is statement 350 executed in each of the following structures?

```
a)  300   FOR K = 1 TO 10
    310   FOR J = 1 TO 10
    350   . . .
    390   NEXT J
    400   NEXT K

b)  300   FOR K = 1 TO 10
    310   FOR J = 1 TO K
    350   . . .
    390   NEXT J
    400   NEXT K

c)  300   FOR K = 1 TO 10
    310   FOR J = K TO 10
    350   . . .
    390   NEXT J
    400   NEXT K

d)  300   FOR K = 1 TO 10
    310   FOR J = K TO 10
    320   IF J > K GO TO 390
    350   . . .
    390   NEXT J
    400   NEXT K
```

e) 300   FOR K = 1 TO 10
    310   FOR J = 1 TO 10
    320   IF J < K GO TO 390
    350   . . .
    390   NEXT J
    400   NEXT K

f) 300   FOR K = 1 TO 10
    310   FOR J = 1 TO 10
    320   IF J < K GO TO 400
    350   . . .
    390   NEXT J
    400   NEXT K

19. The file GUDDLE contains a record for each sale during a week by an organization:

Date,

Account number of customer,

Document number,

Salesperson number,

Product number,

Amount of sale.

Product numbers are five-digit numbers, and there are 60,000 products in the catalog. However, during any week only 400 different products at most are sold. We would like a report of sales for the week for each product, but only products actually sold should be on the report. Write a procedure and program to generate the report using the following strategy:

Keep a table of product numbers and sales amounts. Initially the table is empty. For each record, search the table: If the product number is already in the table, add the sale amount of the current sale; if not, make a new entry in the table to record the sale.

20. Try to write a procedure and program segment to perform a binary search. This is not an easy problem.

21. Question 11 of Chapter 7 asked you to compute federal income tax withheld according to a table, using a CASE structure. The actual table used has more entries than were specified in Chapter 7, and the CASE structure becomes tedious. Arrays give us an alternative: We can store the dividing points between tax brackets 33, 76, 143, . . . , in one array, the base taxes 0, 6.88, 18.94, . . . , in a second array, and the percentages 0.16, 0.18, 0.22, . . . , in a third array. To compute tax withheld for each employee, the strategy would be to search the first array using the search for a match structure (though searching for the bracket), then using the corresponding base tax and percentage from the other arrays. Write a procedure and program segment that follow this strategy.

22. Do a validation analysis, as discussed in Chapter 8, for one of the programs in Chapter 10—Fig. 10.9, for example.

23. Write a program segment that will set to zero all cells of an array D that is declared by

```
60 DIM D(15,8)
```

24. Write a program segment that will generate the grand total of production of all plants for the entire year from the array P in Fig. 10.17.

25. Write a program segment that will compute in turn the total production for each month, from the array P in Fig. 10.17, and store the twelve totals in an array (one-dimensional) Y.

26. Design and write the program outlined in Section 10.4 for generating the file PRODTN from detail records.

27. In execution of the program segment starting at line 240, which A's are added to B(3)?

```
60    DIM A(22,7), B(44)
      .
      .
      .
240   FOR K = 2 TO 6
250   FOR L = 1 TO 20
260   LET B(L) = B(L) + A(L + 2,K)
270   NEXT L
280   NEXT K
```

28. The file SARC contains detail records of a store for the month. Each record contains:

Product number (a number from 1 to 30),

Salesperson number (a number from 1 to 6),

Sale amount.

The records are in no particular sequence.

a) Write a procedure and then a program to show total sales of each product. Modify the procedure and program so that products with no sales are not listed.

b) Write a procedure and then a program that will report the total sales of each product *by each salesperson* as well as the total sales of each product over all salespersons. (This needs a two-dimensional array.)

CHAPTER 11

SYSTEMS ANALYSIS AND DESIGN

We have examined some facets of business data processing systems as we studied how to write programs that could belong in these systems. In this chapter we will explore in an introductory way the evolution and aging of a system and the analysis, design, and development processes that shape and build a system. We will also show some system examples in a more comprehensive way than we were able to do in earlier chapters.

11.1 THE SYSTEM LIFE CYCLE

Every system begins as an idea and a question: "Couldn't we handle these better by . . . ?" The question must be asked of someone, or some group, who can provide an answer. Let us call that person or group the systems analysis team; it will usually be composed of several people. The team's first task is to identify the objectives of the inquiry and define its scope:

"In what ways would you like the operation improved?"

"These other operations performed by departments A and B seem to be related; should we think about changing them, too?"

This is the first phase of the life of a system. We can characterize five phases:

1. Request for a new system, with definition of the objectives and scope of the study;

2. Detailed investigation and analysis;

3. System design;

4. Implementation, including programming, conversion from the old system, documentation, and training;

5. Operation and maintenance.

The second phase usually takes a good deal of work. The systems analysis team must construct a clear and detailed picture of how the operation in question is currently performed: How are the input data presented, on what source documents, when, and in what volumes? How are the data processed, and by whom, step by step, with details of decisions and calculations made and information flow? How does the operation store data and results and present them to people who can use the results? Section 11.2 will explore how the investigation and analysis are carried out.

The third phase is system design. When the systems analysis team knows the requirements on a new system, and knows how the work is currently done and why, they can design a new system. Usually the best way to design a system is to define first the results, the outputs from the system, and then design processing steps that will obtain those results. This design philosophy follows the most effective problem-solving technique, and is most likely to yield a system that is efficient in getting the results desired. The design of a system includes:

- Design of output forms and reports,

- Design of input documents,

- Design of all files created or maintained by the system,

- A systems flowchart showing the relationships among files, programs, and clerical steps,

- Specifications for each computer program,

- Specifications for each step in noncomputer processing of the data.

During the systems design phase, the systems analysis team may produce several different designs. The costs and benefits of each design must be analyzed, and management must make the decision to accept one of the systems designs.

The fourth phase of a system life cycle is the implementation of the system. From the specifications developed during the design phase, the computer programs can be written. The paper forms required for output reports and for input or clerical processes can be reduced to exact formal layouts and printed. When the computer programs are written, they can be tested. First they are tested individually as in Chapter 8, then in combination, following the systems flowcharts, to ensure the compatibility of all programs and files. The programmers and designers must also document the system. Documentation is of several types:

1. Internal documentation of programs, to help programmers understand, maintain, and improve the programs in the future;

2. Operations documentation, to help the staff that must operate the system (run the programs, etc.) do their job;

3. User documentation, to explain to the people who use the system how to prepare the input, how to ensure accuracy and correct errors, when to take each step, and how to interpret and use the results.

Of course, the design specifications are a valuable portion of the documentation, too. Then the programmers (or better yet, the operations staff, after they learn about the system) must train the users in the operation and use of the system.

This training makes extensive use of the documentation, but through trials, walk-throughs, and question-answering opportunities ensure that the people who will use the system understand its features and how best to use them. Finally, often the touchiest part of all is conversion from the old system to the new one. Sometimes the conversion is a gradual one, with pieces of the new system brought into production use one by one. Sometimes the system must be brought into operation all at once, but perhaps with parallel operation of the old system for a time until we are sure that the new system works correctly.

The fifth phase is operation and maintenance. The system has been designed and implemented, and is in use. Most organizations are changing constantly, and their requirements on a data processing system change, too. Some changes are mandated by new legal requirements, others by change in the nature of the business: reorganization, growth, and technological change. Still other changes are requested because with operation of a system comes further understanding of its possibilities and awareness of possible improvements or extensions. Many changes are made in the programs, some in the layout of files, more in output report content, format, frequency, and distribution, fewer in input forms, and still fewer in the general pattern of data flow in the system. If the programmers do a good job, the programs are easy to modify and remain well documented. Some modifications, however, request basic changes in the design of a system; these are accomplished with difficulty if they are really important, and are not implemented if of lesser importance. Eventually, a new idea, the accumulation of modifications desired but not implemented, or the growth of a system to unwieldy proportions, leads management to call for a new study of the area, and the system life cycle begins again.

11.2 THE SYSTEMS ANALYSIS PROCESS

The systems analysis process is mostly a process of gathering information about a system, but the systems analysis team must use some skill in eliciting accurate and comprehensive data and judging the importance of what they are told, while allaying fears of the staff of an upset in their operations and gaining the confidence of the staff in the yet-to-be-designed system. They must find out:

1. The contents of all the various files used or kept by the system, including what entities are described by records in each file, what fields are in each record and how they are coded, and how the file is organized;

2. All of the processing steps in the system, including computer processing, clerical processing, management decisions, which data form

the basis for each processing step, who (or what) performs each step and why, and the sequence in which the steps are done;

3. The origin of each piece of data;

4. The uses of each piece of data, and the uses of the results.

Costs are important too, and the analysis gathers data on the size of each file, the volume of data (usually in records or transactions) processed in each processing step, and (gently) the time spent doing each major processing step.

The systems analysis team gathers most of the data by a series of interviews. It is important first to know the structure of the organization using the system, and to interview carefully representative people who originate data, process data, or use the results of the current system. The interviews should go beyond description of the current system, and find out what each person thinks should be improved. The systems analysis team members performing each interview should make extensive notes, summarize them later, and preferably have the summaries checked by the interviewee. Data, especially about clerical steps and management decision steps, should be checked with a second source and any conflicts in testimony resolved. That, by itself, enables some systems to work better than they had in years!

The systems analysis team also collects samples of all forms and reports used in the system, and goes over them in interviews to be sure that the function of each item in each form or report is understood. The team can obtain copies of computer program listings, and those, of course, show how the computer does its portion of the processing.

The systems analysis team must organize and digest all the data they have collected. A systems flowchart is a good framework. It can be annotated and each form and report tied to its place in the systems flowchart. The interview summaries can be further summarized and organized by processing step consistent with the systems flowchart. Often during the organization of these data the team will realize they are missing this or that detail, or have conflicting understandings of some point; this requires re-interviewing, so the organization of the data is an iterative process.

The skilled systems analyst is always on the lookout for problems. After all, the analyst's objective is to solve problems and improve the system. Therefore, the analyst recognizes difficulties as problems of responsiveness, economy, security, reliability, processing volume, information, or accuracy, and the recognition and classification of problems found will later guide the effort to design the new system.

11.3 REQUIREMENTS ON SYSTEM DESIGN

What must the systems analysis team aim for as they design a new system? Generally, the goal of any system is to support the organization's operations and management decision-making in a reliable, cost-efficient manner, while meeting legal requirements. As we observed in Chapter 1, a data processing system provides information, and it must supply the information requirements at several levels:

1. Support the day-to-day operations of the organization;

2. Enable effective control of the day-to-day operations;

3. Support management decision-making with respect to the organization;

4. Meet reporting requirements outside the organization, either mandated by law, or by licensing or franchising agencies, and so on, or by auditors.

We can be more specific about the requirements, and we can list seven attributes required of any data processing system. These are essentially the same attributes whose lack was recognized as problems during the analysis phase:

1. The system must be responsive, and produce timely information. When a particular set of information is needed, the system must produce it reasonably quickly, and it must be based on reasonably up-to-date data.

2. The system must be comprehensive. It must be able to provide *all* the information necessary to support and control operations and to suggest management decisions. This is unattainable; management may demand at some point the names of all licensed pilots in the engineering department, and if pilot licenses have never before been related to the business of this organization, that information is not likely to be in the system. Nevertheless, we must try to be comprehensive, and maintain the data that are likely to be needed. This is a real problem for systems analysts, because there is substantial cost to collection, storage, and *maintenance* of any data.

3. The information provided must be accurate and reliable. We call a system *reliable* if the same inputs at two different times produce the same results; we call a system *accurate* if those results are correct. Thus reliability is a matter of consistency of treatment, which is more of a problem in clerical processing than in computer processing. This is why the

clerical procedures must be unambiguous and well understood. Accuracy is very important; we have described in earlier chapters the data laundering, reasonability tests, batch control totals, and error reports, and so forth, that are built into systems to help ensure accuracy. Clerical procedures are built around these computer-produced tools; if no action is taken when discrepancies are reported by the computer programs, the batch totals, and so on, are worthless.

4. The system must be capable of handling the volume of data and transactions required. It should be designed to handle perhaps twice the projected growth in volume, since often the growth exceeds the projections. The availability of information—the very success of the system—leads to placing further demands on it.

5. The system must be secure. The need for protection against unauthorized disclosure of information varies greatly among systems, but *all* systems must contain protection against fraud, mischief, or accidental or purposeful damage.

6. Of obvious importance is that the system be economic and efficient. The analysts' skill at devising systems that capture, keep, and process data efficiently is very valuable. It is also important to design a system that can be *implemented* at moderate cost.

7. The system must relate and interface easily with other systems either now in use or likely to be installed in the organization. Practically no system exists with no relation to other systems; payroll systems are related to job accounting, general ledger, and personnel data systems; order processing systems are related to inventory, accounts receivable, and general ledger systems; and the list goes on.

In order to design a system with these attributes, the systems analysts must take full advantage of their knowledge of systems doing similar tasks in other organizations, of the technology available for implementing a system, and of the strengths as well as the weaknesses of the current system. It is a challenging task!

11.4 A SYSTEMS DESIGN EXAMPLE

The XYZ Company is a small wholesaler, which has grown large enough to justify use of a small computer for its accounts receivable from its customers. The system is to be what is called a *balance-forward* type; statements show a line for each transaction in the current month, plus balance forward from the previous month but no transaction detail from previous months. There are only three files kept by the system:

1. The customer master file contains name, address, and current status: balance forward from previous month, payments, credits, and charges in the current month, and some measure of recent delinquency;

2. The transactions received and processed today: charges, credits, payments;

3. The transactions this month to date.

These three files are similar to those described in Chapter 9. The inputs to the system are:

1. Changes to the customer master file: name or address changes, insertion of new customers, and deletion of former customers;

2. Charges, credits, and payments.

The credit manager requires several reports from the system:

1. A daily summary of charges, credits, and payments, with batch totals to facilitate balancing the data in the system against sales and the daily bank deposit;

2. Monthly statements to customers;

3. A monthly summary showing the status and activity of each customer during the month, and especially noting delinquent customers.

In addition, the credit manager wants to be able to inquire and have the current status of any customer displayed at any time. This is necessary if the company is to be responsive to customer inquiries and to manage collections and the extension of further credit in a competent manner.

The daily processing in the system includes both clerical and computer steps. Payments arrive by mail, and also as customers hand checks to XYZ's delivery people. Credits come from delivery people, and also from the sales department in negotiation with customers. Invoices containing charges come from the sales department in batches. Changes to the customer file come mostly from the sales department, but may arrive from other sources, too. First the updates to the customer master file are collected and input to the computer. They are then sorted and applied to the customer master file in the kind of add-change-delete program that we described in Chapter 9. This program also produces a Customer

Change Register showing the old and new contents of each record changed. The clerks must review this register carefully to make sure that all the changes were made properly.

The charges, credits, and payments are all segregated into batches of up to perhaps 40 transactions each, and a total of the transactions in each batch is developed by adding machine. Each batch is entered into the computer using a data capture-and-edit program as described in Chapter 6; the batch number is input with each record. The accumulation of batches is the daily transaction file. The file is sorted by batch number, and a listing of the transactions is produced, including batch totals as added by computer. The batch totals are compared with those manually produced, as a check for errors. Discrepancies are at least noted, and the system may either require that the corrections be applied before further processing, or permit the corrections to be held for the next day's processing.

The next program run posts the transactions to the customer master file; this program is similar to that shown in Fig. 9.20. The transactions must be sorted into sequence by customer number first, however. Then the transactions are merged with the file of transactions to date this month to form a fuller month-to-date transaction file.

In parallel with the computer runs, the daily bank deposit is prepared from the day's remittances. It should balance with the corrected computer-produced summary of payment transactions.

All the files are stored on some kind of disk storage. The last processing step each day is to copy the three major files (customer master, the day's transactions, the transactions this month to date) onto a magnetic tape, and put the tape in the company's vault. The *previous* day's tape is taken from the vault, and taken to the bank for storage in the bank vault. The oldest daily tape in the bank vault can be removed from the vault and reused. This storage policy gives the company good security against various disasters. First, if the computer breaks down, the most recent daily tape and a tape of the programs in the system can load the entire system on a nearby computer, and *at most* we must redo the input and processing for the current day. Most computer breakdowns are fixed quickly, but our company should be prepared. Some breakdowns or accidents wipe out files on disk, so the company may have to use the most recent tape to restore the files on its own computer. If some disaster destroyed the company's entire plant, including the computer and vault, the backup tape in the bank vault safeguards the company's receivables records with loss of at most two days; to lose much more than that could mean financial ruin to the company.

At the end of each month, an additional set of programs is run. The first computes interest or late charges, adds them to the appropriate records in the customer master file, and prints a summary register of the status and activity of all customers this month (inactive customers whose balances are zero may be omitted from the listing). The second program prints the customer statements, using the data in both customer master and transactions month-to-date files. Obviously, this is another program in which the merging principle is used. Finally, a simple program re-initializes the customer master file to begin the new month; Figs. 9.8–9.11 show some of these processes. The next day's transaction file becomes the first transactions month-to-date file of the new month.

The credit manager takes actions based on the monthly summary register, which should be an aging report as well as a summary for general documentation and inquiry support. The credit manager will take steps to attempt collection, and may notify the sales department of problems and enlist their aid in collection, or suspend further credit to a customer.

Later during the month, the credit manager or the clerks need more up-to-date status information than the previous monthly summary register. Therefore, the system must include an inquiry program. This may be an interactive program that displays at a terminal the current status information on a customer in the customer master file, or a sequential run in which customer numbers of several customers are input and the program prints the status information on all customers requested.

There may well be still more clerical steps. For example, it is common to maintain a file folder containing monthly statements and all invoices, and so on, plus any correspondence for each customer. These folders are maintained in alphabetical sequence, and are useful for finding a customer's number when necessary as well as for fielding inquiries of various kinds.

We have described a very simple system, and have left out practically all detail. Yet the vast majority of all processing steps in larger systems are similar to steps in this system.

11.5 MAIN IDEAS

a. A business data processing system follows a life cycle:

1. Request for a new or revised system, with definition of the objectives and scope of the study;

2. Detailed investigation and analysis;

3. System design;

4. Implementation;

5. Operation and maintenance.

b. Systems analysis is a process of gathering information about a current system: how it works, its strengths and problems, and the desires for a new system. Systems analysis is performed through interviews and collection of documents; the systems analyst also plays an important role in gaining receptiveness to the new system.

c. A system should be designed to be:

- Responsive,
- Comprehensive,
- Accurate and reliable,
- Secure,
- Economic and efficient,
- Related easily to other systems.

d. A system supports the day-to-day activities of an organization, assists in the control of the organization's activities, and supports management decision-making. Most systems consist of a daily cycle, which primarily supports and helps to control daily activities, a monthly (and sometimes a weekly) cycle, and irregularly run components, which primarily support managerial control and decision-making.

11.6 QUESTIONS FOR IMAGINATION AND REVIEW

1. Think of some ways in which the structure of an organization affects the design of a system to be used by the organization.

2. Think of problems that systems analysts can *cause*, and ways of preventing or solving them.

3. One of the requirements of a system is that it be economic and efficient. When a proposal to implement a new system is made, one component often is a cost-benefit analysis, which analyzes all the costs of implementing and operating the system and the benefits to be gained. Outline what could be included in the cost-benefit analysis of the XYZ Company's new accounts receivable system.

4. Design a training program for the credit department of the XYZ Company, preparatory to operation of the system described in Section

11.4; assume that accounts receivable processing has previously been manual.

5. A large and growing segment of the data processing industry supplies computer software to companies like XYZ. The software is usually developed first for one particular customer, then generalized to be applicable to other companies. Think of possible problems of adapting XYZ's accounts receivable system to some other company's use, and how you would analyze the advantages and disadvantages of making that adaptation rather than developing a complete system in that company.

6. What data should be carried in an accounts receivable customer master record to give the credit manager the information he or she needs about delinquent customers?

7. What kind of management decisions should be supported by an accounts receivable system? Should additional data, perhaps historical, be kept by the system in order to provide information to support management decisions? If so, what programs must be changed or added in order to maintain these data? To what extent should the system include more regular programs to provide decision-support information, and to what extent can (or must) we rely on special programs written when a need arises?

CHAPTER 12
FUNCTIONS AND STRING OPERATIONS

There are numeric and string operations that are needed commonly enough that they are made available as part of the BASIC system and need not be written by every programmer who needs one. The operations of taking square roots or logarithms are in this category. The subroutines that compute square roots and logarithms are called *functions*, and can be called by the programmer with little fuss. In this chapter we learn about these and other functions and how they can be used.

We will also explore some string operations that will enable us to do more than input, output, move, and compare strings. We will see how strings can be taken apart, combined, and tested for the presence of any given substring. These operations open up large areas of data processing, but we will explore only a few of the possibilities.

12.1 THE CONCEPT AND MECHANISM OF A FUNCTION

If we are asked to compute some statistics, the usual measure of dispersion of data is the standard deviation. To compute the standard deviation of a set of N numbers x_i (perhaps values of some economic index for each of N years), we sum the quantities $(x_i - a)^2$, where a is the mean (average) of the N numbers. After we divide this sum by N, the standard deviation is the square root of the result:

$$d = \sqrt{\frac{\sum_{i=1}^{N} (x_i - a)^2}{N}}.$$

None of this would give us any trouble in a BASIC program except the square root. How do you get a square root from a computer that can only add, subtract, multiply, and divide? The mathematical field called numerical analysis includes the study of how to approximate the computations of such things by the operations of addition, subtraction, multiplication, and division. But if you need a square root, must you find a numerical analyst and program the procedure supplied by the analyst? Surely someone has needed a square root before; can't we borrow the same piece of program used then? Yes indeed. The builders of the BASIC system foresaw the need for square roots and a number of other such operations, and built subroutines to perform the calculations. They are made available to you as *functions*, which can be called as part of any numeric expression. If the sum of squares of differences of the x_i from the average is held as the value of S2, we can compute in BASIC the standard deviation:

```
360   LET D = SQR(S2/N)
```

The operations that perform this statement are as follows:

1. S2 is divided by N.

2. The result is called the *argument* or *parameter* of the function; it is placed in a special location accessible to the SQR subroutine.

3. The SQR subroutine is a section of program supplied as part of the BASIC system. Control is transferred to this section of program by a mechanism equivalent to a GOSUB.

4. The SQR subroutine takes the argument provided in the special location, and computes the square root of the argument; it leaves the result in the special location and returns control (as in a RETURN statement) to the main program.

5. The main program stores the number in the special location as the value of D, and proceeds to the next statement.

   What, then, is involved in using a function? First, we must know the name of the function. Second, we supply the argument to the function in parentheses, following the function name. Third, we may place the function name and argument in any numeric expression, in LET, IF, or other statements that include numeric expressions. For example,

```
230   LET Z = .8 * SQR((T2 − A↑2)/N)
340   IF SQR(H) < T − 3 GO TO 380
450   PRINT "THE SQUARE ROOT OF"; G; "IS"; SQR(G)
```

In a numeric expression, the value of a function may be used anywhere that any value may be used; the following is legal, even though it is unlikely to be anything we want:

```
560   LET Z = SQR(H↑SQR(T − 3) − W/SQR(B * C))
```

As a second example of the use of a function, suppose that we are arranging a loan at simple interest, to be repaid in equal monthly installments. If we already know the principal amount P, the interest rate per month I, and the desired monthly payment M, we would like to know how many months it will take to pay off the loan. A useful formula is

$$(M − P \cdot I)(1 + I)^N = M$$

if we can solve this equation for N. A little manipulation gives

$$(1 + I)^N = \frac{M}{M − P \cdot I}$$

$$\log\left[(1 + I)^N\right] = \log\left(\frac{M}{M − P \cdot I}\right)$$

$$N \log(1 + I) = \log\left(\frac{M}{M − P \cdot I}\right)$$

$$N = \frac{\log\left(\dfrac{M}{M − P \cdot I}\right)}{\log(1 + I)}$$

Since BASIC provides a function named LOG that computes logarithms, we can write a BASIC statement to compute N:

```
620   LET N = LOG(M/(M − P * I))/LOG(1 + I)
```

12.2 THE ABS AND INT FUNCTIONS

In this section we introduce the functions ABS and INT, which are useful for purposes other than special computations.

The ABS function derives the absolute value of its argument. Its definition is

$$\text{abs } (a) = \begin{cases} a \text{ if } a \geq 0, \\ -a \text{ if } a < 0. \end{cases}$$

In effect, the absolute value "strips away" the minus sign, if there is one, from a number, leaving a positive number (or zero). This function is useful for testing whether a number is within some range. If we want to perform some action if the value of G is in the range 6 to 9 (including 6 and 9 themselves), we can do in one IF statement what has taken two in previous examples:

```
400    IF ABS(G − 7.5) > 1.5 GO TO 450
410    perform the action
       .    .
       .    .
       .    .
450    next step
```

The INT function converts its argument to an integer, specifically, the largest integer less than or equal to the argument. In other words, the INT function rounds *down:*

INT(8.3)	is 8
INT(7.9)	is 7
INT(7)	is 7
INT(−7.9)	is −8
INT(−8.3)	is −9
INT(−8)	is −8

We can use this function to round a number to the nearest integer:

```
640    LET S1 = INT(S + .5)
```

produces a value of S1 that is S rounded to the nearest integer. How? Use the definition to see that:

If S is 8.3, S1 will be 8;
If S is 7.9, S1 will be 8;
If S is −8.3, S1 will be −8;
If S is −7.9, S1 will be −8.
But if S is 7.5, S1 will be 8; and
If S is −7.5, S1 will be −7.

With a little more work, we can use the INT function to round a number to two decimal places:

```
650  LET S2 = INT(100 * S + .5)/100
```

or round a number to the nearest thousand:

```
660  LET S3 = 1000 * INT(S/1000 + .5)
```

You should try both of these before you believe such claims!

Still another use for the INT function is to find *remainders* in division. Usually we want the most accurate quotient possible when we program a division, but sometimes we want to perform integer division and obtain a remainder as well as an integer quotient. Suppose N and D are positive integers. The integer quotient is

```
710  LET Q = INT(N/D)
```

Thus if $N = 7$ and $D = 3$, then Q will be computed as 2. The remainder is a little trickier:

```
720  LET R = N - INT(N/D) * D
```

You can verify that if $N = 7$ and $D = 3$, then R will be computed as 1. This is sometimes useful if you need to test, for example, whether an integer K is odd or even; it is even if the remainder upon division of K by 2 is zero, and odd if the remainder is 1:

```
750  IF K - INT(K/2) * 2 = 0 GO TO 780
```

sends control to statement 780 if K is even.

We will mention one more use of the INT function: It can help us pick apart several fields that are stored as one number. Consider the representation and storage of dates as an example. Month is often expressed as a two-digit number, which we can represent as mm. Date is represented by dd, and the last two digits of the year as yy. The entire date can be represented as mmddyy—that is, October 23, 1980, would be represented as 102380. This representation has advantages: It looks reasonable to Americans (though backward to Europeans). It has the disadvantage that comparison of one date with another is difficult: as numbers, 21881 (February 18, 1981) appears to be smaller (earlier?) than 102380. To make valid comparisons, we must separate at least the year from the month and day. The year is simply the remainder upon division by 100, and month and day are represented by the quotient. If E contains a date in this format,

```
900  LET Y = E - INT(E/100) * 100
910  LET M1 = INT(E/100)
```

obtains the year as the value of Y, and the month and day as the value of M1. If we wish, we can separate month from day as well:

```
920   LET M = INT(M1/100)
930   LET D = M1 - M * 100
```

This is necessary if we are accepting such dates from the terminal and attempting to launder them. It would look very sloppy to accept a date like 107080!

One word of caution: There are versions of BASIC in which the INT function rounds *toward zero;* for negative numbers *only* this is different from the behavior we have described:

INT(−7.9) would be −7,

INT(−8.3) would be −8,

INT(−8)   would be −8.

Often our use of the INT function will always supply positive arguments; if your use might supply a negative argument, test your system to see what it does.

12.3 OTHER NUMERIC FUNCTIONS

Every BASIC system has a library of functions, and some of them are fairly standard. We will list some of the more common functions here; your system undoubtedly has others that may be useful to you in special situations.

EXP: The exponential function raises the number e (2.718281828 . . .) to the power given as the argument. The EXP function is useful in problems dealing with exponential growth; the EXP function is also the inverse function of LOG:

EXP(LOG(X)) = X   for positive values of X.

LOG: The logarithm of the argument, to the base e. If you want a logarithm to the base 10, some systems provide that as a function named LOG10 or CLOG. You can also compute $\log_{10}$ of X as LOG(X)/2.302585093. Note that you cannot take the logarithm of a negative number or zero.

SQR: Square root. The argument may not be negative.

SIN, COS, TAN: The trigonometric functions. The arguments must be in radians; if your argument is in degrees, multiply it by 3.14159265/180 to get the equivalent in radians.

ATN: The arctangent. The result is given in radians.

Especially interesting is the RND function, which has no argument at all (in most systems) and produces a random number! Each call produces a new random number. The random numbers are uniformly distributed between 0 and 1 (not inclusive). Now, do you believe that? You shouldn't. If the computer really produced random numbers, we'd call for repair. The RND function actually produces numbers in a sequence of pseudo-random numbers computed according to a formula. The formula is chosen so that the numbers jump around as random numbers would, and pass the statistical tests one would expect actual random numbers to pass. The numbers in the sequence would eventually start repeating, but not until after several million.

The RND function is most useful in programs that simulate some real-world situation. For example, if we are simulating the flow of jobs through a shop in which a job is equally likely to need any of four machines, we can derive the machine number of the next job as

```
INT(4 * RND + 1)
```

The numbers 4 * RND are distributed between 0 and 4 (but less than 4); when we add 1 to those results, we have numbers between 1 and 5. The INT function yields numbers 1, 2, 3, and 4, equally likely.

When a program is run several times, the sequence of random numbers will be the same each time. This can be helpful in debugging and testing a program. If you want to start a new set of random numbers, insert the simple statement

line no.   RANDOMIZE

in the initialization section of your program. This initializes the starting point of your random number sequence based on the date and time of day.

Most BASIC systems also allow you to define your own functions within your program. The explanation of how to do that is beyond the scope of this text, but a little more explanation will help you recognize a situation in which you might want to define a function and help you find the details in your manual when the situation arises. Each function definition begins with a DEF statement that names the function to be defined. The definition you supply is essentially a subroutine. Control is passed to your defined function when the function name appears in a numeric expression being evaluated, and when evaluation of the function is completed according to your definition, control returns to complete the evaluation and execution of the statement containing the expression.

Thus, transfer of control and use of arguments passed to the function are exactly the same as we have seen in the use of library functions. The main differences between your function and a subroutine are:

1. Call by mention in expression, rather than GOSUB;

2. Arguments can be passed to the function;

3. The function must send a value in return.

12.4 STRING OPERATIONS

We have concentrated on numeric operations throughout this text, though we have seen examples that input, move, compare, and output strings as well. Text data *are* important in data processing, and we will learn in this section how to do more operations on strings.

One of the operations necessary is to take apart a string and extract a portion. For example, dates may be represented as mm-dd-yy; the hyphens between month, day, and year make the dates more readable. If the date February 17, 1980, is to be represented as 02-17-80, it must be stored as a string, perhaps D$. As we saw in Section 12.2, we may wish to separate the month, day, and year for validity testing or for comparing two dates. The function MID$ extracts a portion of a string. The function has three parameters:

1. Name of the string,

2. First character position of the portion to be extracted,

3. Number of characters to be extracted.

The characters in a string are in positions numbered starting at position 1, so in the string D$,

- Month is in positions 1 and 2,

- Day is in positions 4 and 5,

- Year is in positions 7 and 8.

We can therefore extract month, day, and year from D$ by

```
310   LET M1$ = MID$(D$,1,2)
320   LET D1$ = MID$(D$,4,2)
330   LET Y1$ = MID$(D$,7,2)
```

The strings M1\$, D1\$, and Y1\$ are each two-character strings that can be compared with other strings; the original string D\$ remains intact.

We must say a little more about the arguments to the MID\$ function. Each of the second and third arguments may be any numeric expression, but there are restrictions on the values of those expressions:

- The second argument, first character position of the portion to be extracted, must be a position within the string, that is, 1 or more, and no greater than the length of the string.

- The third argument, number of characters to be extracted, must be positive.

If the third argument specifies more characters than remain in the string, the remainder of the string is extracted; this is *not* an error condition. For example, if D\$ is "02-17-80", the statement

```
330  LET Y1$ = MID$(D$,7,50)
```

would yield a value of "80" for Y1\$.

Sometimes we need to find the length of a string in order to do further operations correctly. For example, the string A2\$ may contain the city, state, and zip code portions of an address, with one space separating city name, state, and zip code. Examples would be

```
"EUGENE OR 97403"
```

```
"PITTSBURGH PA 15213"
```

If we want to extract state and zip code from an address in order to test or reformat the address, the arguments to MID\$ must depend on the string length. The LEN function yields the length of the string given; if

```
A2$ is "EUGENE OR 97403"
```

then

```
510  LET L1 = LEN(A2$)
```

will store 15 as the value of L1. Presuming that every address has a two-letter state abbreviation and a five-digit zip code, separated by one space, we can extract city, state, and zip code separately from an address by

```
510  LET L1  = LEN(A2$)
520  LET C1$ = MID$(A2$,1,L1 - 9)
530  LET S1$ = MID$(A2$,L1 - 7,2)
540  LET Z1$ = MID$(A2$,L1 - 4,5)
```

By counting, verify that the expressions $L1 - 9$, $L1 - 7$, and $L1 - 4$ are correct.

If we can take strings apart, can we also put them together? Yes; the mechanism for that is not a function but a plus sign. If F$ = "PAT" and L$ = "SMITH", then the result of

```
610  LET N$ = F$ + " " + L$
```

is that N$ is set to the value "PAT SMITH".

Another operation we would like to perform is a search of a string: Does it contain some particular character or sequence of characters? And if so, where is it in the entire string? As one example, we may have names in the form "last, first", as "SMITH, PAT". One good reason for keeping names in this form, of course, is that they can easily be sorted into alphabetical order. However, when we print the names, on payroll checks, for example, we should turn them around and print "PAT SMITH". To do this we must find the comma in the string and use its position in the string in the arguments to MID$ functions that can extract first and last names to be put together in the desired order.

The function that searches a string is named INSTR. It has three arguments:

1. In the string to be searched, the character position at which the search is to begin;

2. The string to be searched;

3. The character or characters (call it a substring) for which we are searching.

The value returned by the function is the character position at which the substring found begins, or 0 if no occurrence of the substring is found. As introductory examples, if S$ = "MISSISSIPPI" and U$ = "ISS",

```
INSTR(1,S$,U$) = 2
INSTR(3,S$,U$) = 5    (finds the second "ISS")
INSTR(6,S$,U$) = 0    (starting at position 6, there is no "ISS")
INSTR(1,U$,S$) = 0    (no "MISSISSIPPI" in "ISS")
```

We can use INSTR in reversing the names. Assume that each name N1$ is stored as last name, comma, one space, and then first name.

```
510  LET P = INSTR(1,N1$,",")
520  IF P = 0 GO TO 570
530  LET F$ = MID$(N1$,P + 2,40)
540  LET L$ = MID$(N1$,1,P - 1)
```

```
550   LET N$ = F$ + " " + L$
560   GO TO 580
570   LET N$ = N1$
580   ...
```

For another use of INSTR, suppose that an array N$ contains names of K employees (or applicants), and an array C$ contains a list of each employee's qualifications, interests, or skills, such as

```
"PILOT, SPOT WELDER, ACCOUNTING, FRENCH"
```

An inquiry program accepts a particular desired skill S$ from a user at a terminal, and is to print the names of all persons whose lists include the specified skill. This piece of the program follows a procedure step:

FOR j from 1 to K

  IF the j'th qualifications list contains the string S$

    THEN print the j'th name

The program segment is simple:

```
410   FOR J = 1 TO K
420   IF INSTR(1,C$(J),S$) = 0 GO TO 490
430   PRINT N$(J)
490   NEXT J
```

One more pair of useful functions converts numbers to strings and strings to numbers. The function STR$ has a numeric value as its argument, and the result is a string containing the representation of the numeric value as it would ordinarily be printed. The function VAL has a string as its argument, and if the string contains a valid representation of a number, the result is the value of that number; if the string cannot be transformed into a number, an error message is printed.

```
310   LET V$ = STR$(5↑2)      sets V$ = "25"
320   LET N = VAL(V$ + "3")      sets N = 253
```

One of the applications of these functions is packing and unpacking data. If we are representing the data in an invoice record, we have a problem with the products ordered; there may be several, so how do we store the quantities, product numbers, and prices so the whole record can be read simply? One of the possible ways is to pack all the quantities ordered into one string Q$, as numbers separated by asterisks. We would store similarly the product numbers in N\$ and the prices in P\$. Thus if a customer ordered

    2 of P1408 at 31.95
    1 of 6175   at   8.20
    4 of 1288   at   3.64

the data could be stored as

    Q$ = "2*1*4*"
    N$ = "P1408*6175*1288*"
    P$ = "31.95*8.20*3.64*"

A program reading an invoice record could read simply Q\$,N\$,P\$ without having to know how many products were ordered in that particular order. The individual quantities, product numbers, and prices can be put in arrays Q1, N1\$, P1, following the procedure shown in Fig. 12.1. The procedure searches Q\$ for the first quantity, and then by resetting L1 to the position just beyond the first asterisk, finds the second quantity (if there is one) on the second trip through the loop. The process ends when the beginning for the next search is found to be beyond the contents of the string. Figure 12.2 shows a program segment that follows the procedure.

The functions we have introduced are named differently in some BASIC systems. There are also minor differences in the actions and the arguments. Most systems also have more functions that operate on

---

1. Set J to 1
         L1 to 1
         L3 to 1
         L5 to 1

2. WHILE L1 ≤ length of Q\$
   2.1 Search for first "*" in Q\$ after position L1, call the position L2
   2.2 Extract portion of Q\$ from positions L1 to L2 − 1, convert the result to a number, store it in Q1(J)
   2.3 Search for first "*" in N\$ after position L3, call the position L4
   2.4 Extract portion of N\$ from positions L3 to L4 − 1, store it in N1\$(J)
   2.5 Search for first "*" in P\$ after position L5, call the position L6
   2.6 Extract portion of P\$ from positions L5 to L6 − 1, convert to a number, store it in P1(J)
   2.7 Set L1 to L2 + 1
           L3 to L4 + 1
           L5 to L6 + 1
   2.8 Increase J by 1

3. Set K = number of items ordered = J − 1

Figure 12.1 Procedure for unpacking order data.

```
200    LET J = 1
210    LET L1 = 1
220    LET L3 = 1
230    LET L5 = 1
300    IF L1 > LEN(Q$) GO TO 400
310    LET L2 = INSTR(L1, Q$, "*")
320    LET Q1(J) = VAL(MID$(Q$, L1, L2-L1))
330    LET L4 = INSTR(L3, N$, "*")
340    LET N1$(J) = MID$(N$, L3, L4-L3)
350    LET L6 = INSTR(L5, P$, "*")
360    LET P1(J) = VAL(MID$(P$, L5, L6-L5))
370    LET L1 = L2 + 1
372    LET L3 = L4 + 1
374    LET L5 = L6 + 1
380    LET J = J + 1
390    GO TO 300
400    LET K = J - 1
```

Figure 12.2 Program segment for unpacking order data.

strings; we have presented a set of operations that are reasonably standard, and powerful enough to enable us to do almost anything we might wish to do with strings.

12.5 MAIN IDEAS

a. A function is a subroutine that may accept one or more arguments and returns a value. It is called by mention in an expression.

b. A BASIC system includes a library of functions supplied that perform commonly desired tasks. Most BASIC systems also let a programmer define functions unique to a program.

c. The INT, ABS, and RND functions perform tasks useful in a variety of programs.

d. Other numeric functions, such as LOG, EXP, SQR, SIN, and ATN, are available when mathematical problems require them.

e. Programs can operate on strings with:

MID$	which extracts a portion from a string,
LEN	which yields the length of a string,
INSTR	which searches a string for occurrence of a substring,
STR$	which converts a number into a string,
VAL	which converts a string into a number,
+	which concatenates two strings into one string.

With these operations, we can unpack strings (such as dates) into components to be tested or recombined.

12.6 QUESTIONS FOR IMAGINATION AND REVIEW

1. Question 3 in Chapter 4 asked for a computation of the number of years it will take a population to reach some target population, given some growth rate. At that time you could construct a WHILE loop to obtain the number of years. But if P is the beginning population, T is the target population, G is the growth rate, and N is the number of years, we can use the equation

$$P(1 + G)^N = T$$

to solve for N, since

$$N \log(1 + G) = \log(T/P).$$

Write a program to find N using this equation.

2. An array A holds N numbers, and B$ contains N corresponding strings. Write a program segment that will print the number in A that is closest to a given number X, and the string in B$ that corresponds to the closest A. Use the ABS function to measure how close two numbers are to each other.

3. In systems in which the INT function rounds toward zero, it can still be used to perform rounding, but you must either make a separate case for negative numbers, or use the ABS function and a function SGN that returns a value

    1   if the argument > 0,

    0   if the argument $= 0$,

  -1 if the argument < 0.

Try to show both ways of rounding a number X to the nearest integer.

4. In an accounting or payroll program, there may be special additional tasks at the end of each calendar quarter. If M is the current month (1–12), write a program segment that will implement the procedure step

    4.3 IF end of quarter (M = 3, 6, 9, or 12)

          THEN execute subroutine 1600

5. If M, D, and Y have been input as month, day, and year, write a procedure and program segment that will test the date for validity:

    $1 \le M \le 12$,

    $1 \le D \le 31$,

    M, D, Y all integers.

Set an indicator I6 to 1 if the date is valid, or to 0 if the date is not valid.

6. If M1, D1, Y1 and M2, D2, Y2 represent two dates, write a procedure and program segment that will set an indicator I7 to 1 if M1, D1, Y1 represent the earlier date, and 2 if M2, D2, Y2 represent the earlier or the same date.

7. If a date is represented in the form mm-dd-yy in a string D$, write a program segment that will convert the date to the form mm/dd/yy in a string D1$.

8. Convert the same string D$ to the form dd-mmm-yy, where mmm is a three-letter abbreviation for the month: JAN, FEB, MAR, etc. *Hint:* You may wish to keep a table of the abbreviations in an array.

9. One way of drawing attention to a report heading is to spread it out by inserting a space between each two letters:

P A Y R O L L   R E G I S T E R.

Write a procedure and program segment that will spread the characters of a string H$, producing the expanded string H1$.

10. Think of other string operations that might be useful, and if you can, write program segments to accomplish those operations.

CHAPTER 13
FORMS LAYOUT AND PRINT CONTROL

Until now we have concentrated on the logic of programs and the kind of information that is printed by a program. The output, with spacing controlled primarily by use of the TAB function, has not looked very professional or businesslike, and it is time to improve the formatting of the output. We will examine first the design of reports and the layout of forms, and then show how we can control spacing of output. The most important features will allow us to line up decimal points in the numbers in a column and specify exactly the number of decimal places to be printed in a number—such as leaving two places for dollars-and-cents amounts.

Finally, we will show yet another programming structure often used in report programs.

13.1 REPORT LAYOUTS

Part of a data processing system design is the design of output forms and
reports that will present information to people in a way that is easiest for
them to use. Action documents, such as checks, invoices, and customer
statements, are usually printed on preprinted forms, such as the one
shown in Fig. 13.1. These forms often go to a number of people, mostly
outside the immediate organization, and the form can place each piece
of information in a context where its meaning is clear and the user can
find the most important pieces of information easily.

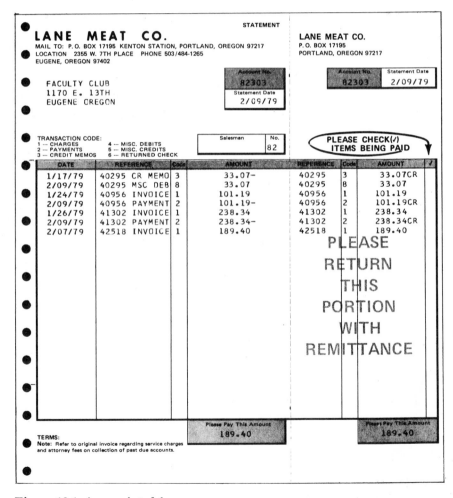

Figure 13.1 A preprinted form.

Control documents, such as payroll registers, error reports, accounts-receivable aging reports, sales reports, edit and balance reports, and customer change registers, are usually produced on ordinary computer paper, and adequate headings are printed by the programs that produce the reports. These reports are usually kept inside the organization for the use of a relatively few people, and the convenience of using standard paper rather than loading more preprinted (and expensive) forms (and aligning them properly) outweighs any advantages of extra readability of preprinted forms. Special reports produced to support particular management decision-making also are printed on ordinary paper.

Preprinted forms are designed on forms such as the one shown in Fig. 13.2, which shows space for the 132 columns and 66 lines, since most computer printers can print 132 characters per line and ordinary paper is 66 lines (11 inches, 6 lines to the inch) long. Reports to be printed on ordinary paper are designed on similar forms, and Fig. 13.3 shows a portion of a report layout and the portion of a printed report that follows that layout. The programmer uses the report layout as a part of the specifications for a program, and writes the program to produce the report according to the layout. For display of results on a video screen a similar form, called a screen layout, is used.

13.2 FORMATTING NUMERICAL OUTPUT IN BASIC

A programmer who wants to print a good-looking report needs more tools than we have presented in the earlier chapters. Clarity and readability call for the programmer to:

- Line up the decimal points in columns of numbers,

- Force some designated number of decimal places to be printed,

- Insert commas in large numbers.

We will show first the BASIC facilities to exercise this control, and then some other features for format control. First we describe how to specify the format of one number, and then show how to get a number printed according to that format.

On a report layout form we specify the maximum number of digits to be printed to the left of the decimal point, the position of the decimal point (if any), and the number of digits to be printed after the decimal

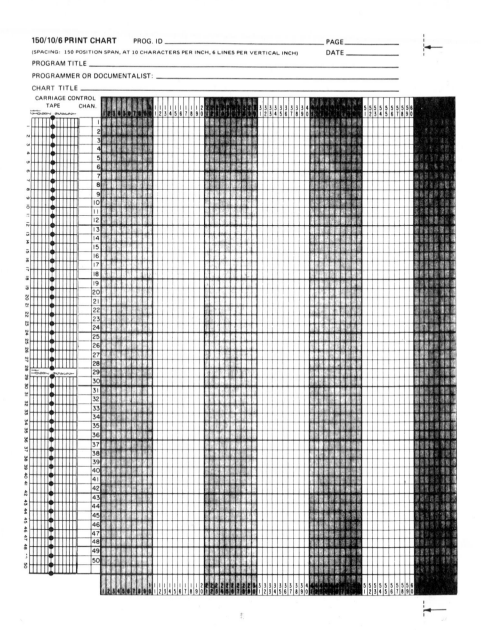

Figure 13.2 A report layout form.

Fold back at dotted line.

 Fold in at dotted line.

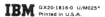

IBM   GX20-1816-0 U/M025*
Printed in U.S.A.

NOTE: Dimensions on this sheet vary with humidity.
Exact measurements should be calculated or scaled
with a ruler rather than with the lines on this chart.

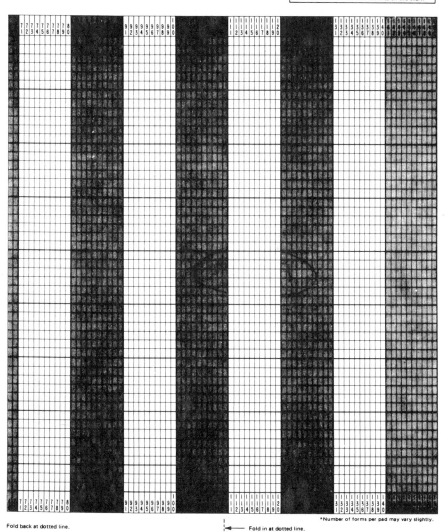

*Number of forms per pad may vary slightly.

Fold back at dotted line.

Fold in at dotted line.

CONNECT TIME (MINUTES)	CPU TIME (SEC)	K-CORE SECONDS	L-KCORE (SEC)	HPQ UNITS	CHARS /100	AMOUNT
XXX	XXXXX	XXXXX	XXXX	XXXX	XXXXX	XXX.XX
XXX	XXXX	XXXXX	XXXX	XXXX	XXXXX	XXX.XX
XXX	XXXXX	XXXXX	XXXX	XXXX	XXXXX	XXX.XX
	TOTAL FOR CLASS:					XXXXX.XX

PROJECT #:   XXXXX

CONNECT TIME (MINUTES)	CPU TIME (SEC)	K-CORE SECONDS	L-KCORE (SEC)	HPQ UNITS	CHARS /100	AMOUNT
4	8	96	0	0	29	0.54
37	14	202	0	0	108	2.04
68	13	89	0	0	306	3.21
1	3	19	0	0	16	0.16
1	4	30	0	0	8	0.18
1	2	19	0	0	6	0.12
1	3	26	0	0	8	0.15
23	24	385	0	0	331	2.90
68	76	1246	0	0	1040	9.09
3	3	22	0	0	29	0.26
13	12	186	0	0	150	1.43
44	48	804	0	0	544	5.47
1	3	21	0	0	20	0.18
7	27	369	0	0	64	1.65
15	20	302	0	0	155	1.89
10	30	481	0	0	164	2.35
	TOTAL FOR CLASS:					31.62

CONNECT TIME (MINUTES)	CPU TIME (SEC)	K-CORE SECONDS	L-KCORE (SEC)	HPQ UNITS	CHARS /100	AMOUNT
1	4	30	0	0	4	0.07
3	2	18	0	0	6	0.11
24	45	918	0	0	135	1.36
23	18	297	0	0	284	1.54
	TOTAL FOR CLASS:					3.08

PROJECT #:   25256

Figure 13.3 A report layout and corresponding report.

point: xxxx.xx specifies up to four digits (or three digits and a minus sign) to the left of the decimal point, and two digits after the decimal point. We can specify the same thing in a *numeric format* in BASIC as

####.##. Using the format ####.##, numbers will appear as follows:

18	as	18.00,
−285	as	−285.00,
31.6	as	31.60,
.06	as	0.06,
2.138	as	2.14.

The numbers 10000 and −1200 cannot be printed using this format, since they require more digits than allowed by the format. Note that when digits must be lost on the right, the number is *rounded*. We can also specify formats without a decimal point: The format ##### provides for numbers up to five digits (or negative numbers up to four digits), as follows:

18	as	18,
−285	as	−285,
31.6	as	31,
.06	as	0,
1478	as	1478,
−3125	as	−3125,
66323	as	66323.

Note that fractions are *not* rounded to the nearest integer, but truncated! Various systems do various odd things about rounding or truncating, and vary also in how many digits of a number will be stored or printed; when such details matter to you, check the behavior of your system by testing.

There are several ways of using numeric formats in a BASIC program; we will show one that is standard among several common versions of BASIC. The format is written in an *image* statement, so called because it shows the image of a line to be printed. The image statement consists of the usual line number, a colon (:) which identifies the statement as an image statement, and the image of a line to be printed. Two possible image statements are

```
800   :#####
810   :####.##
```

An image statement is nonexecutable, and may appear anywhere in the program before the END statement; it is *referred to* by a PRINT statement that specifies the image and the number to be printed:

```
240   PRINT USING 800, A
250   PRINT USING 810, B
```

The USING clause specifies the image statement to be used.

Each character after the colon in an image statement represents a character (beginning at the leftmost printable position) in the output line. Figures 13.4(a) and (b) show the correspondence between characters in the image statement and characters printed in the output line. The vertical line under the colon in each image statement represents the edge of the printable portion of the output line.

We may print several numbers on one line; to do so we must include several formats in one image statement, and a list of variables (or numbers or expressions) in the PRINT statement that uses the image. Spaces between formats in an image statement are reproduced into the output line, and there must be at least one space between the formats in an image. Figure 13.4(c) shows an image that includes two formats, with five spaces between the formats. The five spaces are reproduced into the output line, and each format controls the printing in corresponding positions in the output line. The PRINT statement that uses an image statement *may not* use any spacing control other than the image: TABs may not be included, and the commas or semicolons between the variables in

```
 240   PRINT USING 800, A    (A = 1478)
 800   :#####
Output:  |   1478
```

(a)

```
 250   PRINT USING 810, B    (B = 2.138)
 810   :####.##
Output:  |    2.14
```

(b)

```
 310   PRINT USING 820, A, B
 820   :#####     ####.##
Output:  |   1478       2.14
```

(c)

```
 310   PRINT USING 820, A, B
 820   :    KWH USED: #####     CHANGE FROM LAST YEAR ####.#%
Output:  |   KWH USED:   1478    CHANGE FROM LAST YEAR    2.1%
```

(d)

Figure 13.4 Image statements and printed output lines: (a) an image statement with integer format; (b) an image statement with decimal places in its format; (c) an image statement including two formats; (d) an image statement including text characters.

the PRINT statement are separators only, without their usual function in controlling printer spacing.

We may also include characters in an image statement besides formats and spaces. These characters are also reproduced directly in their corresponding positions in the output line; do you see why it is called an *image* statement? Figure 13.4(d) shows a modification of Fig. 13.4(c); the numeric format portions of the image statement control the output of A and B, and other characters are copied with no change into the output line.

Because characters that are not part of a format are reproduced directly into the output, we and the system must be very sure which characters are part of a format and which are not. This brings us to the rule that every numeric format in an image statement must begin with at least two number signs (#). Thus,

    ##   ##.#   #####.##

are all valid numeric formats, while

    #   #.###

are not valid numeric formats. The single # is recognized as a text character and copied into the output line. Similarly, in the characters #.###, the first # *and the period* are recognized as text characters, and the remaining ### are recognized as an *integer* format! The result, therefore, would be

    110   PRINT USING 830, W   (W = 2.183)

    830   :#.###

                ↓

    Output: |#. 2

In numbers that are likely to be large, we would like to have commas printed to make the numbers easier to read, such as

    8,794,600.

We can specify the insertion of commas by inserting a comma anywhere in a numeric format after the first two # symbols. More than one comma may be included in the format, but one comma serves as an indicator that commas are to separate groups of three digits before the decimal point. The format must include enough # symbols and commas to correspond to the total length of the field needed on the output line. Thus, if a format is to allow seven digits and two commas to be printed in an integer format,

##,#####

is too small because it allows for only eight characters altogether in the output. Especially if the number may be negative, an appropriate format would be

##,#######

Of course, commas are actually printed only if the number to be printed is large enough to justify them. For example, repeated execution of statement 730 in a loop with different values of S could print a column as follows:

730   PRINT USING 850, S

850   :##,#######

          ↓

Output: | 326

        | 44,720

        | −817

        | 6,543,218

        |−1,628,750

We will describe one more feature of numeric formats. The previous example showed negative numbers, which are normally printed with the minus sign preceding the first digit. Minus signs may not be noticed if printed this way, and a common practice is to put minus signs after the number. We can specify that by putting a minus sign at the end of the format. We can modify the image used in the preceding example, with results as follows:

730   PRINT USING 850, S

850   :##,######−

          ↓

Output: | 326

        | 44,720

        | 817−

        | 6,543,218

        | 1,628,750−

Numeric print formats can also be specified to print a "floating" dollar sign, which will immediately precede the first digit of a printed number, or to print a series of asterisks (*) preceding significant digits of a number. These and perhaps other features can be found in the manual for your BASIC system when you need them.

You may want to ask what the computer does when asked to print a number too large to be printed within the format provided. Most BASIC systems print an ampersand (&) followed by the value of the number as it would be printed unformatted. Further characters in that line are pushed to the right since this number uses more spaces on the line than expected. For example,

```
450     PRINT USING 860, 16.3, 18.2
460     PRINT USING 860, 4389.23, 18.2
860     :##.#    ##.#
                  ↓
Output: | 16.3     18.2
        | &4389.23    18.2
```

We complete this section with an example, modification of the program in Fig. 7.4, which prints a table of values accumulated at interest for 5, 10, and 15 years at various interest rates. The statements 100–120 and 240, which print the actual lines in the table, can be replaced as shown in Fig. 13.5. Note that the image statement is placed at line 125 and its colon positioned directly under the opening quotes in statements 100 and 110, which print headings. This gives us good visual correspondence between the headings and the formats for the columns.

13.3 FORMATTED OUTPUT INCLUDING STRINGS

If we try to modify more programs to make the output nicer, we run into a problem. In Fig. 7.6, for example, each output line printed by the main processing loop includes values of strings—social security number and employee name—as well as values of numeric variables. So we need a way to print values of string variables in formatted output. Many versions of BASIC give us three options in formatting output of a string:

1. Left-justify the string in the space allocated;

2. Center the string in the space allocated;

3. Right-justify the string in the space allocated.

```
10   REM   PRINT TABLE OF VALUES OF $100
15   REM   COMPOUNDED QUARTERLY FOR 5, 10, 15 YEARS
20   REM   AT INTEREST RATES 3%, 3.25%, ..., 12%
25   REM   G STRUBLE     JAN 1980
30   REM     MODIFIED VERSION OF FIG. 7.4
40   REM     I  = ANNUAL INTEREST RATE
42   REM     V1 = VALUE AFTER 5 YEARS AT INTEREST RATE I
44   REM     V2 = VALUE AFTER 10 YEARS
46   REM     V3 = VALUE AFTER 15 YEARS
100      PRINT "          TABLE OF VALUES OF $100"
110      PRINT "  RATE      5 YEARS      10 YEARS      15 YEARS"
125           :##.####     ####.##      ####.##       ####.##
200      FOR I = .03 TO .121 STEP .0025
210      LET V1 = 100 * (1+I/4)^20
220      LET V2 = 100 * (1+I/4)^40
230      LET V3 = 100 * (1+I/4)^60
240      PRINT USING 125, I, V1, V2, V3
250      NEXT I
970  END
```

```
               TABLE OF VALUES OF $100
   RATE      5 YEARS      10 YEARS      15 YEARS
 0.0300      116.12       134.83        156.57
 0.0325      117.57       138.22        162.50
 0.0350      119.03       141.69        168.66
 0.0375      120.52       145.25        175.05
 0.0400      122.02       148.89        181.67
 0.0425      123.54       152.62        188.54
 0.0450      125.08       156.44        195.66
 0.0475      126.63       160.35        203.05
 0.0500      128.20       164.36        210.72
 0.0525      129.80       168.47        218.67
 0.0550      131.41       172.68        226.91
 0.0575      133.04       176.99        235.46
 0.0600      134.69       181.40        244.32
```

Figure 13.5 Program using numeric images.

A string format begins with a single apostrophe ('), and continues with repeated L, C, or R, which specify left-justification, centering, or right-justification, respectively. For example,

    'LLLL

is a format that specifies left-justification of a string within a five-character field (note that the apostrophe, as well as each L, designates a character position). If the string to be printed is more than five characters long, the leftmost five characters are printed, and others are lost, as follows:

```
270      PRINT USING 910, "OIL"
280      PRINT USING 910, "GASOLINE"
910         :'LLLL
```

             ↓

Output: | OIL
         |
         | GASOL

Unlike numeric formats, a string format may be a single character. Obviously, if a single-character format (') can print only one character of a string, in one designated position, one need not worry whether that character is centered or justified right or left!

String formats are included in image statements in the same way that numeric formats are. The programmer must be careful to print only strings with string formats and only numbers with numeric formats.

Figure 13.6, a modification of Fig. 7.6, uses formatted output. It prints column headings; a line for each employee, including strings that contain social security number and name; and numeric output showing hours worked, hourly wage, gross pay, tax withheld, and net pay. Finally, the program prints totals of gross pay, taxes withheld, and net pay. The grouping of the three image statements makes it easy to line up headings over their columns and the totals under their respective columns. The second portion of Fig. 13.6 shows the output of the program.

Formatted output can be written to a file as well as printed. All that is necessary is to put the file access number in the print statement:

```
580   PRINT #2, USING 840, A, B, C
```

The output is formatted according to the image statement 840 just as if it were to be printed, and that line is written to the file. One word of caution, however: The QUOTE statement cannot cause quotes to be inserted around strings written to a file as formatted output, so the programmer may have to put the quote marks in the image statement:

```
630   PRINT #2, USING 850, P$, D$, Q
850   :'LLLLLL    "'LLLLLLLLLLLLLLLL"   #####
```
To file: | XR   "TEGWID, LARGE   "   391

13.4 REPORTS USING CONTROL BREAKS

In this section we introduce a logic structure known as *control breaks*. If we want a payroll register with a total of each department, the input file should be sorted by department. After the data on all employees in a department have been printed and the employees' hours and gross wages have been added to totals, the program must print those totals and reset them to zero so the next employees' data will form totals for the next department. This requires the program to keep the department of the last employee, to compare with the department of each employee read. When the department of the current employee is different from the department of the last employee processed, the last employee must have been the last of a department, so the department totals should be printed

```
10   REM   PAYROLL REGISTER
15   REM      MODIFICATION OF FIG. 7.6
20   REM   G STRUBLE   JAN 1980
30   REM      T1 = TOTAL OF GROSS PAY
32   REM      T2 = TOTAL OF TAXES WITHHELD
34   REM      T3 = TOTAL OF NET PAY
36   REM      S$ = SOCIAL SECURITY NUMBER
38   REM      N$ = EMPLOYEE NAME
40   REM      D  = EMPLOYEE'S DEPARTMENT
42   REM      H  = HOURS WORKED BY THE EMPLOYEE
44   REM      W  = EMPLOYEE'S HOURLY WAGE
46   REM      E$ = EXEMPTION CODE: "EXEMPT" = NO OVERTIME PAID,
48   REM                          "OV" = ELIGIBLE FOR OVERTIME PAY
50   REM      E  = NUMBER OF PERSONAL EXEMPTIONS
52   REM      Y  = WAGES PAID YEAR-TO-DATE SUBJECT TO FICA TAX
54   REM      G  = GROSS PAY COMPUTED
56   REM      T  = TAX COMPUTED
58   REM      N  = NET PAY
70       FILES PAYR
100      LET T1 = 0
110      LET T2 = 0
120      LET T3 = 0
125      LET H1$ = "  SSN            NAME               HRS    WAGE    GROSS
     TAX      NET"
130                    :'LLLLLLLL 'LLLLLLLLLLLLLLLLLLLLL ##.# ##.## ###.##
     ###.##   ###.##
135              :                           TOTALS         #####.## #
     ####.## #####.##
150      PRINT H1$
200      IF END #1 GO TO 400
210      INPUT #1, S$, N$, D, H, W, E$, E, Y
218 REM  COMPUTE GROSS PAY
220      IF H <= 40 GO TO 260
230      IF E$ = "EXEMPT" GO TO 260
240      LET G = H * W + .5 * (H-40) * W
250      GO TO 270
260      LET G = H * W
268 REM  COMPUTE TAX WITHHELD
270      IF G > E * 15 GO TO 300
280      LET T = 0
290      GO TO 310
300      LET T = .14 * (G - E*15)
308 REM  COMPUTE NET PAY, PRINT, AND ADD TO TOTALS
310      LET N = G - T
320      PRINT USING 130, S$, N$, H, W, G, T, N
340      LET T1 = T1 + G
350      LET T2 = T2 + T
360      LET T3 = T3 + N
370      GO TO 200
400      PRINT
410      PRINT USING 135, T1, T2, T3
970  END
```

SSN	NAME	HRS	WAGE	GROSS	TAX	NET
524364759	BAYLOR, PAT	40.0	6.25	250.00	30.80	219.20
169834558	PATUCCO, CHRIS	37.5	8.00	300.00	39.90	260.10
522750088	WU, LESLIE	44.0	7.50	345.00	39.90	305.10
246619055	BAKER, WILSON	24.0	7.00	168.00	13.02	154.98
677527444	SCHMIDT, COLLETTE	41.0	9.12	373.92	48.15	325.77
564093456	FERNANDEZ, RAFAEL	40.0	9.50	380.00	42.70	337.30
	TOTALS			1816.92	214.47	1602.45

Figure 13.6 Program using numeric and string formatted output.

and reset before processing (printing and adding) the data on the current employee. If, for example, the first department contains two employees, the sequence of operations would be:

1. Set totals to zero

2. Read first record

3. Print first record, add to totals

4. Read second record

5. Since departments in first two records are equal, print second record, add to totals

6. Read third record

7. Since departments in second and third records are *not* equal, print department totals, reset totals to zero

8. Print third record, add to totals

The totals printed in Step 7 are the totals of the first two employees and, therefore, of the first department. After Step 8, the variables containing totals contain only the data from the third record and, therefore, the totals (as far as we have read records yet) for the second department. Thus the general action for each record is

> Read the record
>
> IF department number is different from previous department number,
>
>> Print totals
>>
>> Reset to zero
>>
>> Set "previous department number" to department from current record
>
> Print the current record, add it to totals

The step that compares department numbers and then prints and resets totals is called a control break. We must be careful not to attempt a control break just after reading the *first* record, since there is then no previous department number to compare.

Figure 13.7 shows the procedure for this program. Note that Step 6 is necessary to print the totals for the last department. Because of the necessity of treating the first record separately from the main loop (because no test for control break) and of Step 6 for printing totals of the last department, practically every action appears twice in the procedure.

---

1. Initialize totals to zero
2. Read first record
3. Print first record, add to totals
4. Set previous department to current department
5. WHILE there are records,
   5.1 Read a record
   5.2 IF department $\neq$ previous department
       THEN Print totals
           Reset totals to zero
           Set previous department to current department
   5.3 Print record, add to totals
6. Print totals

Figure 13.7 Procedure for a report with control break by department.

This should suggest that subroutines are useful; if any of the actions are complex, they can be written once as a subroutine and called from both places in the program where that action is needed.

Figure 13.8 shows a program that follows this procedure. Three subroutines are used; note that subroutine 1200 calls subroutine 1000. We assume that each record in the file PAYRG contains social security number, name, department, number of hours worked, and gross wages. These fields are sufficient to illustrate the logic of the process and provide yet another example of formatted output.

The control break logic can be used in many situations. Listing transactions in an edit report and showing the totals for each batch is a similar process. Sometimes the individual records (called *detail lines* on the report) are not printed. Sometimes logic using control breaks on two or even more fields is necessary; sales may be totaled by state, for example, and by district within each state. Such programs are a little tricky to write, but with careful footwork you should be able to do it successfully, since the logic really is the same at both levels of control breaks.

13.5 MAIN IDEAS

a. One of the tasks in system design is the layout of forms and reports. The planning is done on layout forms, and programs that produce reports are written from those layout forms.

b. Formatted output in BASIC requires *image statements*, which specify the format of printed lines. These image statements are referred to by USING phrases in PRINT statements.

```
10   REM   PRODUCE REPORT INCLUDING DEPARTMENT TOTALS
20   REM   G STRUBLE    FEB 1980
36   REM      S$ = SOCIAL SECURITY NUMBER
38   REM      N$ = EMPLOYEE NAME
40   REM      D  = EMPLOYEE'S DEPARTMENT
42   REM      H  = HOURS WORKED BY THE EMPLOYEE
44   REM      G  = GROSS PAY
46   REM      T1 = DEPARTMENT TOTAL OF HOURS WORKED
48   REM      T2 = DEPARTMENT TOTAL OF GROSS PAY
50   REM      D1 = DEPARTMENT FROM PREVIOUS RECORD
55   REM   USES SUBROUTINES
57   REM      1000 TO INITIALIZE TOTALS
59   REM      1100 TO PRINT RECORD, ADD TO TOTALS
61   REM      1200 TO PRINT AND RESET TOTALS
70       FILES PAYRG
100      GOSUB 1000
110      INPUT #1, S$, N$, D, H, G
120      GOSUB 1100
130      LET D1 = D
195  REM   MAIN PROCESSING LOOP
200      IF END #1 GO TO 300
210      INPUT #1, S$, N$, D, H, G
220      IF D = D1 GO TO 240
230      GOSUB 1200
240      GOSUB 1100
250      GO TO 200
295  REM   PRINT LAST DEPARTMENT TOTALS
300      GOSUB 1200
310      GO TO 9970
995  REM   SUBROUTINE TO INITIALIZE TOTALS TO ZERO
1000     LET T1 = 0
1010     LET T2 = 0
1090     RETURN
1095 REM   SUBROUTINE TO PRINT A RECORD, ADD TO TOTALS
1100     PRINT USING 8010, S$, N$, D, H, G
1110     LET T1 = T1 + H
1120     LET T2 = T2 + G
1190     RETURN
1195 REM   SUBROUTINE TO PRINT AND RESET TOTALS
1200     PRINT USING 8020, D1, T1, T2
1210     PRINT
1220     GOSUB 1000
1230     LET D1 = D
1290     RETURN
8010:'LLLLLLLL  'LLLLLLLLLLLLLLLLLLLL  ##    ##.#    ###.##
8020:       TOTALS FOR DEPARTMENT ##           ####.#  #####.##
9970 END


524364759  BAYLOR, PAT               4    40.0    250.00
169834558  PATUCCO, CHRIS            4    37.5    300.00
       TOTALS FOR DEPARTMENT   4         77.5    550.00

522750088  WU, LESLIE                5    44.0    345.00
       TOTALS FOR DEPARTMENT   5         44.0    345.00

246619055  BAKER, WILSON             6    24.0    168.00
677527444  SCHMIDT, COLLETTE         6    41.0    373.92
564093456  FERNANDEZ, RAFAEL         6    40.0    380.00
       TOTALS FOR DEPARTMENT   6        105.0    921.92
```

Figure 13.8 Program for a report with control break by department.

c. An image statement can specify the formats under which numbers and strings are to be printed, as well as text characters (including spaces).

d. *Numeric formats* can specify a particular number of decimal places, total number of characters allocated to a field, and placement of commas and trailing minus sign. *String formats* specify length of the field, and centering or left- or right-justification.

e. The logic structure *control break* enables summarization of data by a key such as department number. The central idea is comparison, as each record is read, of its key with the key of the previous record.

13.6 QUESTIONS FOR IMAGINATION AND REVIEW

1. In Fig. 13.5 it appears that the report heading TABLE OF VALUES OF $100 is more-or-less centered. Rewrite statement 100 to take advantage of the centering that the computer can do of character strings.

2. In Fig. 13.5, interest rates are printed as

```
0.0300
0.0325
etc.
```

Rewrite statements 240 and 125 so that the rates are printed as

```
3.00%
3.25%
etc.
```

3. Draw a report layout for the report produced by the procedure in Fig. 10.2; include report and column headings. Then modify the program in Fig. 10.3 to produce the report according to your layout.

4. Draw a report layout for the tax bills discussed in Section 10.1, and modify the program in Fig. 10.5 to produce the bills according to your layout. You may wish to do this either assuming a preprinted form on which your program need only print the data on each property, or assuming that your program should print the entire text on plain paper. It would be instructive to try it both ways!

5. The payroll register printed by Fig. 13.6 should include a report heading, and the report heading should include a date. Modify the pro-

gram so that it will first ask the user at the terminal for the date to put
on the report, and then (after spacing several lines) begin the report with
a report heading including the date supplied.

6. We have described formatting a report to a user's terminal. This
sometimes makes no sense: If the terminal is a video screen, the report
may flash by too quickly to be read, with no copy for later reference or
action; if the terminal is a teletype, printing is so slow that the report
seems to be (forgive the expression) interminable. Larger systems usually have faster printers, and a report like a payroll register should be
printed by that printer. A common mechanism is to write the report to a
file, formatted exactly as it should appear on paper, and later call for the
file to be copied to the printer.

    a) Modify the program in Fig. 13.6 to write the report into a file.

    b) Investigate how you could copy a file to the printer using your
        computer.

7. The formatted output features enable the printing of a minus sign
after a number, but in many accounting applications we prefer CR, to
indicate Credit, after the number. Some BASIC systems provide formatted output features including CR. If your system does not have such
a feature, show how CR or a string containing two spaces could be stored
as the value of a string variable as a result of testing a number; this
variable could be used to print CR after a numeric value rather than
printing a minus sign.

8. Modify the program in Fig. 13.8 to print final totals of all employees
at the end of the report. A program could add data to the variables that
accumulate the final totals either (a) as each employee is processed, or
(b) as each department total is being printed, just before the department
totals are reset to zero.

9. As an extension of the ideas in Question 8, suppose the file PAYRG
used in Fig. 13.8 also includes a plant number, and the records are in
sequence by plant and by department within each plant. Modify the program in Fig. 13.8 to print department totals and plant totals. This requires control breaks on plant and on department; the program must
compare plant numbers first, but cause department totals to be printed
first. Why?

10. The concept of the control break can also be adapted to print page
headings at the top of each page of a report. The program must maintain
a counter of lines printed on the current page, incrementing this counter

each time a line is printed. Then in place of a comparison between, say, department and previous department, the program must compare the line counter with a desired maximum. When the line counter exceeds this maximum, the program spaces to the top of a new page (possibly printing and resetting page totals first), prints page headings, possibly increments a page counter, and resets the line counter to zero. Modify the program in Fig. 13.6 to print the headings at the top of each page.

GLOSSARY

Action documents Computer output on paper, such as checks and invoices, used directly in facilitating the day-to-day work flow in an organization.

Address The number that identifies a location in a computer's main storage.

Application A use of a computer; therefore, *application* has been used to mean an information processing system or subsystem such as accounts receivable.

Argument See **Parameter.**

Arithmetic and logic section The portion of a computer that does arithmetic and logical manipulations, including conversions between representations, on operands.

Array A list or block of numbers or strings. A number or string in the array is accessed by the array name and one or more subscripts.

Assembly language Generally, a symbolic representation of machine language.

BASIC Beginner's All-purpose Symbolic Instruction Code.

BASIC mode Control level in which the user has access to commands in the BASIC subsystem of the operating system.

Batch processing Data are gathered into batches, fed to a computer, and processed in batches, and the results for the entire run are then printed and returned to the user.

Binary A number system using base 2. Especially efficient for computers since all digits are 0 or 1.

Bit Contraction of binary digit. Storage that will hold a binary 1 or 0. Sometimes used to refer to a digit rather than the storage that holds a digit.

Block A continuously recorded set of data on a magnetic tape or disk.

Branch instruction An instruction that breaks sequential execution of instructions and designates the location from which the next instruction will be executed. Synonym: **jump instruction.**

Bug An error in a computer program.

Business data processing Data processing using business data, usually financial data.

Business information system An information processing system used in business.

Byte Physical storage (usually main storage) that will store one printable character. In many computers, a byte is 8 bits.

Call A function or subroutine is called by a transfer of control to the function or subroutine. The function or subroutine will return control when finished.

Cell A location that holds one number or string in an array.

Central processing unit Abbreviated cpu. A computer's control section, arithmetic and logic section, main storage, and input/output section except for the input and output devices and controllers.

COBOL COmmon Business Oriented Language

COM Computer Output on Microfilm (or microfiche) Computer output formatted as for printing but photographed onto either rolls or sheets of microfilm.

Command A direction given by the user at a terminal that requests immediate action by the operating system. A command acts on a program, a file, or the user's status.

Compile To translate a program in a higher-level language (e.g., BASIC) into machine language. A **compiler** is a program that does the translation.

Conditional branch An instruction that executes a branch if a particular condition is satisfied.

Control break The step in a program that compares values of data elements in each two successive records and takes special actions when the two values are unequal. By extension, the logic structure using control breaks.

Control key A terminal key, held down while hitting another key, that designates a control function rather than a printable character.

Control section The portion of a computer's circuitry that directs the operation of the computer. Among other tasks, it retrieves and decodes instructions, and makes decisions as to what instruction to execute next.

Control structure The pattern of flow of control in a segment of a program or a procedure.

Control total A total computed before execution of a program, to be compared with a total generated by the program to verify the correctness of the program execution or data entered.

Conversational   See **Interactive.**

CRT (cathode ray tube) terminal   A terminal that displays the record of interaction between the user and the computer on a screen.

Cursor   Indicator of the location on a CRT screen at which the next character (input or output) will be displayed.

Data   Facts used as a basis for processing.

Data capture and edit   A program that accepts data, tests the data for validity, displays an error message for any invalid data element (and perhaps gives the user the immediate opportunity to correct invalid data), and usually writes the data to a file.

Data element   A piece of data: a number or a character string. Synonym: **field** or **data field.**

Data key   In a search, the data field that is compared to the search key.

Data processing   Processing (reading, writing, moving, calculating) data by an electronic digital computer, resulting in information, and manual procedures that prepare the data for computer processing and use the information that results from the processing.

Data processing system   The equipment used in data processing: a computer and auxiliary equipment. See also **Information processing system.**

Debugging   Finding and correcting errors (**bugs**) in computer programs.

Desk check   Simulated execution on paper of a computer program, using sample data.

Detail line   In a report, a line printed from the data in an individual record.

Direct-access file   A file organized to permit reading or writing of any record, regardless of which record was last read or written.

Direct-access storage   Storage devices that permit access to each record directly, without regard to the location of the previous record accessed.

Disk drive   The mechanism that rotates, reads, and writes, a disk or disk pack.

Disk pack   A stack of disks with magnetic coating, mounted rigidly on a spindle, used for a computer's secondary storage.

Diskette   A low-cost magnetic disk unit used especially in small computers.

Edit   To alter or correct a program. Also, an edit program tests data for validity and reports invalid data.

Executable   An executable statement is translated into machine-language instructions that are executed when the program is run.

Execution cycle   The portion of computer operation in which the computer, having found out what operation to perform (see **Instruction cycle**) does the operation.

Execution phase   The computer executes the machine language program translated from the user's program in, say, BASIC. Data are processed only during the execution phase.

Expression   A formula for deriving a value. An expression is composed of one or more variables and constants, and, if necessary, operators to combine them into one value.

Field   See **Data element.**

File   A collection of similar data stored together. Also, a collection of data on individual entities in some population. A program may also be a file.

File access number   The number by which INPUT, PRINT, SCRATCH, QUOTE, and IF END statements in BASIC refer to a file. Called a **channel number** in some systems.

File space   Secondary storage space set aside for a user's programs and data files.

Floating-point   Number representation, and arithmetic using that representation, that represents each number by a set of leading significant digits and an indicator of where the decimal point should be. Sometimes called **scientific notation.**

Floppy disk   See **Diskette.**

Flow diagram   See **Program flowchart.**

Format   In a BASIC image statement, the specification for printing one data element.

Formatted screen   Display formatted on a CRT terminal using the ability of a terminal to set the location of the cursor under program control.

Function   In BASIC, a subroutine that is called by use of its name in a numeric or string expression. The value of one or more numbers or strings is usually passed to the subroutine as parameters, and the function returns a value.

Grandfather-father-son backup   The current version of a data file and the two most recent previous versions (father and grandfather) are kept.

Graph plotter   A device that, under computer control, draws graphs on paper.

Hard-copy terminal   A terminal that prints the record of interaction between the user and the computer.

Higher-level language   A language in which each statement is generally translated into several machine-language instructions. BASIC and COBOL are examples.

Indexed sequential file   A file in sequence on some key field, with an index so that access to any record is sequential within a segment of the file determined by the index.

Indicator   In machine language, a special location in the computer's control section that records the result of a test or the status of a device. In BASIC, a variable used by a program for the same purpose.

Information   Knowledge resulting from the processing of data.

Information processing   Essentially synonymous with **data processing.**

Information processing system Computer programs, input forms, output forms and reports, and the procedures using them; also a synonym for **data processing system.**

Initialization Assigning initial values to variables. Initialization of variables is necessary before values of those variables can be used.

Input/output section The portion of a computer that performs input from input devices (including secondary storage) and output to output devices.

Instruction The basic unit of control over a computer's process. Executed from its location in main storage, an instruction specifies an operation to be carried out and the locations of its operands.

Instruction counter A register in a computer's control section that always contains the address of the next instruction to be executed.

Instruction cycle The portion of computer operation in which the control section fetches an instruction from main storage and decodes it to see what operation to perform. The instruction cycle is followed by the execution cycle, and then the instruction cycle for the next instruction.

Interactive Involving conversational interaction between a user at a terminal and a computer. The computer responds to the user's messages within a short time, before the user types in the next message. Synonym: **conversational.**

Internal sorting techniques A class of techniques that sort a set of data while the data are all in internal storage. Exchange sorting methods are an example.

Internal storage A computer's main storage that holds programs and data. Bytes or words in internal storage are accessed directly by addresses in instructions.

Interpreter A translator that essentially translates each statement from a higher-level language into machine language, then executes that machine language before going on to translate the next statement.

Job control cards In a batch processing system, cards that tell the operating system what programs to execute, where to find the input data files, and where to place the resulting files.

Job scheduler The portion of the operating system that assigns devices, file space, and workspace to a user, and activates programs for a user.

Jump See **Branch instruction.**

Keyword A word that indicates what kind of action is to be taken by a BASIC statement.

Large-scale integration (LSI) Techniques, mostly photographic, for etching entire circuits onto small chips.

Library A set of programs and/or files kept in a computer's secondary storage. Usually, the programs in a library are available to many users of the computer.

Line number A unique number attached to a statement in a BASIC program.

Loop   A sequence of instructions or statements whose execution is repeated.

Machine language   Representation of programs in which they are actually executed. In machine language, instructions have numeric operation codes and operand addresses.

Magnetic core   A set of iron rings whose magnetic polarities can be set to represent binary digits 0 and 1. Used for a computer's main storage.

Magnetic disk   See **Disk pack; Disk drive.**

Main storage   A computer's internal storage, in which each byte or word has an address, and can be accessed in a microsecond or so.

Master file   Contains all the relatively stable data on each entity (employee, customer, product, etc.) in a population; some master files contain current status data as well.

Merge   To combine two files in sequence on the same key. The combined file will include all records from the two files, in sequence by the key. The term is extended to any similar processes that coordinate the input of two files the way a merge does. Synonym for this extended definition: **zipper strategy.**

Microcomputer   A computer based on a microprocessor. The price of the computer is under $10,000.

Microfiche   A sheet of microfilm, which can hold a number of pages of data and an index to assist in the data retrieval.

Microprocessor   The entire arithmetic and control sections of a computer, etched onto a chip by large-scale integration techniques.

Microsecond   One millionth of a second.

Millisecond   One thousandth of a second.

Minicomputer   Generally, a computer with a price range of $10,000 to $100,000.

Monitor mode   Control level in which the user has access to general operating system utility commands, and can enter any of various subsystems, such as BASIC mode.

On-line   Connected directly to a computer.

Operand   A piece of data to be used in an operation.

Operating system   An integrated set of programs that controls all processing done by the computer.

Operation code   The portion of an instruction that specifies what operation (e.g., add, jump, output) is to be performed.

Parameter   A value passed to a function for use by the function. Synonym: **argument.**

Password   An identification of a computer user, required as part of the authorization procedure. When typed at a terminal, the password is not displayed.

Plotter   See **Graph plotter.**

Precedence of operators   A rule specifying the sequence in which operations are performed in evaluating an expression.

Procedure   A finite set of steps or instructions that can be mechanically interpreted and carried out by some agent.

Program   A sequence of machine-language instructions, or statements in another computer language, that performs a complete task.

Program flowchart   Diagrammatic representation of a procedure, showing flow of control by directed arrows. Synonym: **flow diagram.**

Program verification   A series of statements about a program that demonstrate its correctness. Also called **program validation.**

Programming   Writing programs.

Prompt message   A message displayed at a terminal to tell the user what input to type in next.

Pseudocode   A restricted language used to express procedures.

Pseudo-random numbers   A sequence of numbers computed according to a formula but having the properties that random numbers would be expected to exhibit.

Random access   Synonym for **direct access.**

Read mode   A path is established for a program to read records from a file.

Real-time   The computer reacts quickly enough to control the system providing the computer input.

Record   The portion of a file that contains the data on one entity in a population. A record is composed of one or more data elements or data fields.

Relation   One of $<, <=, =, >=, >, <>$ or $\#$.

Scroll   Mode of CRT screen display in which the current line is always at the bottom of the screen, and each line moves up one position to make room for a new line.

Search key   A value to search for.

Secondary storage   Storage, usually magnetic disk or tape, that holds programs and data files. Accessed through the operating system and input and output instructions, which normally access a block of bytes or words.

Semiconductor storage   Microminiature patterns of impure silicon configured into capacitors, resistors, and transistors, for a computer's inexpensive, very compact, fast-access main storage.

Sentinel value   A value of a data element (or, by extension, a record) that will be taken to mean, by convention, end of data or some other special condition.

Sequential access   Records are written in sequence according to the sequential physical characteristics of the device, and read in the same sequence in which they are written.

Sequential file   A file whose records can only be written or read sequentially.

Serial sorting techniques   A class of techniques that sort a set of data by treating them sequentially, usually reading them (several times) from files. The sort-by-merge technique is an example.

Simple variable   A variable that is not subscripted, and therefore not a cell in an array.

Sort key   A data field used to put in sequence a set of data.

Special analyses   Processing in addition to normal business information system operations, to answer specific questions that contribute to management decisions.

Statement   An action is specified in a higher-level or assembly language by a statement. A statement is usually a line in a program; in BASIC, each statement has a line number, and contains a keyword.

String variable   A variable whose value is a string of characters.

Structured programming   Writing procedures or programs, using a restricted set of control structures (in this text, WHILE, IF-THEN, IF-THEN-ELSE, LOOP-EXIT, FOR, and subroutine calls). Using these structures facilitates top-down programming, and makes programs easier to develop, verify, understand, and maintain.

Structured walk-through   Oral explanation of how a program works. The explanation should follow the top-down structure of the program itself, and should include enough interaction so that the listener or listeners have a thorough understanding of the program.

Subroutine   A more-or-less self-contained section of program that can be executed from some other section. After each execution of the subroutine, control returns to the section that called the subroutine.

Subscript   A value that designates which cell of an array is to be accessed. Synonym: **index.**

Supervisor   The portion of the operating system that manages time-sharing and input-output requests of programs in execution. Synonym: **monitor.**

Syntax   The grammatical rules defining what statements in a language are permitted.

Systems flowchart   A diagrammatic representation of the processing steps in a business information system, showing input documents, files, programs, reports, and clerical steps, and the relationships among these components.

Terminal   A device for a user to communicate with a computer. The communication is usually interactive, involving a keyboard and either a typing unit or a CRT screen.

Text file   In BASIC, a file in which every line has a line number. Programs are text files.

Time slice   The maximum period of time that a time-sharing system will allow a program to execute before going on to service other users.

Time-sharing   A mode of computer operation in which processes initiated by several terminals share the use of a computer; each process takes a turn in actual execution for a small time interval.

Top-down programming   A technique of writing programs or procedures in which the process is defined in terms of major steps, and then each step is refined or decomposed into simpler and more detailed steps.

Track   On a magnetic disk, the portion that can be accessed while the read/write heads are held stationary.

Transaction code   A data element that designates the type of transaction represented by a record.

Translation phase   The computer translates the user's program into machine language.

Translator   A program that translates a program written in a higher-level or assembly language into machine language.

Unconditional branch   An instruction that executes a branch regardless of any conditions or data.

Variable   Symbolic name for a main storage location whose contents can be changed during execution of a program.

Video terminal   See **CRT terminal.**

Word   Storage required to hold a number, several characters, or an instruction.

Workspace   Main storage allocated to a user while the user is active.

Write mode   A path is established for a program to write records into a file.

SOLUTIONS TO ODD-NUMBERED QUESTIONS

CHAPTER 2

5. 05200 Compare A and B
   05201 If indicator shows A > B, branch to 06468
   05202 Compare C and 16
   05203 If indicator shows equality, branch to 06468

CHAPTER 3

1. Batch-processing operating systems perform the same functions as time-sharing operating systems, though the communication between operating system and user is different. Management of disk space and access is the same. Job management is similar, but the batch operating system takes its direction from job control cards rather than commands from a terminal. The task of running programs is quite similar. The management of time-sharing has its counterpart in batch operating systems, since many batch operating systems also keep several programs in execution and cycle among them; this is usually called *multiprogramming*.

3. One possible convention to prevent students from duplicating file names is to require that the first two (or three?) letters of every file name be the student's initials. An instructor may have to check the class roster, however, and give special instructions to, say, James Smith, to use the initials QS to avoid confusion with Jennifer Smith's files.

CHAPTER 4

1. 1. Obtain number of people
   2. Compute base fare = 2 + 0.50 (number of people − 1)

3. Compute tax $= 0.06 \times$ base fare
4. Compute total fare $=$ base fare $+$ tax
5. Print total fare

Steps 2, 3, and 4 could be combined into

2. Compute total fare $= 1.06 \ (1.50 + 0.50 \times$ number of people$)$

3. 1. Obtain current population, target population, growth rate
2. Set number of years n to 0
   growing population to current population
3. WHILE growing population $<$ target population
   3.1 Multiply growing population by $(1 +$ growth rate$)$
   3.2 Add 1 to n
4. Print number of years n

See Fig. S.1 for the corresponding flowchart.

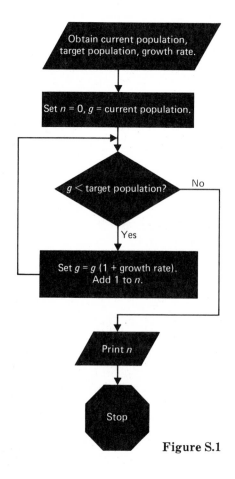

Figure S.1

5. a) Step 1 loan amount $= 1000$
annual interest rate $= 0.09$
monthly payment $= 6$
Step 2 monthly interest rate $= 0.09/12 = 0.0075$
Step 3 $6 < 0.0075 \times 1000$; therefore
Step 3.3 Print "insufficient monthly payment"

b) Step 1 loan amount $= 1000$
annual interest rate $= 0.09$
monthly payment $= 230$
Step 2 monthly interest rate $= 0.09/12 = 0.0075$
Step 3 $230 > 0.0075 \times 1000$; therefore
Step 3.1 Print column headings
Step 3.2 loan amount $1000 > 0$; therefore
Step 3.2.1 month's interest $= 1000 \times 0.0075 = 7.50$
Step 3.2.2 $230 < 1000 + 7.50$
Step 3.2.3 loan reduction $= 230 - 7.50 = 222.50$
Step 3.2.4 Print 1000, 7.50, 230, 222.50
Step 3.2.5 loan amount $= 1000 - 222.50 = 777.50$
Step 3.2 $777.50 > 0$; therefore
Step 3.2.1 month's interest $= 777.50 \times 0.0075 = 5.83$
Step 3.2.2 $230 < 777.50 + 5.83$
Step 3.2.3 loan reduction $= 230 - 5.83 = 224.17$
Step 3.2.4 Print 777.50, 5.83, 230, 224.17
Step 3.2.5 loan amount $= 777.50 - 224.17 = 553.33$
Step 3.2 $553.33 > 0$; therefore
Step 3.2.1 month's interest $= 553.33 \times 0.0075 = 4.15$
Step 3.2.2 $230 < 553.33 + 4.15$
Step 3.2.3 loan reduction $= 230 - 4.15 = 225.85$
Step 3.2.4 Print 553.33, 4.15, 230, 225.85
Step 3.2.5 loan amount $= 553.33 - 225.85 = 327.48$
Step 3.2 $327.48 > 0$; therefore
Step 3.2.1 month's interest $= 327.48 \times 0.0075 = 2.46$
Step 3.2.2 $230 < 327.48 + 2.46$
Step 3.2.3 loan reduction $= 230 - 2.46 = 228.54$
Step 3.2.4 Print 327.48, 2.46, 230, 228.54
Step 3.2.5 loan amount $= 327.48 - 228.54 = 98.94$
Step 3.2 $98.94 > 0$; therefore
Step 3.2.1 month's interest $= 98.94 \times 0.0075 = 0.74$
Step 3.2.2 $230 > 98.94 + 0.74$; therefore
monthly payment $= 98.94 + 0.74 = 99.68$
Step 3.2.3 loan reduction $= 99.68 - 0.74 = 98.94$
Step 3.2.4 Print 98.94, 0.74, 99.68, 98.94
Step 3.2.5 loan amount $= 98.94 - 98.94 = 0$
Step 3.2 $0 = 0$; therefore
Stop

7. Insert in the procedure in Fig. 4.7:

   a) a second part of Step 2: Set $n = 0$

   b) Step 3.2.6   Set $n = n + 1$

   c) Step 3.3   Print n

   Renumber the former Step 3.3 as 3.4.

9. 1. Obtain exam score
   2. IF exam score ≥ 70
        THEN Print P
        ELSE Print N

11. 1. Obtain sales for month
    2. Set compensation $= 1200$
    3. IF sales for month $> 20,000$
         THEN add 0.05 (sales for month $- 20,000$) to compensation
    4. Print compensation

CHAPTER 5

1.   26   single letter names
    260   letter followed by a digit
     26   letter, $
    260   letter, digit, $
    $\overline{572}$ valid variable names. Half are string variables, half numeric.

3. 310   valid; prints
   ON A CLEAR DAY, YOU CAN SEE PEOPLE STRAINING THEIR EYES
   320   valid; prints
   142.87   21.4
   330   invalid; no comma or semicolon between variable names
   340   invalid; needs quotes around WAGE $=$
   350   valid; prints
   PEOPLE STRAINING THEIR EYES   21.4   A 2
   360   valid; prints
   INVOICE AMOUNT 142.87
   Unnumbered statement invalid. Since it has no number, it is interpreted
   as a command, and is not a valid command.
   380   valid; prints
   2.00 2   142.87 AF$A;F$;2.00
   390   valid; prints
   (A + B9)/2 = 82.135

5. 180   K = 1
   190   T = -0.9
   200   F$ = "YES"

3. Assumptions:

a) The first year's depreciation is charged during the year of purchase;

b) Total depreciated value in 1980 is calculated after the 1980 depreciation is charged.

The procedure and program are stated in terms of a "current year," which is set to 80. Thus the year can easily be changed.

1. Set total original value, total depreciation, total depreciated value to zero
   Set current year to 80
2. WHILE there are records
   2.1 Read a record
   2.2 Add original value to total original value
   2.3 IF year purchased + useful life < current year
           THEN 2.3.1 Compute current depreciation = Original value/useful life
                2.3.2 Compute current value = current depreciation × (year purchased + useful life − current year − 1)
           ELSE 2.3.3 Set current depreciation to zero
                2.3.4 Set current value to zero
   2.4 Add current depreciation to total depreciation
       Add current value to total depreciated value
3. Print total original value, total depreciation, total depreciated value

See Fig. S.6 for the program.

5. Assume the sentinel mark is the string "STOP", and that it is part of an entire record. The changes required are:

Delete statement 200

Insert:

```
215   IF P$ = "STOP" GO TO 300
960   DATA "STOP", "0", 0, 0
```

Change statement 230 to

```
230   GO TO 210
```

By placing the sentinel record at line 960, just before the END statement, we enable easy insertion of other records (DATA statements) at 530, 540, . . . , without having to move the sentinel record.

7.

Workspace	File space	Terminal listing
a) LAB8 (empty)	no change	
b) CCCC (empty)	no change	
c) ZZZZ	AAAA, BBBB, CCCC, ZZZZ	

```
210    F$ = "7"
220    Invalid; 7 is a number, and cannot be a value of F$
230    Invalid; "1" is a string, and cannot be a value of T
240    X = −4
250    YO = −36. But be careful; some systems may evaluate −Y
       first, so the result could be +36
260    Invalid. Since the multiplication sign × is omitted, S − 3 is
       treated as a subscript. Chapter 10 explains further.
270    Y2 = (6 − 2)*(6 − 3)↑2 = 4*3↑2 = 4*9 = 36
280    Invalid; both Y22 and 22Y are invalid
290    Invalid; parentheses not paired
300    Invalid; two consecutive operators *− not allowed
```

7. A PRINT statement is executable, and therefore can print messages and values of variables as the program is executed. A REM statement is nonexecutable, and only appears in the program listing, with no effect on program execution.

9.

```
150    valid; go to 460
160    not valid; only one relation permitted
170    not valid; strings and numbers cannot be compared
180    not valid; need quotes around YES
190    valid; go to 460
200    invalid; destination of GO TO must be a line number
210    Invalid; THEN and GO TO should not both be present
```

11. a) `400   IF B <= T GO TO 480`
b) `620   IF Y$ <> "STOP" GO TO 350`
c) `1050  IF 3*K > (Q − 4)↑2 GO TO 2000`

13. See Fig. S.2.

```
10   REM    CHAPTER 5    QUESTION 13
20   REM    G STRUBLE    JAN 1980
30   REM       Q = QUANTITY ORDERED
32   REM       P = PRICE PER UNIT
100      LET K = 4
200      LET T = 0
300      IF K <= 0   GO TO 400
310      PRINT "TYPE QUANTITY ORDERED";
320      INPUT Q
330      PRINT "TYPE PRICE PER UNIT";
340      INPUT P
350      LET T = T + Q*P
360      LET K = K − 1
370      GO TO 300
400      PRINT "T ="; T
970   END
```

Figure S.2 Solution program for Chapter 5, Question 13.

15. Procedure:

   1. LOOP
     1.1 Obtain miles per gallon
     1.2 EXIT WHEN miles per gallon = 0
     1.3 Obtain price per gallon
     1.4 Compute cost = 157/miles per gallon × price per gallon
     1.5 Print cost

Program: See Fig. S.3.

```
10   REM   CHAPTER 5 QUESTION 15   COST OF GASOLINE THE DALLES TO TILLAMOOK
20   REM   G STRUBLE   JAN 1980
30   REM       M = MILES PER GALLON
32   REM       P = PRICE PER GALLON
34   REM       C = COST OF 157-MILE TRIP
100      PRINT "TYPE MILES PER GALLON";
110      INPUT M
120      IF M = 0   GO TO 970
130      PRINT "TYPE PRICE PER GALLON";
140      INPUT P
150      LET C = 157/M * P
160      PRINT "COST FOR THE TRIP =";  C
162      PRINT
190      GO TO 100
970   END
```

Figure S.3 Solution program for Chapter 5, Question 15.

17. Insert:

```
  54   REM N = NUMBER OF MONTHS
 210      LET N = 0
 465      LET N = N + 1
 970      PRINT "NUMBER OF MONTHS FOR REPAYMENT = ";N
 990      END
```

CHAPTER 6

1. a) Procedure printing one address on a line:

   1. WHILE there are records
     1.1 Read a record
     1.2 Print name, address, city, state, zip
     1.3 Print two blank lines

For the program, see Fig. S.4.

b) To print two names and addresses across the page, we must read two records, then print both. We must also make arrangements for printing the last record in case there are an odd number of records.

```
10   REM   PRINT NAMES AND ADDRESSES
20   REM   G STRUBLE   JAN 1980
30   REM       C$ = CUSTOMER NUMBER
32   REM       N1$ = NAME
34   REM       A1$ = ADDRESS
36   REM       C1$ = CITY, STATE, ZIP
38   REM       P  = PURCHASES
40   REM       D$ = DATE LAST PURCHASE
70      FILES CUST
100      IF END #1   GO TO 970
110      INPUT #1, C$, N1$, A1$, C1$, P, D$
120      PRINT N1$
130      PRINT A1$
140      PRINT C1$
150      PRINT
160      PRINT
190      GO TO 100
970   END
```

Figure S.4 Solution program for Chapter 6, Question 1(a).

   1. WHILE there are records
     1.1 Read a record
     1.2 IF there is another record
        THEN read a second record
        ELSE set second record to null strings
     1.3 Print names, addresses, cities, states, zips
     1.4 Print two blank lines

For the program, see Fig. S.5.

```
10   REM   PRINT NAMES AND ADDRESSES IN TWO COLUMNS
20   REM   G STRUBLE   JAN 1980
30   REM       C$ = CUSTOMER NUMBER
32   REM       N1$, N2$ = NAMES,
34   REM       A1$, A2$ = ADDRESSES,          FROM TWO RECORDS
36   REM       C1$, C2$ = CITIES, STATES, ZIPS   "   "   "
38   REM       P  = PURCHASES
40   REM       D$ = DATE LAST PURCHASE
70      FILES CUST
100      IF END #1   GO TO 970
110      INPUT #1, C$, N1$, A1$, C1$, P, D$
120      IF END #1   GO TO 150
130      INPUT #1, C$, N2$, A2$, C2$, P, D$
140      GO TO 180
150      LET N2$ = " "
160      LET A2$ = " "
170      LET C2$ = " "
180      PRINT N1$; TAB(32); N2$
190      PRINT A1$; TAB(32); A2$
200      PRINT C1$; TAB(32); C2$
210      PRINT
220      PRINT
290      GO TO 100
970   END
```

Figure S.5 Solution program for Chapter 6, Question 1(b).

	Workspace	*File space*	*Terminal listing*
d)	ZZZZ	AAAA, BBBB, CCCC, TTY (copy of BBBB)	
e)	ZZZZ	no change	BBBB
f)	ZZZZ	no change	error message; ZZZZ is not in file space
g)	CCCC (old ZZZZ)	no change	
h)	CCCC (old ZZZZ)	no change	error message; duplicate name CCCC
i)	DRAW (old AAAA)	AAAA, BBBB, CCCC, DRAW (copy of AAAA)	
j)	ZZZZ	AAAA, BBBB, CCCC, DRAW (copy of AAAA)	

```
10    REM   COMPUTE DEPRECIATION IN CURRENT YEAR, TOTAL VALUE
20    REM   G STRUBLE   JAN 1980
30    REM       P1$, P2$, P3$ = FIRST 3 FIELDS OF RECORD, UNUSED IN PROGRAM
32    REM       P = YEAR PURCHASED
34    REM       V = ORIGINAL VALUE
36    REM       L = USEFUL LIFE
38    REM       V9 = TOTAL ORIGINAL VALUE
40    REM       D  = CURRENT YEAR DEPRECIATION
42    REM       D9 = TOTAL DEPRECIATION
44    REM       Y  = CURRENT YEAR
46    REM       C  = CURRENT VALUE
48    REM       C9 = TOTAL CURRENT VALUE
70       FILES EQUIP
100      LET V9 = 0
110      LET D9 = 0
120      LET C9 = 0
130      LET Y = 80
200      IF END #1  GO TO 350
210      INPUT #1, P1$, P2$, P3$, P, V, L
220      LET V9 = V9 + V
230      IF P + L <= Y GO TO 270
240      LET D = V / L
250      LET C = D * (P + L - Y - 1)
260      GO TO 290
270      LET D = 0
280      LET C = 0
290      LET D9 = D9 + D
300      LET C9 = C9 + C
310      GO TO 200
350      PRINT "TOTAL ORIGINAL VALUE ="; V9
360      PRINT "TOTAL DEPRECIATION IN"; Y; "="; D9
370      PRINT "TOTAL DEPRECIATED VALUE IN"; Y; "="; C9
970   END
```

Figure S.6 Solution program for Chapter 6, Question 3.

CHAPTER 7

1. 300   IF *condition a* GO TO 330
   310   IF *condition b* GO TO 400
   320   GO TO 340
   330   IF *not condition b* GO TO 400
   340   *action 2*

   .
   .
   .

   390   GO TO 500
   400   *action 1*

   .
   .
   .

   500   *next step*

3. 410   LET V = (V + D) * (1 + I/12)

5. Initial procedure:

   1. Set k to 1
   2. WHILE k ≤ 50
       2.1 Read a record
       2.2 Compute average inhabitants/household in tract
       2.3 Print record and average
       2.4 Add 1 to k

   See the program in Fig. S.7.

   a) Insert Step 2.5:
       2.5 Read two records

       Modify the program of Fig. S.7 by adding

   250   INPUT #1, T$, P9, H9
   260   INPUT #1, T$, P9, H9

```
10    REM   SUMMARIZE 50 CENSUS TRACT RECORDS
20    REM   G STRUBLE   JAN 1980
30    REM       T$ = CENSUS TRACT NUMBER
32    REM       P  = POPULATION IN TRACT
34    REM       H  = NUMBER OF HOUSEHOLDS
36    REM       K  = COUNTER
38    REM       A  = AVERAGE PEOPLE/HOUSEHOLD IN TRACT
70        FILES SMPL
100       LET K = 1
200       IF K > 50   GO TO 970
210       INPUT #1, T$, P, H
220       LET A = P / H
230       PRINT T$; TAB(12); P; TAB(22); H; TAB(32); A
240       LET K = K + 1
290       GO TO 200
970   END
```

Figure S.7 Program for the initial task of Chapter 7, Question 5.

b) Expand Step 1 by adding
   Set total population, total households to zero
   Add steps
   2.6 Add population to total population
   2.7 Add households to total households
3.   Print total population/total households

Change statement 200 to

```
200   IF K > 50 GO TO 300
```

Add statements

```
110   LET P1 = 0
120   LET H1 = 0
270   LET P1 = P1 + P
280   LET H1 = H1 + H
300   PRINT "AVERAGE PER HOUSEHOLD IN SAMPLE = ";P1/H1
```

This average printed is *not* the same as an average of the averages. Consider only two tracts:
  pop. = 1900, households = 190, average = 10
  pop. = 20, households = 10, average = 2
The average population per household in the entire sample is 1920/200 =
9.6, but the average of the averages is 6.0.

c) The WHILE clause in the procedure becomes
   WHILE there are records *and* k ≤ 50

   Step 2.5 must read
   2.5 IF there are two more records
         THEN read two records

The program is changed by adding

```
205   IF END #1 GO TO 300
245   IF END #1 GO TO 270
255   IF END #1 GO TO 270
```

7. a) 7 times

   b) 4 times $(K = 1, 3, 5, 7)$

   c) 4 times $(K = 1, 3, 5, 7)$

   d) 6 times $(K = 0.5, 1.5, 2.5, 3.5, 4.5, 5.5)$

   e) 0 times

   f) 2 times $(K = 1, 0)$

   g) 1 time $(K = 2)$

   h) 1 time $(K = 2)$

9. Modify the procedure of Fig. 7.5:
   Expand Step 1 to set totals of regular wages and overtime wages to zero
   Expand Step 2.2.1 to

2.2.1 IF hours worked ≤ 40 *or* employee is exempt

   THEN 2.2.1.1 gross pay = hours $\times$ wage
   2.2.1.2 IF hours worked ≤ 40

               THEN add hours worked $\times$ wage to regular total
               ELSE add 40 $\times$ wage to regular total
                    add (hours worked $-$ 40) $\times$ wage to
                    overtime total

   ELSE 2.2.1.3 gross pay = hours $\times$ wage + 0.5 $\times$ (hours $-$ 40) $\times$ wage

       add 40 $\times$ wage to regular total
       add 1.5 $\times$ (hours $-$ 40) $\times$ wage to overtime total

The totals printed in Step 3 will include regular and overtime totals.

Modify the program of Fig. 7.6 by adding the statements

```
54    REM T4 = TOTAL OF REGULAR WAGES (HOURS <= 40)
56    REM T5 = TOTAL OF OVERTIME WAGES (ON HOURS > 40)
130      LET T4 = 0
140      LET T5 = 0
244      LET T4 = T4 + 40 * W
246      LET T5 = T5 + 1.5 * (H - 40) * W
262      IF H <= 40 GO TO 266
263      LET T4 = T4 + 40 * W
264      LET T5 = T5 + (H - 40) * W
265      GO TO 270
266      LET T4 = T4 + H * W
430      PRINT "TOTAL REGULAR WAGES =" ; T4
440      PRINT "TOTAL OVERTIME WAGES =" ; T5
```

The Step 2.2.1 above can be recast as a CASE structure; try it!

11. 2. Case 1: wage ≤ 33: DO tax $= 0$
    Case 2: wage ≤ 76: DO tax $= 0.16 \times$ (wage $- 33$)
    Case 3: wage ≤ 143: DO tax $= 6.88 + 0.18 \times$ (wage $- 76$)
    Case 4: wage ≤ 182: DO tax $= 18.94 + 0.22 \times$ (wage $- 182$)
    Case 5: ELSE DO tax $= 27.52 + 0.24 \times$ (wage $- 182$)
   3. IF tax $>$ exemptions $\times$ 14.40
      THEN subtract exemptions $\times$ 14.40 from tax
      ELSE set tax to zero

See Fig. S.8 for the program segment following this procedure.

13. It would seem that an end-of-file condition could signal search failure in Step 4 of Fig. 7.10, but this criterion fails if the *last* record in the file is the record desired. Therefore the test in Step 4 must be the test for search key = data key.

15. In statement 230 of Fig. 7.13, if year-to-date wages Y of the current record are the same as the highest found so far Y1, the IF statement

```
52   REM      G = GROSS WAGES
54   REM      E = EXEMPTIONS
56   REM      T = TAX
200     IF G <= 33   GO TO 250
210     IF G <= 76   GO TO 260
220     IF G <= 143 GO TO 270
230     IF G <= 182 GO TO 280
240     GO TO 290
250     LET T = 0
257     GO TO 300
260     LET T = 0.16 * (G - 33)
267     GO TO 300
270     LET T = 6.88  +  0.18 * (G - 76)
277     GO TO 300
280     LET T = 18.94  +  0.22 * (G - 143)
287     GO TO 300
290     LET T = 27.52  +  0.24 * (G - 182)
300     IF T > E * 14.40   GO TO 330
310     LET T = 0
320     GO TO 400
330     LET T = T - E * 14.40
```

Figure S.8 Program segment for Chapter 7, Question 11.

branches to 270; thus the first of tied employees is the one kept and reported. If the equal sign is removed from statement 230, the last of tied records will be reported.

To report *all* employees tied for highest year-to-date wages requires a much greater change. We must pass through the entire file before we know what the highest year-to-date wage is. We may try to keep in main storage all records tied for highest, something that is not easy even when we learn about arrays in Chapter 10. The simpler alternative is to make a second pass through the file, reporting at that time all records that match the highest year-to-date wage.

17. Consider a program that is to search for an optimum record, and all records are acceptable candidates. After the first record has been read, it should be recorded as the best so far. If so, the variables holding the best record so far can be initialized by reading the first record directly into them.

   This can be a simplification in some programs. It is balanced sometimes by extra work to compute the criterion variable, for example, current depreciated value in the program of Question 16. It can also make program modification difficult, if a restricted category is required after the program is first written.

19. The procedure is very similar to Fig. 7.10:
   1. Obtain serial number (search key) from terminal
   2. Set data key = "STOP" (different from search key)
   3. WHILE search key $\neq$ data key *and* there are records left to read
      3.1 Read a record (including data key)

4. IF search key = data key
    THEN 4.1 Compute current value = original price × (useful life −
               age) / useful life
              4.2 IF current value < 0
                   THEN set current value to zero
              4.3 Print description, location, age, current value
    ELSE 4.4 Print message that the search has failed

The program is in Fig. S.9.

```
10    REM   FIND PIECE OF EQUIPMENT WITH GIVEN SERIAL NUMBER
20    REM   G STRUBLE   JAN 1980
30    REM      K$ = SERIAL NUMBER (SEARCH KEY)
32    REM      S$ = SERIAL NUMBER (DATA KEY)
34    REM      D$ = DESCRIPTION
36    REM      L$ = LOCATION
38    REM      P  = ORIGINAL PRICE
40    REM      A  = AGE
42    REM      L  = USEFUL LIFE
70       FILES EQUIP
100      PRINT "TYPE SERIAL NUBER OF DESIRED EQUIPMENT";
110      INPUT K$
200      LET S$ = "STOP"
300      IF K$ = S$  GO TO 400
310      IF END #1  GO TO 400
320      INPUT #1, S$, D$, L$, P, A, L
350      GO TO 300
400      IF K$ = S$  GO TO 430
410      PRINT "SERIAL NUMBER NOT ON FILE"
420      GO TO 970
430      LET V = P * (L - A) / L
440      IF V >= 0  GO TO 460
450      LET V = 0
460      PRINT D$; TAB(40); L$
470      PRINT "AGE ="; A; TAB(20); "CURRENT VALUE ="; V
970   END
```

Figure S.9 Program for Chapter 7, Question 19.

CHAPTER 8

1. a) An unending loop of statements 200 and 340–370 would result after
    the file was completely processed.

   b) The last record would be read but not processed. Execution would
    appear normal otherwise.

   c) No change. The case H = 40 gives the same results whether handled
    by statement 240 or 260.

   d) No change. This is an equivalent expression.

   e) Negative taxes would be computed for employees whose taxes should
    be zero.

   f) Employees whose tax = 0 would not be listed. Furthermore, their
    wages would not be added to the gross wages total, and since net pay

is not computed, the net pay for the *previous* employee would be added again to the net pay total.

g) With the first change, hours worked and hourly wage are interchanged, so employees will not be paid correctly for overtime work. The second change will cause the program to try to read a string (exemption code) into a numeric variable E, and the program will stop at that point. The third change sends exemption code into E1$, and E$ is not initialized. When E$ is tested in statement 230, the program will either stop or use an inappropriate value, which would cause no employees to be recognized as exempt.

7. a) Social security number should be nine digits.

b) There is really nothing we can do with a name.

c) Department number should be one of existing departments; if there are 15 departments, the number can be checked for the range 1–15.

d) Hours worked should be nonnegative, and less than some reasonable limit, perhaps 80 for a week.

e) Hourly wage should be not less than a statutory minimum, if applicable, and less than some reasonable limit, say, $25.00.

f) Exemption code should be either "EXEMPT" or "OV".

g) Number of exemptions should be nonnegative, and less than some reasonable limit, such as 12.

h) Wages paid year-to-date should be nonnegative, and less than some reasonable limit.

The procedure of Fig. 7.5 can be changed by slipping a new Step 2.2 after 2.1 and before the current Step 2.2.

2.2 Launder the record read

    2.2.1 IF social security number is not nine digits
         THEN print error message
    2.2.2 IF department number < 1 *or* department number > 15
         THEN print error message
    2.2.3 IF hours worked < 0 *or* hours worked > 80
         THEN print error message
    2.2.4 IF hourly wage < 3.25 *or* hourly wage > 25
         THEN print error message
    2.2.5 IF exemption code ≠ "EXEMPT" *and* exemption code ≠ "OV"
         THEN print error message
    2.2.6 IF number of exemptions < 0 *or* number of exemptions > 12
         THEN print error message
    2.2.7 IF wages year-to-date < 0 or wages year-to-date > 80,000
         THEN print error message

A program segment implementing this step is shown in Fig. S.10. The statements 218 and up would have to be renumbered accordingly to ac-

```
220    IF LEN(S$) = 9  GO TO 240
230    PRINT "SOC. SEC. NO.": S$; " INCORRECT LENGTH"
240    IF D < 1   GO TO 260
250    IF D <= 15  GO TO 270
260    PRINT S$; TAB(12); N$; " INVALID DEPARTMENT"; D
270    IF H < 0   GO TO 290
280    IF H <= 80  GO TO 300
290    PRINT S$; TAB(12); N$; " HOURS WORKED INVALID"; H
300    IF W < 3.25  GO TO 320
310    IF W <= 25   GO TO 330
320    PRINT S$; TAB(12); N$; " HOURLY WAGE INVALID"; W
330    IF E$ = "EXEMPT"  GO TO 360
340    IF E$ = "OV"   GO TO 360
350    PRINT S$; TAB(12); N$; " EXEMPTION CODE INVALID "; E$
360    IF E < 0   GO TO 380
370    IF E <= 12   GO TO 390
380    PRINT S$; TAB(12); N$; " NUMBER OF EXEMPTIONS INVALID"; E
390    IF Y < 0   GO TO 410
400    IF Y <= 80000   GO TO 420
410    PRINT S$; TAB(12); N$; " WAGES YEAR-TO-DATE INVALID"; Y
420    ...
```

Figure S.10 Program for Chapter 8, Question 7.

commodate this insertion; we will learn in Chapter 9 how the program segment could be made a subroutine, perhaps numbered with line numbers 700 to 890 and a GOSUB statement inserted at line 215, to avoid renumbering the old statements 220 on.

This procedure modification uses the record even if found invalid. If the desire is to bypass processing a record if it contains invalid fields, the overall procedure could become

1. Set totals to zero
2. WHILE there are records left
   2.1 Read a record
   2.2 Set error indicator to zero
   2.3 Check individual fields
       (as a part of the THEN clause for each error found, include a step
          Set error indicator to 1)
   2.4 IF error indicator = 0
          THEN process the record
3. Print totals

The THEN clause of Step 2.4 includes Steps 2.2 to 2.6 of the original procedure of Fig. 7.5. Modify the program to implement this change; it's not as big a change as it looks!

CHAPTER 9

1. If the SCRATCH statement were renumbered 115, it would clear the contents of the output file before each record is copied into the file. The result is that the new file would contain *the last* record of the old file, then the

records entered at the terminal. If the SCRATCH statement were renumbered 140, it would *never* be executed, since there is no way for control to reach it. Anyway, the program would halt with an error message the first time a record was sent to the new file.

5. 1. Set new file for writing
   2. WHILE there are records in BIGWIG
      2.1 Read a record
      2.2 IF charges this month $\neq$ 0
          THEN write record to new file

The program is shown in Fig. S.11.

```
10   REM   PRODUCE SPECIAL FILE FROM BIGWIG.   ACTIVE CUSTOMERS ONLY.
20   REM   G STRUBLE   BIGGLE-WIGGLE STORE   JAN 1980
30   REM       N  = ACCOUNT NUMBER
32   REM       N$ = CUSTOMER NAME
34   REM       A$ = CUSTOMER ADDRESS
36   REM       C$ = CUSTOMER CITY, STATE, ZIP
38   REM       L  = CREDIT LIMIT
40   REM       B  = BALANCE AT BEGINNING OF CURRENT MONTH
42   REM       C1 = NUMBER OF CHARGES    IN CURRENT MONTH
44   REM       C2 = DOLLAR TOTAL OF CHARGES CURRENT MONTH
46   REM       C3 = DOLLAR TOTAL OF CREDITS CURRENT MONTH
48   REM       P  = DOLLAR TOTAL OF PAYMENTS CURRENT MONTH
70       FILES BIGWIG, SPECL
80       SCRATCH #2
90       QUOTE #2
100      IF END #1   GO TO 970
110      INPUT #1, N, N$, A$, C$, L, B, C1, C2, C3, P
120      IF C1 = 0   GO TO 140
130      PRINT #2, N, N$, A$, C$, L, B, C1, C2, C3, P
140      GO TO 100
970  END
```

Figure S.11 Program for Chapter 9, Question 5.

7. The two programs take longer to execute than one combined program. There are operational reasons, too; it is easier to remember to run one program than two every month, and we would not have to worry about running the two in their proper sequence. On the other hand, a more complex program may be harder to debug and maintain than two simpler ones. Furthermore, we may want to print the statement data more than once, perhaps for internal information even in the middle of a month; if the program that prints the data also clears the month's detail, extra printings are at least more dangerous.

9. 1. Set file for writing
   2. LOOP
      2.1 LOOP
          2.1.1 Obtain social security number
          2.1.2 **EXIT WHEN** social security number is nine digits or "STOP"

```
10    REM    CAPTURE AND EDIT PAYROLL DATA
20    REM    G STRUBLE   JAN 1980
30    REM       S$ = SOCIAL SECURITY NUMBER
32    REM       H1 = REGULAR HOURS
34    REM       H2 = OVERTIME HOURS
36    REM       X  = VALUE OBTAINED BY SUBROUTINE
38    REM       P$ = PROMPT MESSAGE TO BE USED BY SUBROUTINE
50    REM    USES SUBROUTINE 700 TO OBTAIN NUMERIC VALUE X
70        FILES PAYCAP
80        SCRATCH #1
100       PRINT "TYPE SOCIAL SECURITY NUMBER";
110       INPUT S$
120       IF LEN(S$) = 9   GO TO 200
130       IF S$ = "STOP"   GO TO 200
140       PRINT "9 DIGITS, OR TYPE STOP WHEN DONE"
150       GO TO 100
200       IF S$ = "STOP"   GO TO 970
300       LET P$ = "REGULAR HOURS"
310       GOSUB 700
320       LET H1 = X
330       LET P$ = "OVERTIME HOURS"
340       GOSUB 700
350       LET H2 = X
360       PRINT #1, S$, H1, H2
370       PRINT
390       GO TO 100
698   REM    SUBROUTINE, PROMPTING WITH P$, OBTAINING VALUE X
700       PRINT "TYPE "; P$;
710       INPUT X
720       IF X < 0   GO TO 740
730       IF X <= 40   GO TO 760
740       PRINT "VALUE MUST BE WITHIN 0 TO 40"
750       GO TO 700
760       RETURN
970   END
```

Figure S.12 Program for Chapter 9, Question 9.

      2.1.3 Display error message

2.2 EXIT WHEN social security number = "STOP"

2.3 SET P$ to "REGULAR HOURS"

2.4 Obtain numeric field, store as value of regular hours

2.5 Set P$ to "OVERTIME HOURS"

2.6 Obtain numeric field, store as value of overtime hours

2.7 Write record

The program, shown in Fig. S.12, assumes that both fields are to be edited for the same range. If the allowed ranges are different, the range limits may be sent as parameters to the subroutine, like the prompt message P$.

13. Suppose that the master file PAYM contains, for each employee,

Social security number

Name

Hourly wage

Wages year to date

and the file CURRP contains, for each employee,

```
10   REM   ADD WAGES FOR CURRENT PERIOD TO YEAR-TO-DATE WAGES
12   REM   IN MASTER FILE PAYM, PRODUCING UPDATED FILE UPAYM
30   REM      K1$ = RECORD KEY (SOC. SEC. NO.) FROM MASTER RECORD
32   REM      K2$ = RECORD KEY (SOC. SEC. NO.) FROM CURRENT PERIOD RECORD
34   REM      H9$ = HIGH-VALUES, LARGER THAN ANY SOC. SEC. NO.
70        FILES PAYM, CURRP, UPAYM
100       LET H9$ = "ZZZZZZZZZZ"
200       IF K1$ <> H9$  GO TO 220
210       IF K2$ = H9$   GO TO 9970
220       IF K1$ >= K2$  GO TO 260
225  REM  CASE 1:  MASTER SSN < CURRENT PERIOD SSN
260       IF K1$ > K2$  GO TO 300
265  REM  CASE 2:  SSNS MATCH
295  REM  CASE 3:  CURRENT PERIOD SSN < MASTER SSN
```

(a)

```
965  REM   SUBROUTINE TO READ MASTER RECORD
970  REM      K1$ = SOC. SEC. NO.
972  REM      N1$ = NAME
974  REM      W1  = HOURLY WAGE
976  REM      Y1  = WAGES YEAR TO DATE
1000      IF END #1  GO TO 1030
1010      INPUT #1, K1$, N1$, W1, Y1
1020      GO TO 1040
1030      LET K1$ = H9$
1040      RETURN
1465 REM   SUBROUTINE TO READ PAY RECORD CURRENT PERIOD
1470 REM      K2$ = SOC. SEC. NO.
1472 REM      W2  = HOURLY WAGE
1474 REM      H2  = HOURS WORKED
1476 REM      G2  = GROSS PAY CURRENT PERIOD
1500      IF END #2  GO TO 1530
1510      INPUT #2, K2$, W2, H2, G2
1520      GO TO 1540
1530      LET K2$ = H9$
1540      RETURN
1995 REM   SUBROUTINE TO WRITE A MASTER RECORD
2000      PRINT #3, K1$, N1$, W1, Y1
2010      RETURN
2995 REM   SUBROUTINE TO UPDATE YEAR-TO-DATE WAGES
3000      LET Y1 = Y1 + G2
3010      RETURN
3995 REM   SUBROUTINE TO PRINT ERROR MESSAGE
4000      PRINT "NO MASTER RECORD FOR SSN "; K2$
4010      PRINT K2$, W2, H2, G2
4020      RETURN
```

(b)

Figure S.13 Program for Chapter 9, Question 13. (a) Statements to modify the program of Fig. 9.18. (b) Subroutines to complete the program.

Social security number
Hourly wage
Hours worked this pay period
Gross pay this pay period

These are representative of actual file contents, and sufficient for an illustration. The procedures for the three processing subroutines are very simple:

2000:
Write a master record into a new master file
3000:
Add gross pay this pay period to wages year to date
4000:
Print error message: no master file record

The program modifications (to Fig. 9.18) and subroutines are shown in Fig. S.13.

15. One reason for not permitting replacement of fields such as account balance is that between the time we learn a correction is needed and the time it could be applied by an add-change-delete update, other transactions change the numbers. For example, the account balance may be $182.09, and we discover a 90-cent error resulting from transposing digits in a transaction. The balance should be $181.19. We prepare an update to change the balance to $181.19. But before that update is applied, another transaction, not itself erroneous, increases the balance to $259.63. If we apply the update and change the balance to $181.19, we have undone the intervening transaction! If we put in an adjustment of $0.90 instead, the balance would become $258.73, which corrects the effect of the erroneous transaction but leaves intact the correct subsequent transaction. The second major reason is that the transactions should all be journalized and form an auditable record. A clear adjustment transaction of $0.90 can be journalized too, and correct the record of transactions.

17. The add-change-delete program writes a new "A" record before reading another transaction that might modify the record. To allow a record being added to be modified by "C", updates in the same run would require the following.

a) Sort the updates so "A" updates precede other updates for the same key.

b) An "A" update is *not* immediately written when its key is found to be less than the current master record key. It is moved to a special set of variables to be held while the next update record is read.

c) Each update record must be compared not only with the current master record but also with the special set, because it might update either.

d) Before writing a record into the new file, our program must see whether the record held in the special set should be written first.

This at least doubles the complexity of the program, and it is not usually done. We find it acceptable to report attempted updates to a brand new record as erroneous, and resubmit them to be processed during the next update run.

19. The data-capture-and-edit program will have the following main organization:

1. Prepare file for writing
2. LOOP

2.1 Obtain Account number or "STOP"
2.2 EXIT WHEN Account number = "STOP"
2.3 Obtain transaction code "A", "C", or "D"
2.4 CASE 1: transaction code = "A": DO
        2.4.1 Obtain customer name
        2.4.2 Obtain address
        2.4.3 Obtain city, state, zip
        2.4.4 Obtain credit limit
        2.4.5 Write a record
    CASE 2: transaction code = "C": DO
        2.4.6 Obtain field code "CN," "CA," "CC," or "CL"
        2.4.7 Obtain field value
        2.4.8 Write a record
    CASE 3: ELSE DO:
        2.4.9 Write a record

Each of the "Obtain" steps that can include laundering of the input will be itself a LOOP-EXIT structure. This program will write a record with six fields in Step 2.4.5, a record with four fields in Step 2.4.8, and a record with two fields in Step 2.4.9; thus each record will have the correct length for its transaction code.

    The program is in Fig. S.14. It could still be improved. Note that a credit limit entered in a "C" transaction is not validated; it could be, since we could test the field code and use a different input segment if the field code is CL. Actually, that suggests that statements 1400–1450 be made into a subroutine, called from the two possible places that should input and validate the credit limit. Can you make the improvement?

21. At the end of each month the BIGMTD file should be taken out of the daily grandfather-father-son backup cycle. Perhaps the company will have a monthly cycle of these full-month transaction tapes, and release a tape of transactions three months ago. More likely, full-month transaction tapes would be kept longer. An empty tape conceptually is the correct month-to-date transaction tape at the beginning of the month. Any of the merge-type programs can accept a file containing no records, and do the right thing with the nonempty file. This is true of master or transaction files. The programs even perform properly if *both* input files are empty, but the results are not very interesting!

CHAPTER 10

1. Leaving out the multiplication sign before a parenthesized expression makes the compiler use the parenthesized expression as a subscript. The value of $4*J - 6$ may even be a possible subscript value. If $J = 3$, for example, statement 260 will store the value of $A(6)$ in B. In most systems, the cell $A(6)$ exists even if A has not been dimensioned, and the value is zero. Since it is thus possible to make such an error without having it caught either at translation or execution time, we must be especially careful to prevent this type of error.

```
10   REM   DATA-CAPTURE-AND-EDIT FOR ADD-CHANGE-DELETE UPDATES
12   REM      OF THE FILE BIGWIG
20   REM   G STRUBLE        BIGGLE-WIGGLE    JAN 1980
30   REM       K$ = ACCOUNT NO.
32   REM       T$ = TRANSACTION CODE
34   REM       N$ = CUSTOMER NAME
36   REM       A$ = ADDRESS
38   REM       C$ = CITY, STATE, ZIP
40   REM       L  = CREDIT LIMIT
42   REM       F$ = FIELD CODE
44   REM       V$ = FIELD VALUE
70       FILES BIGACD
80       SCRATCH #1
90       QUOTE #1
100      PRINT
105      PRINT "TYPE ACCT. NO.";
110      INPUT K$
120      IF K$ = "STOP"  GO TO 200
130      IF LEN(K$) <> 4  GO TO 160
140      IF K$ < "1000"  GO TO 160
150      IF K$ <= "4999"  GO TO 200
160      PRINT "ACCT. NO: 4 DIGITS, VALUE 1000-4999, OR STOP"
170      GO TO 105
200      IF K$ = "STOP"  GO TO 9970
300      PRINT "TYPE TRANSACTION CODE";
310      INPUT T$
320      IF T$ = "A"  GO TO 400
330      IF T$ = "C"  GO TO 400
340      IF T$ = "D"  GO TO 400
350      PRINT "TYPE A, C, OR D"
360      GO TO 300
400      IF T$ = "A"  GO TO 1100
410      IF T$ = "C"  GO TO 1600
420      GO TO 1900
1095 REM   CASE 1:   TRANSACTION CODE = "A"
1100     PRINT "TYPE CUSTOMER NAME";
1110     INPUT N$
1200     PRINT "TYPE CUSTOMER ADDRESS";
1210     INPUT A$
1300     PRINT "TYPE CITY, STATE, ZIP";
1310     INPUT C$
1400     PRINT "TYPE CREDIT LIMIT";
1410     INPUT L
1418 REM   VALIDATE CREDIT LIMIT
1420     IF L < 0  GO TO 1440
1430     IF L <= 10000  GO TO 1500
1440     PRINT "CREDIT LIMIT 0-10000"
1450     GO TO 1400
1500     PRINT #1, K$, T$, N$, A$, C$, L
1510     GO TO 100
1595 REM   CASE 2:   TRANSACTION CODE = "C"
1600     PRINT "TYPE FIELD CODE";
1610     INPUT F$
1618 REM   VALIDATE FIELD CODE
1620     IF F$ = "CN"  GO TO 1700
1630     IF F$ = "CA"  GO TO 1700
1640     IF F$ = "CC"  GO TO 1700
1650     IF F$ = "CL"  GO TO 1700
1660     PRINT "FIELD CODE: CN, CA, CC, OR CL"
1670     GO TO 1600
1700     PRINT "TYPE FIELD VALUE";
1710     INPUT V$
1800     PRINT #1, K$, T$, F$, V$
1810     GO TO 100
1898 REM   CASE 3:   TRANSACTION CODE = "D"
1900     PRINT #1, K$, T$
1910     GO TO 100
9970 END
```

Figure S.14 Program for Chapter 9, Question 19.

3. This task can be done either by adding a third step to the procedure of Fig. 10.2, very similar to Step 2, or by letting the same pass through the array in Step 2 handle the additional task as well. We would add a step:

2.2.2 IF Sales for K'th salesperson $< 0.5 \times$ average
    THEN write record containing names and sales

We must of course add somewhere the step that prepares a file for writing.

   We follow the second strategy, and use the control structure of Step 2 to consider all salespersons. The statements we must modify in the program of Fig. 10.2 are

```
 70   FILES SLSMO, WORSE
220   IF S(K) < 2 * A GO TO 232
```

Statements added are

```
 80   SCRATCH #2
 90   QUOTE #2
232   IF S(K) >= A/2 GO TO 240
235   PRINT #2, N$(K), S(K)
```

5.
```
400   FOR K = 1 TO G/2
410   LET T = W(K)
420   LET W(K) = W(G + 1 − K)
430   LET W(G + 1 − K) = T
440   NEXT K
```
This works for G odd or even. If G is odd, the middle cell is left in place. If it were interchanged (the FOR limit $G/2 + 0.5$), it would be interchanged with itself, which is one of the more creative ways of doing nothing.

7.
```
700   FOR K = M TO 1 STEP − 1
710   PRINT Q$(K)
720   NEXT K
```

9. First, the program to capture the data for the file RATES from the terminal:

   1. Prepare file RATES for writing
   2. LOOP
       2.1 Obtain district number or "STOP"
       2.2 EXIT WHEN "STOP" is typed in
       2.3 Obtain tax rate
       2.4 Write record

The program is shown in Fig. S.15.

   Second, a program the assessor can use in assigning new rates to all districts. Such a program is needed once a year.

   1. Prepare file NEWR for writing
   2. WHILE there are records in RATES
       2.1 Read a record

```
10   REM   PROGRAM TO BUILD THE FILE OF TAX DISTRICTS AND RATES
20   REM   NORGE GUDDLE   FEB 1980
30   REM      D$ = DISTRICT NUMBER
32   REM       R = TAX RATE
70      FILES RATES
80      SCRATCH #1
90      QUOTE #1
200     PRINT "TYPE STOP OR DISTRICT NUMBER";
210     INPUT D$
220     IF D$ = "STOP"  GO TO 970
230     PRINT "TYPE TAX RATE";
240     INPUT R
248 REM  VALIDATE RATE:  ACCEPT IF IN RANGE 0 TO 0.10
250     IF R < 0   GO TO 270
260     IF R <= .10  GO TO 300
270     PRINT "RATES MUST BE IN RANGE 0 - .10"
280     GO TO 230
300     PRINT #1, D$, R
305     PRINT
310     GO TO 200
970  END
```

Figure S.15 Program for Chapter 10, Question 9, part 1.

    2.2 Display district number
    2.3 Obtain new rate from terminal
    2.4 Write a record: old district, new rate

The program is shown in Fig. S.16.

11. Change statements 410 and 460 to:

    410   FOR J = 1 TO M
    460   NEXT J

Delete statements 420 and 470.

```
10   REM   PROGRAM TO ACCEPT AND FILE NEW TAX RATES FOR ALL DISTRICTS
20   REM   NORGE GUDDLE   FEB 1980
30   REM      D$ = DISTRICT NUMBER
32   REM       R = RATE READ FROM FILE
34   REM      R1 = NEW RATE
70      FILES RATES, NEWR
80      SCRATCH #2
90      QUOTE #2
100     IF END #1 GO TO 970
110     INPUT #1, D$, R
120     PRINT D$; TAB(25);
130     INPUT R1
140     IF R1 < 0  GO TO 160
150     IF R1 <= .1  GO TO 200
160     PRINT "RATES MUST BE IN RANGE 0 - 0.10"
170     GO TO 120
200     PRINT #2, D$, R1
210     GO TO 100
970  END
```

Figure S.16 Program for Chapter 10, Question 9, part 2.

13. Yes. How do we decide?

a) The main business of statement 200 is to specify how many times the main loop is to be performed. Any statement that specifies $M - 1$ times does that properly.

b) The FOR statement at 210 specifies how many times the inner loop is to be performed, and also the range of subscripts. The original statement 210 specifies 1 to $M - 1$ the first time, 1 to $M - 2$ the second time, . . . , 1 to 1 the last time. The proposed modification does that, too.

15. We need store only the scores in an array, not the names. The mean can be computed during the reading of the data. The procedure can be as follows:

1. Set total $= 0$
   $K = 1$
2. WHILE there are records
   2.1 Read a score into K'th cell
   2.2 Add score to total
   2.3 Increase K by 1
3. Set number of scores to $K - 1$
   Compute and print mean
4. Sort the scores into sequence
5. Compute and print median

The last step, computing the median from the sorted scores, needs some explanation. How are we to know whether we have an even or an odd number of scores? We could set a switch after we read each record, sort of like "She loves me, she loves me not." Then, depending on the final setting of that switch, we set the mean to the single middle score in the sorted array or to the average of the middle two. The program shown in Fig. S.17 uses instead the property that a fractional number used as a subscript is truncated. If N is odd, subscripts $(N + 1)/2$ and $(N + 2)/2$ will both access the middle score, the one with subscript $(N + 1)/2$. If N is even, the same two expressions used as subscripts will access the scores with subscripts $N/2$ and $(N + 2)/2$. Try it! As we study the INT function in Chapter 12, we will find a more straightforward way of doing this task.

17. The first segment executes the body of the loop once for each value of K. The value of J is 1 less than the value of K. The second segment executes the body of the loop M times for each value of K; during these M executions, J takes on all values 0 to $M - 1$.

19. The procedure:

1. Set number of entries to 0
2. WHILE there are records in GUDDLE
   2.1 Read a record
   2.2 Search the table for the product number

```
10   REM   COMPUTE MEAN AND MEDIAN OF UP TO 300 SCORES
20   REM   G STRUBLE    FEB 1980
30   REM      ARRAY S CONTAINS SCORES
32   REM      N$ = NAME
34   REM      T = TOTAL OF SCORES, TEMPORARY LOCATION
36   REM      N = NUMBER OF SCORES
38   REM      A = MEAN
40   REM      M = MEDIAN
42   REM      K, J USED AS COUNTERS AND SUBSCRIPTS
60      DIM S(300)
70      FILES SCORE
98  REM   1. INITIALIZE
100     LET T = 0
110     LET K = 1
198 REM   2. LOAD ARRAY AND COMPUTE TOTAL OF SCORES
200     IF END #1, GO TO 300
210     INPUT #1, N$, S(K)
220     LET T = T + S(K)
230     LET K = K + 1
240     GO TO 200
298 REM   3. COMPUTE AND PRINT MEAN
300     LET N = K - 1
310     LET A = T / N
320     PRINT "MEAN OF"; N; "SCORES ="; A
398 REM   4. SORT SCORES INTO ASCENDING SEQUENCE
400     FOR J = N TO 2 STEP -1
410     FOR K = 1 TO J-1
420     IF S(K) <= S(K+1)   GO TO 460
430     LET T = S(K)
440     LET S(K) = S(K+1)
450     LET S(K+1) = T
460     NEXT K
470     NEXT J
498 REM   5. COMPUTE AND PRINT MEDIAN
500     LET M = .5 * (S( (N + 1)/2 ) + S( (N + 2)/2 ))
510     PRINT "MEDIAN ="; M
970  END
```

Figure S.17 Program for Chapter 10, Question 15.

2.3 CASE 1: Product is in the table: DO
            Add sales to amount in table
    CASE 2: Number of entries = 400: DO
            Print message
    CASE 3: ELSE DO:
            Add 1 to number of entries
            Store product number, sales in cell (numbers of entries)
  3. FOR J from 1 to number of entries
        Print product number, sales

Actually, it would be a good idea to sort the entries in the table in Step 3 before printing them. The program (without a sort step) is shown in Fig. S.18.

21. The arrays we set up will be W, which will contain wage brackets; T, which will contain the base tax amount for each bracket; and P, which

will contain the percentage of tax on the wages within the bracket. Using the table of Chapter 7, Question 11, the contents of the arrays would be:

$W(1) = 0$	$T(1) = 0$	$P(1) = 0$
$W(2) = 33$	$T(2) = 0$	$P(2) = 0.16$
$W(3) = 76$	$T(3) = 6.88$	$P(3) = 0.18$
$W(4) = 143$	$T(4) = 18.94$	$P(4) = 0.22$
$W(5) = 182$	$T(5) = 27.52$	$P(5) = 0.24$

The portion of the procedure that computes the tax on an employee's

```
10    REM   GENERATE REPORT OF PRODUCTS SOLD
20    REM   NORGE GUDDLE   FEB 1980
30    REM       ARRAY P$ CONTAINS PRODUCT NUMBERS
32    REM       ARRAY S CONTAINS SALES TOTALS
34    REM       D = DATE            FROM GUDDLE
36    REM       A = ACCT. NO        FROM GUDDLE
38    REM       D$ = DOCUMENT NO.   FROM GUDDLE
40    REM       N = SALESPERSON NO. FROM GUDDLE
42    REM       P1$ = PRODUCT NO.   FROM GUDDLE
44    REM       S1 = SALE AMOUNT    FROM GUDDLE
46    REM       E = CURRENT NO. OF ENTRIES
48    REM       J = SUBSCRIPT USED IN SEARCH
50    REM       K = INDICATOR: RESULT OF SEARCH
60        DIM P$(400), S(400)
70        FILES GUDDLE
100       LET E = 0
200       IF END #1   GO TO 350
210       INPUT #1, D, A, D$, N, P1$, S1
220       GOSUB 400
228 REM   CASE STRUCTURE
230       IF K <> 0   GO TO 290
240       IF E = 400  GO TO 310
250       LET E = E + 1
260       LET P$(E) = P1$
270       LET S(E) = S1
280       GO TO 340
290       LET S(K) = S(K) + S1
300       GO TO 340
310       PRINT "TABLE FULL.  PRODUCT "; P1$; " SALES"; S1
340       GO TO 200
348 REM   PRINT TABLE
350       PRINT
360       PRINT "PROD. NO."; TAB(16); "SALES"
370       FOR J = 1 TO E
380       PRINT P$(J); TAB(16); S(J)
390       NEXT J
395       GO TO 970
397 REM   SEARCH SUBROUTINE
400       LET K = 0
410       FOR J = 1 TO E
430       IF K <> 0  GO TO 490
440       IF P$(J) <> P1$   GO TO 460
450       LET K = J
460       NEXT J
490       RETURN
970   END
```

Figure S.18 Program for Chapter 10, Question 19.

```
698 REM  FIND TAX TO BE WITHHELD
700     LET K = 5
710     FOR J = 1 TO 4
720     IF K <> 5  GO TO 760
730     IF G > W(J+1)  GO TO 750
740     LET K = J
750     NEXT J
760     LET T1 = T(K) + P(K)*(G - W(K))
770     IF T1 > 14.40 * E  GO TO 790
780     LET T1 = 0
785     GO TO 800
790     LET T1 = T1 - 14.40 * E
800     ...
```

Figure S.19 Program segment for Chapter 10, Question 21.

gross wage is:

1. Set indicator K = 5
   Set subscript J = 1
2. WHILE J ≤ 4 *and* K = 5
   2.1 IF gross wage ≤ wage bracket (J + 1)
       THEN set K = J
   2.2 Increase J by 1
3. Compute Tax = T(K) + P(K) × (gross wage − wage bracket (K))
4. IF Tax > 14.40 × number of exemptions
   THEN Reduce tax by 14.40 × number of exemptions
   ELSE Set tax to zero

The program segment (assuming the arrays are already loaded) is shown in Fig. S.19.

This, of course, should be generalized to use a variable as the number of brackets. Wherever 5 and 4 appear in the procedure, they should be replaced by number of brackets and number of brackets −1, respectively.

23. Some people like to indent the contents of FOR-NEXT loops; it helps to show visually the control structure. We do that in the programs of Figs. S.20 and S.21, as examples.

25. 1. FOR M from 1 to 12
   1.1 Set total for month (subscripted by M) to zero
   1.2 FOR J from 1 to 20
       1.2.1 Add production (J, M) to total for month

The program is shown in Fig. S.21.

```
198 REM  SET TO ZERO ALL CELLS OF D, DIM 15, 8
200     FOR J = 1 TO 15
210       FOR K = 1 TO 8
220         LET D(J,K) = 0
230       NEXT K
240     NEXT J
```

Figure S.20 Program segment for Chapter 10, Question 23.

```
198 REM   COMPUTE TOTAL PRODUCTION FOR EACH MONTH, ALL PLANTS
200     FOR M = 1 TO 12
210       LET Y(M) = 0
220       FOR J = 1 TO 20
230         LET Y(M) = Y(M) + P(J,M)
240       NEXT J
250     NEXT M
```

Figure S.21 Program segment for Chapter 10, Question 25.

27. $A(5, 2), A(5, 3), A(5, 4), A(5, 5), A(5, 6)$

Numbers are added to $B(3)$ only when $L = 3$. When L is 3, the first subscript of the cells of A to be added is $L + 2 = 5$. The second subscript, K, ranges from 2 to 6.

CHAPTER 12

1. 1. Obtain current population P, target population T, growth rate G
   2. Compute N as $\log(T/P)/\log(1 + G)$
   3. Print N

The program is shown in Fig. S.22.

If we want to print N as an integer number of years, we should round N *up,* so should print, say, $INT(N + 0.999)$.

3. The point is that if INT rounds toward zero, we must *subtract* 0.5 from negative numbers before taking the INT function in order to get a rounding effect. Try some examples to verify that. The first strategy is to distinguish negative numbers as a special case:

```
200   IF X < 0 GO TO 230
210   LET R = INT (X + .5)
220   GO TO 240
230   LET R = INT(X − .5)
240   next step
```

```
10    REM   COMPUTE NO. OF YEARS TO REACH A TARGET POPULATION
20    REM   JAMES G BLAINE          FEB 1980
30    REM      P = CURRENT POPULATION
32    REM      T = TARGET POPULATION
34    REM      G = GROWTH RATE
36    REM      N = NUMBER OF YEARS
100     PRINT "TYPE CURRENT POPULATION";
110     INPUT P
120     PRINT "TYPE TARGET POPULATION";
130     INPUT T
140     PRINT "TYPE GROWTH RATE";
150     INPUT G
200     LET N = LOG(T/P) / LOG(1+G)
300     PRINT "GROWTH TO THE TARGET POPULATION WILL TAKE"; N; "YEARS"
970   END
```

Figure S.22 Program for Chapter 12, Question 1.

```
400     LET I6 = 1
410     IF M < 1   GO TO 430
420     IF M <= 12   GO TO 440
430     LET I6 = 0
440     IF D < 1   GO TO 460
450     IF D <= 31   GO TO 470
460     LET I6 = 0
470     . . .
```

Figure S.23 Program segment for Chapter 12, Question 5.

The second strategy is to round a nonnegative number, then restore the sign:

```
200   LET R = SGN(X) * INT(ABS(X) + .5)
```

5. 1. Set indicator I6 to 1
   2. IF M < 1 *or* M > 12
      THEN set I6 to 0.
   3. IF D < 1 *or* D > 31
      THEN set I6 to 0.

This strategy considers the data valid ("innocent"?) until it is found invalid ("guilty"?). This is not by any means the only possible way to do the task. A program segment following this procedure is shown in Fig. S.23.

7. 400   LET D1$ = MID$(D$,1,2) + "/" + MID$(D$,4,2) +
   "/" + MID$(D$,7,2)

9. 1. Set H1$ to first character of H$.
   2. Set J to 2.
   3. WHILE J ≤ length of H$
      3.1 Concatenate space and J'th character of H$ at end of H1$
      3.2 Add 1 to J

```
300   LET H1$ = MID$(H$,1,1)
310   FOR J = 2 TO LEN(H$)
320   LET H1$ = H1$ + " " + MID$(H$,J,1)
330   NEXT J
```

CHAPTER 13

1. Figure S.24 shows the image statements and the PRINT statements that print headings. Only statement 100 is changed and statement 130 added; the others are shown so we see how these statements relate to the spacing of the column headings and the table.

```
100     PRINT USING 130, "TABLE OF VALUES OF $100"
110     PRINT "  RATE      5 YEARS      10 YEARS      15 YEARS"
125     :##.####    ####.##      ####.##      ####.##
130     :'CCCCCCCCCCCCCCCCCCCCCCCCCCCCCCCCCCCCCCCCCCC
```

Figure S.24 PRINT and image statements for Chapter 13, Question 1.

3. Figure S.25 shows a possible report layout. Figure S.26 shows a program, a modification of Fig. 10.3, which implements the report layout.

5. Statement 150 is replaced by the segment shown in Fig. S.27.

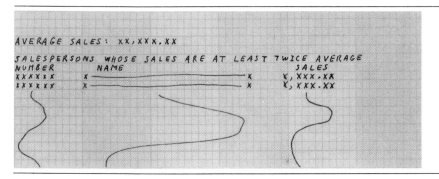

Figure S.25 Report layout for Chapter 13, Question 3.

```
10    REM   PRINT NUMBERS AND NAMES OF SALESPERSONS
12    REM   WHOSE SALES ARE AT LEAST TWICE THE AVERAGE
20    REM   G STRUBLE    FEB 1980
30    REM       ARRAY N:   SALESPERSON NUMBERS
32    REM       ARRAY N$:  SALESPERSON NAMES
34    REM       ARRAY S:   SALES FOR THE MONTH
36    REM       T = TOTAL SALES
38    REM       K = COUNTER AND SUBSCRIPT OF SALESPERSONS
40    REM       M = NUMBER OF SALESPERSONS
42    REM       A = AVERAGE SALES PER SALESPERSON
60        DIM N(200), N$(200), S(200)
70        FILES SLSMO
98    REM   1. READ DATA INTO ARRAYS, FIND AVERAGE SALES
100       LET T = 0
110       LET K = 1
120       IF END #1 GO TO 170
130       INPUT #1, N(K), N$(K), S(K)
140       LET T = T + S(K)
150       LET K = K + 1
160       GO TO 120
170       LET M = K - 1
180       LET A = T / M
190       PRINT USING 250, A
198   REM   2. PRINT HEADINGS
200       PRINT
210       PRINT "SALESPERSONS WHOSE SALES ARE AT LEAST TWICE AVERAGE"
220       PRINT "NUMBER        NAME                             SALES"
240           :######    'LLLLLLLLLLLLLLLLLLLLLLLLLL    ##,###.##
250           :AVERAGE SALES: ##,###.##
298   REM   3. LIST SALESPERSONS
300       FOR K = 1 TO M
320       IF S(K) < 2 * A  GO TO 340
330       PRINT USING 240, N(K), N$(K), S(K)
340       NEXT K
970   END
```

Figure S.26 Program for Chapter 13, Question 3.

```
140                 :                      PAYROLL REGISTER
     'RRRRRRRRRRRR
145      PRINT "TYPE DATE FOR REPORT HEADING";
150      INPUT D$
160      FOR J = 1 TO 10
161      PRINT
162      NEXT J
170      PRINT USING 140, D$
175      PRINT
180      PRINT H1$
```

Figure S.27 Statements for Chapter 13, Question 5. To replace statement 150 in Fig. 13.6.

7. We can print CR after a number to indicate that the number is negative by the following kind of segment:

```
700   LET X8$ = " "
710   IF X >= 0 GO TO 730
720   LET X8$ = "CR"
730   PRINT USING 790, ABS(X), X8$
790   :     #####.##'L
```

9. The procedure of Fig. 13.7 is changed to:
   1. Initialize department and plant totals to zero
   2. Read first record
   3. Print first record, add to department totals
   4. Set previous plant and department to current plant and department
   5. WHILE there are records
      5.1 Read a record
      5.2 IF plant ≠ previous plant
          THEN Print department totals
                Add department totals to plant totals
                Reset department totals to zero
                Set previous department to current department
                Print plant totals
                Reset plant totals to zero
                Set previous plant to current plant
      5.3 IF department ≠ previous department
          THEN Print department totals
                Add department totals to plant totals
                Reset department totals to zero
                Set previous department to current department
      5.4 Print record, add to department totals
   6. Print department totals
      Add department totals to plant totals
      Print plant totals

The program of Fig. 13.8, revised to follow this procedure, is shown in Fig. S.28.

```
10   REM   PRODUCE REPORT INCLUDING DEPARTMENT AND PLANT TOTALS
20   REM   G STRUBLE    FEB 1980
36   REM      S$ = SOCIAL SECURITY NUMBER
38   REM      N$ = EMPLOYEE NAME
39   REM      P  = EMPLOYEE'S PLANT NUMBER
40   REM      D  = EMPLOYEE'S DEPARTMENT
42   REM      H  = HOURS WORKED BY THE EMPLOYEE
44   REM      G  = GROSS PAY
46   REM      T1 = DEPARTMENT TOTAL OF HOURS WORKED
47   REM      T3 = PLANT TOTAL OF HOURS WORKED
48   REM      T2 = DEPARTMENT TOTAL OF GROSS PAY
49   REM      T4 = PLANT TOTAL OF GROSS PAY
50   REM      D1 = DEPARTMENT FROM PREVIOUS RECORD
52   REM      P1 = PLANT FROM PREVIOUS RECORD
55   REM   USES SUBROUTINES
57   REM      1000 TO INITIALIZE DEPARTMENT TOTALS
58   REM      1050 TO INITIALIZE PLANT TOTALS
59   REM      1100 TO PRINT RECORD, ADD TO TOTALS
61   REM      1200 TO PRINT AND RESET DEPARTMENT TOTALS
63   REM      1300 TO PRINT AND RESET PLANT TOTALS
70      FILES PAYRG
100     GOSUB 1000
105     GOSUB 1050
110     INPUT #1, S$, N$, P, D, H, G
120     GOSUB 1100
130     LET D1 = D
140     LET P1 = P
195 REM   MAIN PROCESSING LOOP
200     IF END #1 GO TO 300
210     INPUT #1, S$, N$, P, D, H, G
220     IF P = P1  GO TO 250
230     GOSUB 1200
240     GOSUB 1300
250     IF D = D1  GO TO 270
260     GOSUB 1200
270     GOSUB 1100
280     GO TO 200
295 REM   PRINT LAST DEPARTMENT AND PLANT TOTALS
300     GOSUB 1200
305     GOSUB 1300
310     GO TO 9970
995 REM   SUBROUTINE TO INITIALIZE DEPARTMENT TOTALS TO ZERO
1000    LET T1 = 0
1010    LET T2 = 0
1040    RETURN
1045 REM  SUBROUTINE TO INITIALIZE PLANT TOTALS TO ZERO
1050    LET T3 = 0
1060    LET T4 = 0
1090    RETURN
1095 REM  SUBROUTINE TO PRINT A RECORD, ADD TO DEPARTMENT TOTALS
1100    PRINT USING 8010, S$, N$, P, D, H, G
1110    LET T1 = T1 + H
1120    LET T2 = T2 + G
1190    RETURN
1195 REM  SUBROUTINE TO PRINT AND RESET DEPARTMENT TOTALS
1200    PRINT USING 8020, D1, T1, T2
1210    PRINT
1214    LET T3 = T3 + T1
1216    LET T4 = T4 + T2
1220    GOSUB 1000
1230    LET D1 = D
1290    RETURN
1295 REM  SUBROUTINE TO PRINT AND RESET PLANT TOTALS
1300    PRINT USING 8030, P1, T3, T4
1310    PRINT
1320    GOSUB 1050
1330    LET P1 = P
1390    RETURN
8010:'LLLLLLLL   'LLLLLLLLLLLLLLLLLLLL  ##  ##     ##.#    ###.##
8020:     TOTALS FOR DEPARTMENT          ##  ####.#  #####.##
8030:     TOTALS FOR PLANT              ##      ####.#  #####.##
9970  END
```

Figure S.28 Program for Chapter 13, Question 9.

INDEX